Industrialisation and Globalisation

In a refreshingly accessible style, John Weiss presents a survey of industrialisation in developing countries since 1945, as well as offering a study of the predominant theories of industrial growth in the Third World. This authoritative text analyses:

- the possibility of different paths to industrialisation
- the dominant Neoclassical view and the challenges to this orthodoxy
- the importance of small scale industry
- the importance of technological change for industrialisation.

At a time when globalisation is becoming an increasingly controversial phenomenon, this book offers a powerful argument that, despite potential difficulties with market access, integration with world markets offers developing countries the opportunity for future growth via industrialisation.

Industrialisation and Globalisation will be vital reading for students and academics involved in development economics as well as being indispensable to policy-makers.

John Weiss is Professor of Development Economics at the University of Bradford, UK. He is the author of several books on economic development including *Industry in Developing Countries*, also published by Routledge and most recently (with Steve Curry) *Project Analysis in Developing Countries*.

Industrialisation and Globalisation

Theory and evidence from developing countries

John Weiss

Routledge
Taylor & Francis Group

LONDON AND NEW YORK

First published 2002 by Routledge
2 Park Square, Milton Park, Abingdon, Oxon, OX14 4RN

Simultaneously published in the USA and Canada
by Routledge
605 Third Avenue, New York, NY 10017

Routledge is an imprint of the Taylor & Francis Group, an informa business

© 2002 John Weiss

Typeset in Goudy by Wearset Ltd, Boldon, Tyne and Wear

British Library Cataloguing in Publication Data
A catalogue record for this book is available from the British Library

Library of Congress Cataloging in Publication Data
A catalog record for this book has been requested

ISBN13: 978-0-415-18018-4 (hbk)
ISBN13: 978-0-415-45863-4 (pbk)

To my wife and family

Contents

Figures

Tables

Preface

This book arose out of an intention to revise my earlier work *Industry in Developing Countries*, first published in hardback by Croom-Helm in 1988 and in paperback by Routledge in 1990. Most of that work was originally written in the mid-1980s, so that a great deal of new material has emerged since then. Hence all chapters of the original book have now been rewritten. The focus of the original has been retained however, in that the approach combines evidence with a discussion of alternative theoretical frameworks or paradigms. The distinction between Neoclassical, Structuralist and Radical schools of thought has been retained as a means of organising discussion around potentially complex issues. However, these distinctions were always oversimplifications, hopefully justifiable for expositional purposes, and many working in this area would feel uncomfortable at being labelled in this rather crude manner.

The new book has drawn on my own work on industrialisation, some of which was conducted with doctoral students at Bradford University and some with colleagues, chiefly in recent years Hossein Jalilian and Michael Tribe. Responsibility for errors is, of course, mine.

My family have always been a wonderful source of support and at the time of completing this manuscript were suffering considerably more than usual from my absence for professional reasons. I can only hope that it is all worth it.

1 Industrialisation since 1960

An overview

This chapter summarises some of the basic data on the industrialisation that has taken place in developing countries since 1960. The conventional grouping 'developing countries' is very heterogeneous, covering countries with very different population sizes, income levels, resource endowments, and political and social cultures. Most statistical compilations work with income level as a criteria for membership of this group, although a relatively low share of industry in total economic activity is often assumed to be a key characteristic of such countries.[1]

The simplest definition of a developing country is one with an income per capita of below a certain level, although the precise level of income has no objective basis. As they are currently striving to reach 'developed' or mature economy status, they differ in significant ways from richer economies. The term 'developing countries' is, in part, a relic from the early work on development, which attempted to explain and generalise about the problems of what were seen as a distinct category of economy. More recent literature, however, has distinguished various sub-categories within this group and acknowledges that the generic term 'developing countries' now carries little analytic content. At one extreme there are economies that, even if their average incomes remain low by the standards of developed economies, have relatively sophisticated economic structures; these are now often referred to as 'newly industrialised economies' (NIEs). On the other hand there are many economies, principally in sub-Saharan Africa and South Asia, where incomes remain extremely low, poverty is widespread and economic change is very slow. These are often referred to in statistical publications as 'least developed economies'. Between these extremes are a range of other economies about which it is difficult to generalise. In addition, the ex-Soviet Republics and the Eastern European economies of the ex-Soviet bloc are now labelled 'transition economies' in the light of the social and political changes that have occurred since the disintegration of the Soviet Union. In some of these transitional economies, particularly in Central Asia, incomes are low and many of their economic problems resemble those once seen as the preserve of developing countries. This book does not address the concerns of these transitional economies directly.

In international statistical compilations, the industry sector is generally defined to cover not only manufacturing, but also construction, mining and public utilities. The focus here is primarily on manufacturing, but some sources give information only on industry in aggregate so that on occasions reference cannot be made to manufacturing specifically. As is discussed in later chapters, manufacturing is often seen as the most dynamic part of the industrial sector and given a leading role in development strategies. The United Nations and the World Bank have both collected a substantial amount of comparative material on manufacturing in developing countries and this evidence is drawn on heavily in this chapter. However, at the outset it is important to note frankly some of the limitations of this data.

It is well known that economic data on developing countries can leave much to be desired, but there is a problem related specifically to the statistical coverage of manufacturing. This arises from the fact that, by definition, statistics refer to the 'enumerated' or 'formal' sector; that is, to enterprises large enough to be covered by censuses of production. The activities of small workshops and household units of below a minimum size – that is, the 'informal sector' – will either go unrecorded, or their output and employment will be estimated crudely. For many poor or developing countries, therefore, manufacturing statistics will underestimate total activity and will give a biased indication of its composition. It is normally the case that small-scale informal sector production has a much lower output per worker than in formal manufacturing. This means that small units are much more important in terms of their share in manufacturing employment than in manufacturing output, so that errors of under-recording are likely to be greatest in employment statistics.[2]

The period covered here is from 1960 to the late-1990s, and since 1960 the world economy has gone through several phases with the relatively high growth years of the 1960s, when output and trade expanded at historically high levels, a recession in the mid-1970s after the first oil price shock, a brief period of recovery in the late-1970s, followed by a more prolonged and severe recession after 1980. After recovery in the mid-1980s the remaining years of the twentieth century saw a rapid growth in capital and, to a lesser extent, trade flows in a process now described conventionally as 'globalisation'. It is well known that the level of economic activity in developed economies has a major impact on growth prospects in developing countries, particularly through changes in export demand. Developing country exports of manufactures, in particular, have grown impressively during the 1980s and 1990s at an average of around 13% annually in value terms, and private capital flows to these countries have also increased substantially.[3]

Over this period of approximately forty years, the evidence is strong that a substantial degree of industrialisation has taken place in many developing countries. Although countries conventionally classed in this group still provide only a relatively small share of world manufacturing output, this share has risen and manufacturing has assumed a more central role in many of these economies.[4] In surveying the broad picture of industrial development since 1960 the discussion here is organised around two main issues:

- The extent to which the industrialisation of developing countries over this period has changed the economic structure of these economies;
- The extent to which industrial development has occurred unevenly particularly within the group of developing countries.

Industrialisation and structural change

In many developing countries growth of national income and manufacturing output since 1960 has been high by most standards of comparison; whether in relation to historical rates in these countries before 1960, in relation to rates currently achieved by developed economies, or in relation to the growth performance of the developed economies at earlier stages of their industrialisation. Table 1.1 gives the growth of manufacturing production in the aggregate groupings of developing and developed countries for several periods after 1963. Data on transitional economies of Eastern Europe are also given for comparison. The impact of the first oil shock is apparent since, in both groups, growth is lower after 1973, but in all periods developing countries achieved a higher rate of growth of manufacturing; 8% per year 1963–73, and around 6% per year thereafter. It should be noted that at no stage in the nineteenth and early-twentieth centuries did manufacturing output in the UK, the USA or France grow by such annual rates for any sustained period.[5] The transitional, previously centrally planned, economies, which grew so rapidly in the 1960s saw a collapse of investment and production from the late 1980s onwards and have been experiencing a major reduction in their manufacturing capacity.

Having noted the broad magnitude of manufacturing growth in developing countries as a group, it is important to consider the impact of this growth on economic structure. Industrialisation is normally interpreted as a process whereby the share of industry in general, and of manufacturing in particular, in total economic activity is increased. A large number of studies have shown a clear tendency for industrialisation, defined in this way, to be associated with

Table 1.1 Annual average growth of manufacturing production by economic grouping[a] (constant prices)[b]

	Developing countries (%)	Developed countries (%)	European transitional economies[c] (%)
1963–73	8.0	5.5	9.8
1973–95	5.6	2.0	0.5
1980–90	5.1	2.8	2.5
1990–99	6.5	2.2	−5.9

Sources: Pre-1973, UNIDO (1983: 24); post-1973, UNIDO database.

Notes
a See sources for definitions of economic groupings.
b Data up to 1973 are at 1975 prices, and data post-1973 are at 1990 prices.
c Including Russia, but excluding ex-Yugoslavia.

rising incomes. In other words, as incomes per capita increase, so too does the share of manufacturing in national income. There is also evidence of an S-shaped relation, with the manufacturing share falling after a certain level of income is passed. The implication is that as income rises beyond a threshold level there will be a proportionate shift in domestic expenditure towards services rather than manufactures. Exporting can postpone a structural shift away from manufacturing for a time, but there is evidence that it will not be postponed indefinitely.[6] Naturally this statistical association cannot prove causation, and the issue of whether it is the increasing role of manufacturing in economic activity which causes higher incomes per capita, or vice versa, is one to which we will return. However, an increase in the share of manufacturing in national income is conventionally taken as an important statistical measure of structural change at the macro-economic level. If one considers the sectoral composition of national income for developing countries as a group, one finds that, over the period since 1960, there has been a rise in the share of manufacturing, services and others at the expense of agriculture. The increase for manufacturing is around 9 percentage points, from 15% of GDP in the early 1960s to 24% in the mid-1990s, which is slightly above the developed country average.[7] This is only the first of many statistical comparisons, however, where the use of the aggregate category 'developing countries' can obscure important trends within the group. Development of manufacturing within the group of developing countries differentiated by geographical region is illustrated in Table 1.2, this time using World Bank data.

The contrast between production structures in the lower income regions of Africa and South Asia and the higher income areas of East Asia is clear. In East Asia the share of manufacturing has been rising dramatically in response to high rates of growth in manufacturing and now exceeds the share in the developed economies. Further, it is considerably higher than would be predicted for the income level and size of the countries concerned.[8] In Latin America the manufacturing share has been falling since the early 1970s although, on average, it is still above that in the lower income economies of Sub-Saharan Africa and South Asia. In terms of recent growth in manufacturing, the dramatic performance in East Asia (including China) of over 10% annually since the early 1980s and the lower, but still highly creditable, growth of around 7% annually in

Table 1.2 Manufacturing: share in GDP and growth by region

	Share in GDP (%)		Annual growth (%)		
	1980	*1998*	*1966–98*	*1980–90*	*1990–98*
East Asia and Pacific	31	31	10.5	10.2	10.9
Latin America and Caribbean	29	22	3.5	1.2	3.1
South Asia	16	19	5.6	7.0	7.6
Sub-Saharan Africa	16	19	3.6	1.7	1.2

Source: World Bank (2000).

South Asia must be contrasted with much slower growth in Latin America and Sub-Saharan Africa. In many countries in the latter region growth has failed even to keep pace with population increase, so that, in per capita terms, manufacturing value-added has fallen since the early 1980s.

Employment growth

Another approach to economic structure is to examine the share of different sectors in total employment. It can be argued that this is a more important indicator of structural change, since one of the main aims of a policy of structural transformation will be to shift employment from low to high productivity activities. This implies that the change in the proportion of the workforce in developing countries engaged in manufacturing or industry in general, where productivity is high relative to the rest of economy, will be an important measure of structural change. Estimates of the proportion of the labour force engaged in manufacturing in developing countries are particularly prone to error due to the lack of coverage in surveys of small-scale household or workshop units, noted earlier. It is normally argued that this omission is particularly significant in terms of employment since, whilst in many developing countries un-enumerated producers may contribute only a relatively small proportion of output, they can provide a much more significant proportion of manufacturing employment.

The share of either industry or manufacturing in total employment is often substantially less than their share in national income, due to the low productivity of agriculture in many developing countries. Here, unlike the value-added data just discussed, there is little evidence of a significant rise in the employment share of manufacturing in the majority of developing countries. Table 1.3 illustrates this trend using World Bank sources.[9] Data on employment in manufacturing alone are not available from this source, hence industrial employment figures are given. For comparison, data are also shown on three of the fast growing East

Table 1.3 Sectoral employment share by region and selected countries

	Agriculture		Industry	
	1980	1990	1980	1990
Sub-Saharan Africa	72	68	9	9
South Asia	70	64	13	16
Latin America and the Caribbean	34	25	25	24
East Asia[a]	73	70	14	15
Korea	37	18	27	35
Singapore	2	0	44	36
Hong Kong	1	1	50	37

Source: World Bank (1997) Table 4.

Note
a Excludes Korea, Singapore and Hong Kong.

Asian economies, where the pattern of change has differed from the normal one for developing countries. Agriculture still remains by far the most important employer in all but higher income developing countries. The employment shift towards industry was particularly dramatic in the case of South Korea (henceforth Korea), although in the other two higher income economies shown, Hong Kong and Singapore, employment patterns in the 1980s moved away from manufacturing with the growing skill-intensity of production and the emergence of important international service activities in these economies.

Specifically regarding employment, developing countries as a group increased their share of world manufacturing employment by around 11 percentage points from the mid-1970s to the early 1990s, although most of the proportionate increase occurred by the mid-1980s; see Table 1.4. The differences between Tables 1.3 and 1.4 largely reflect the share of non-manufacturing industrial employment in mining and construction.

Nonetheless, in the context of employment growth, it is frequently asserted that manufacturing has generated relatively few new jobs, despite the substantial industrialisation that has taken place since 1960. On the basis of recorded employment statistics up to the 1980s, this view was questionable. For developing countries as a group, manufacturing employment appears to have grown by around 4% per year during the 1960s and 1970s; a creditable performance in historical terms. For example, if one takes as a point of comparison the experience of developed countries in the latter part of the nineteenth century, the rough data available suggest that their annual growth of industrial employment was roughly half this figure.[10] Manufacturing employment growth appeared to slow somewhat after 1980 to an average of around 3.5% annually between 1980 and 1995. This growth was very unevenly distributed with employment falls in a number of countries and rapid growth in others. From the UNIDO database in sixty-eight developing countries with adequate data from 1980 to 1995 it appears that approximately 41 million new manufacturing jobs were created. However roughly three quarters of these, approximately 32 million, were in one country, China. Over the same period there were net job losses in manufacturing in sixteen of the sixty-eight countries and very low employment growth of below 1% annually in another twelve countries.[11] In

Table 1.4 Developing country shares in world manufacturing employment by region (%)

Region	1975	1985	1993
Developed countries	72.6	62.0	61.2
Developing countries	27.4	38.0	38.8
East Asia	7.2	12.0	10.0
Africa	1.9	3.5	3.7
West Asia	1.6	2.0	2.1
South Asia	7.2	9.0	10.1
Latin America	9.5	10.5	12.0

Source: UNIDO cited by Amsden (2001) Table 9.5.

Latin America in particular the numbers employed in manufacturing have fallen significantly during the 1990s as part of enterprise restructuring.[12]

The basic problem is not always the number of additional jobs created in industry relative to output expansion in the sector. Even where this is high, the number of these additional jobs relative to both the annual increase in the labour force and the number of workers in low productivity activities in agriculture and services remains only modest. Again a comparison with late-nineteenth-century experience may put the problem in perspective. In the 1960s, at a time of high employment growth in developing countries, the industrial sector was able to absorb annually only around 22% of the total increase in the labour force; the comparable estimate for a group of now developed economies in the 1880s is nearly twice this, at 42%.[13] In many countries the substantial expansion of industrial and manufacturing output, which has occurred since 1960, is still inadequate to generate the jobs required to absorb a high proportion of the new entrants to the labour force, let alone to offer work to large numbers of the under-employed.

Composition of manufacturing

Structural change cannot be viewed simply in terms of the share of manufacturing or industry in total output or employment. It is important to know whether there has been a shift in the composition of output produced within manufacturing; in particular whether developing countries have moved from what is sometimes termed 'first-stage import-substitution', (involving the replacement of imports by local production of light consumer goods with relatively simple technologies and no significant economies of scale), to the production of intermediates and consumer and producer durables. A diversified industrial structure which is capable of supplying a significant proportion of its own requirements of industrial inputs and capital goods is seen by many as a prerequisite of a self-sustaining programme for long-run growth. In this context structural change within manufacturing can be defined as a shift away from light, relatively labour-intensive industrial activities, towards heavy, more capital-intensive ones, and away from light consumer goods towards industrial intermediates, and durables, both capital and consumer goods.[14]

To illustrate the changes in industrial structure that have taken place in developing countries over this period, Table 1.5 shows the share of different manufacturing branches or categories in world output of that category. In addition, branches are placed in three groups depending on the extent to which they increased their share of world output over the period 1975–95. Branches where developing countries' gains have been greatest include footwear, textiles and clothing, which are the main labour-intensive 'easy' import-substitute activities, but also heavy industrial activities like iron and steel, petroleum refining and non-ferrous metals.

However, rather than focussing on the factor intensity of production, or the uses to which output is put, the technological dynamism of different branches,

Table 1.5 Developing country shares in world output and their change by branch (1975–95)

10% or more gain	0–9% gain	Loss
Footwear (43.8)	Pottery, china, and earthenware (25.7)	Plastics (12.8)
Iron and steel (28.3)	Rubber products (21.5)	Printing and publishing (7.6)
Textiles (36.4)	Industrial chemicals (16.7)	Tobacco manufactures (30.2)
Non-ferrous metals (20.8)	Glass and glass products (17.8)	
Wearing apparel (29.2)	Beverages (27.3)	
Leather and fur products (34.0)	Electrical machinery (14.1)	
Petroleum refining (36.7)	Transport equipment (12.6)	
Miscellaneous petroleum and coal products (24.0)	Metal products (15.0)	
Other non-metallic minerals (26.2)	Non-electrical machinery (9.6)	
	Paper and paper products (13.5)	
	Furniture and fixtures (13.6)	
	Food (18.6)	
	Professional and scientific goods (6.2)	
	Wood and cork products (6.2)	
	Other chemical products (19.0)	

Source: UNIDO cited in Amsden (2001) Table 9.7.

Note
Gain and loss refer to change in share of world output over the period. Within each group branches are ranked by descending order of change. Figures in parentheses are the share of each branch in total world output of that branch in 1995. China is excluded from all figures.

in the sense of their potential for technical change, quality improvement and cost reduction, offers an alternative criteria by which to analyse industrial structure. Table 1.6 provides a simple indication of the changing technological composition of manufacturing. It uses a simple definition of technological dynamism to dis-aggregate manufacturing structure into low, medium and high technology activities.[15] The main drawback with this form of comparison, however, is that within particular branches of manufacturing, activities can be carried out at different levels of technological complexity. Hence a given value-added in electronics, for example, can be related to assembly or to genuine product development. In statistical compilations both will show up as output under the same activity. With this qualification in mind, Table 1.6 gives the average shares of these three groups in manufacturing value-added for developed

Table 1.6 Composition of manufacturing output by technology (% share)

	Developed		NIEs		Second NIEs		Other developing	
	1980	1997	1980	1997	1980	1997	1980	1997
Low technology	55	44	58	51	73	69	78	76
Medium technology	24	25	26	29	20	21	16	19
High technology	21	31	16	20	7	10	6	5

Source: Calculated from data in UNIDO database.

Note
NIEs are Hong Kong, Taiwan, India, Korea, Singapore, Argentina, Brazil, Mexico. Second tier NIEs are Indonesia, Malaysia, Philippines, Thailand, Colombia, Turkey.

economies, a group of relatively more industrialised developing countries – what are termed 'newly industrialised economies' (NIEs) – a group of second-tier or follower NIEs, who have developed relatively large manufacturing sectors more recently, and all other developing countries.

The pattern in Table 1.6 is clear. High technology activities have grown relative to others in all country groupings except for the non-NIE developing countries. Outside of the group of industrialised economies, low technology activities still predominate, particularly in the second tier NIEs and other developing countries. As a group, the NIE are moving towards the structure of the industrialised economies, although as yet they have not specialised as far in high technology activities.

The implication is of a change in industrial structure amongst developing countries away from reliance on low technology, simple manufactures. However this shift has been taken much further in some countries than others and still is insufficient in most cases to come close to the focus on high technology activities found in the developed economies.

Composition of exports

The final broad indicator of structural change considered here is the composition of exports. Heavy reliance on the export of a small number of primary commodities was a key characteristic of many developing countries pre-1960, and a rising share of manufactures in total exports can be seen as desirable, not only to diversify the means of earning foreign exchange, but also as evidence of the international competitiveness of new manufacturing activities.

One of the dominant characteristics of world trade patterns since 1960 has been the growth of manufactured exports from developing countries. For developing countries as a group manufactured exports grew at just under 12% per year in volume terms 1965–73, accelerating to just over 14% per year 1973–80. Since 1980 growth of manufactured export volumes from developing countries has been around 12% annually.[16] In all periods this growth exceeded substantially that of total world merchandise trade. Hence as a consequence of this

Table 1.7 Developing country manufactured exports

	Manufactures/Total exports (%)		Annual growth 1980–98 (%)
	1980	1998	
East Asia and Pacific	45	82	15.8
Latin America and Caribbean	20	49	11.6
Middle East and North Africa	6	17	3.4
South Asia	54	78	10.2
Sub-Saharan Africa	12	n.a.	n.a.

Source: Calculated from data in World Bank (2000).

Note
Growth rates are in US$ values; n.a. is 'not available'.

rapid growth the share of manufactures from developing countries in their total exports and in world trade in manufactures increased. Thus from a relatively low base the developing country share of world exports of manufactures has grown to nearly 25%. Table 1.7 gives the average annual share of manufactures in total exports for groups of countries classified by region. In all cases, except Sub-Saharan Africa, there is evidence of a clear trend towards a rising share over time. By the early 1990s, even in many low-income or least developed countries, manufactures were over a quarter of exports. Although success in exporting manufactures has been very unevenly spread between developing countries, a point to which we will return shortly, even in many countries which remain highly dependent upon primary exports there has been some diversification, in the sense that they have become less dependent upon their single most important primary export.[17]

Although developing country exporters now account for around half of world exports of footwear and textiles, an examination of the commodity composition of manufactured exports from developing countries reveals that growth has occurred across a range of products, not simply the more traditional labour-intensive exports.[18] Rapid export growth has also been achieved in products like consumer electronics, chemicals, iron and steel, machinery and transport equipment, so the pattern of exports from developing countries is shifting towards greater technological complexity as well as capital-intensity. This can be seen by drawing on data on the trend in world manufactured exports classified by level of technological sophistication. A four-fold classification can be used that distinguishes between exports that are:

- resource-based products involving processing of agricultural products, minerals, energy resources and so forth;
- low technology products such as textiles, footwear, garments, sports goods, toys, furniture, based on mature, relatively simple, often labour-intensive technologies;

Table 1.8 World manufactured exports by technology category

	Annual growth 1985–98 (%)		Developing country share in world exports (%)	
	Developed	Developing	1985	1998
Resource based	7.0	6.0	26.3	23.7
Low technology	8.5	11.7	26.7	34.5
Medium technology	8.5	14.3	8.3	15.3
High technology	11.3	21.4	10.7	27.0
Total	8.8	12.5	16.4	23.3

Source: Lall (2000a) Table 2.

Note
Growth rates and shares are in terms of US$ values.

Table 1.9 Distribution of developing country manufactured exports by technology category (%)

Year	Resource based	Low technology	Medium technology	High technology
1985	38	30	21	11
1998	18	27	26	29

Source: Lall (2000a) Table 5.

- medium technology products, such as automobiles, chemicals, basic metals, machinery and simple electronics, with more complex but not rapidly changing technologies, strong learning effects in operations and sometimes economies of scale in production;
- high technology products, such as pharmaceuticals, complex electronics, aircraft and precision instruments, where technologies are both complex and rapidly changing, with high skill requirements.[19]

As shown in Table 1.8, within world trade in manufactures it is the high technology goods that have grown most rapidly over the last twenty years. Further, developing countries have seen a major expansion in their exports of high technology goods and, as Table 1.9 shows, in the aggregate in the late-1990s, less than half of their exports were still in the technologically less complex resource based and low technology goods.

Parts of the production process of high technology goods are often divisible and not all production locations require high skills and good technological infrastructure, thus international sourcing can be practised as part of globalisation. The major rise in such exports from developing countries seen in Tables 1.8 and 1.9 arises primarily through the transfer of parts of their production, usually involving lower Research and Development (R and D) activity and skill levels, to lower wage economies. The components and parts produced in these operations are then exported for completion or final assembly elsewhere. NIEs in East Asia have been at the forefront of this re-location process, so that in countries like Singapore, Malaysia, Philippines, Thailand and Taiwan well over one-third of manufactured exports are classed in the high technology category. For the Philippines and Singapore the proportion is over 60%. Developing countries, chiefly the NIEs, now account for around one-third of world exports of electronics, which is the industry where this sourcing process has been developed furthest. On the other hand, in many countries, including large countries like India, Pakistan and China, the bulk of manufactured exports are still in the lower technology categories, so that the highly impressive growth of high technology exports has been concentrated very unevenly between countries.[20]

To summarise, therefore, by any of the indicators conventionally used to gauge structural change at the macro level, as a group, developing countries have shown important structural shifts. The share of manufacturing in total production has risen, as has its share in total exports. Although one can question the accuracy of some of these statistics, the general conclusion is clear, despite setbacks in more recent years in some countries, manufacturing, and industry in general, have played a much larger role in developing countries since 1960.

Uneven industrial development

As pointed out earlier, the group of developing countries is very heterogeneous. In 1960, at the beginning of the period with which we are concerned, there was a significant inequality between developing regions and countries in terms of both income and manufacturing output, and this gap has widened in many cases with a wide disparity in growth between different countries and regions. Table 1.2 has summarised some of the changes since the late 1960s.

Real manufacturing growth has been very rapid in East Asia and China, where the newly industrialised economies are located. In some countries in sub-Saharan Africa, it has been below the rate of population increase, so that real value-added per capita has declined. In South Asia, although growth has been around 5% per year, this is still sufficiently above population increase for value-added per capita to double in twenty-five years. In Latin America and the Caribbean growth has been low at just below 3% annually, largely due to the difficulties caused by the debt and adjustment crises many countries of the region faced in the 1980s. Finally it is worth noting the continued gap in productivity levels as reflected in the very large difference in average per capita value-added between countries and regions.[21]

As might be expected there have also been disparities within regions, so that the additional manufacturing output and exports produced by developing countries since 1960 has been highly concentrated in a relatively small number of countries. Apart from China with over a quarter of developing country manufacturing production, the other five main producers in order of the absolute size of their manufacturing sectors are Korea, Brazil, Taiwan, India and Mexico. In 1995, if one excludes China from the comparison, these five countries, with roughly 37% of the population of developing countries, had 48% of manufacturing value-added.[22]

Although, as we have noted above, many developing countries expanded their exports of manufactured goods over this period, the bulk of the increase was again concentrated in a few countries. Data for the mid-1970s, for example, indicate that the ten chief developing country exporters took over 75% of all manufactured exports from the group. The four major East Asian exporters, Hong Kong, Taiwan, Korea and Singapore, accounted for over 45%. By the late 1990s, the top ten exporters took over 80% of all manufactured exports from developing countries. Further, this tendency towards export concentration rises with the technological sophistication of the goods concerned, so that in the high technology category, 96% of all developing country exports come from the leading ten exporting economies. The leading five exporters – Singapore, Taiwan, Korea, Malaysia and China – account for over 70% of developing country exports of these goods.[23]

Newly industrialised economies

The uneven spread of manufacturing and export growth within the group of developing countries has led to efforts to reclassify countries into 'the more dynamic' and 'the rest'. In recognition of the fact that some of these countries might already have reached the stage at which they could be termed 'industrialised', the more advanced of these have been christened 'newly industrialised economies' (NIEs). Unfortunately there are no commonly agreed criteria for membership of this group. One approach, where export growth has been rapid, is to define NIEs as those countries with a successful export-oriented strategy for manufacturing; another includes as NIEs those countries where manufacturing has reached some threshold share of GDP – typically either 20% or 25%.[24] The countries most frequently included in lists of NIEs are probably Hong Kong, Singapore, Korea, Taiwan, Argentina, Brazil, Mexico, India, China, Turkey, with Malaysia, Indonesia and Thailand sometimes included as well.[25]

Different countries are included in this list for different reasons. The first four, Hong Kong, Singapore, Korea, Taiwan, are the original 'Gang of Four' whose dramatic performance since the 1960s first alerted observers to the prospect of rapid industrial expansion in initially low income countries. These are now sometimes referred to as the 'first-tier' NIEs in recognition of their earlier start on the process of export-oriented industrialisation. In fact recent World Bank statistics now classify Hong Kong, Singapore and Korea in the category of high income countries due to the levels of income per capita they have achieved. Taiwan is excluded from these statistics for political reasons, but its income per head is higher than Korea.

Argentina, Brazil and Mexico are economies with a long history of industrial development and the latter, in particular, have large domestic markets. Similarly India and China are often included as NIEs on the grounds of the very large scale of their industrial sectors. Further, in the case of China its very rapid growth in recent years has meant that it has accounted for a significant propor-tion of the additional manufacturing value-added created outside Europe and North America. Turkey is also an economy with a lengthy history of industrial-isation and a relatively large internal market. Finally, the three East Asian economies of Malaysia, Indonesia and Thailand have achieved significant export growth in recent years and, as a consequence, have been described as second-tier NIEs that have followed the path of manufactured export growth first set out by their first tier regional neighbours.[26]

Data on some of the structural characteristics and economic performance of these countries is given in Table 1.10. Together they have around one-third of the population of all developing countries, including China. However this relat-ively high proportion is strongly influenced by the inclusion of India and China. From Table 1.10 it is difficult to identify common characteristics shared by the countries most frequently cited as NIEs. With the exception of Argentina all have had a growth rate of manufacturing since the mid-1970s in excess of that in the groups of both developed and developing economies. Despite this poor performance, Argentina is normally included in lists of NIEs on the grounds of the absolute size and relative technological sophistication of its manufacturing sector.

The role of manufacturing in the economies of the NIEs varies markedly between the countries in Table 1.10. In terms of its share in GDP, all countries in the table, with the exception of Hong Kong, have a share above 15%. In a majority of cases the share of manufacturing in the NIEs is either close to or greater than that in the higher income economies. The low and declining share of manufacturing in the economy of Hong Kong is largely due to the shift of many manufacturing activities from the island to mainland China, rather than a process of de-industrialisation. For exports, manufactures exceed 50% of total exports in all cases except Indonesia and Argentina, where oil and other primary exports are of major importance. In a number of cases manufactures now provide the bulk of exports.[27] Manufacturing value-added per capita varies substantially between countries from over US$6000 in Singapore to US$70 in India. However, in all cases, apart from Singapore, Korea and Hong Kong, the per capita figures are very low in comparison with developed economies, but nonetheless they are generally high by the standards of most other developing countries. Singapore now has a per capita figure which exceeds the average for higher income economies.

A diversification, as well as an expansion, of manufacturing is a characteris-tic of NIEs. Some evidence of this is given in Table 1.10 by the share of high technology branches in total manufacturing. In two countries, Singapore and Malaysia, the shares of these branches are well above those in the higher income group (although much of this is likely to be assembly operations for parts and components made elsewhere) whilst in three other NIEs, Hong Kong, Korea and Taiwan, the shares are broadly similar to those in the higher income economies. For other countries in the table, however, structural change in manufacturing in the direction of these branches has been carried much less far

Table 1.10 NIEs: economic characteristics and performance

Countries	Manufacturing share in GDP (%) 1998	Manufacturing value-added per capita US$ 1998	High technology branches in total manufacturing^a 1995 (%)	Manufactured goods in total exports (%) 1998	High technology exports in total manufactured exports^b (%) 1998	Manufacturing annual growth 1980–90 (%)	Manufacturing annual growth 1990–98 (%)
Argentina	19	1253	8	35	n.a.	-0.8	4.3
Brazil	23	1078	17	55	8	1.6	2.5
Mexico	20	821	8	85	30	1.5	3.6
Hong Kong	7	1738	26	95	26	n.a.	n.a.
Korea	31	2142	26	91	30	13.0	6.9
Taiwan	n.a.	n.a.	24	n.a.	37	n.a.	n.a.
Singapore	23	6064	53	86	60	6.6	6.7
India	16	70	15	74	7	7.4	8.0
China	37	286	19	87	20	10.4	14.7
Malaysia	29	946	36	79	52	8.9	10.8
Indonesia	25	115	5	45	10	12.6	8.8
Thailand	32	582	10	71	35	9.5	7.7
Turkey	16	501	10	77	6	7.9	5.9
High income economies	21	5344	27	82	18	n.a.	2.5

Source: World Bank (2000) *World Development Indicators 2000*, except for share of high technology branches, which comes from UNIDO database, and high technology export data, which comes from Lall (2000a).

Notes

n.a. is 'not available'.
a High technology branches are defined here as International Standard Industrial Classification branches 382, 383, and 385.
b High technology exports are defined in Lall (2000a).

and they are 10% or less of total manufacturing in five countries, including, surprisingly given their income levels and history of industrialisation, Mexico, Argentina and Turkey.

The trade pattern of the NIEs illustrates clearly the extent to which their development since 1960 has differentiated them from other developing countries.[28] The NIEs have been the main exporters of manufactures from developing countries. However, as we have noted above, there is a clear differentiation between countries included in the table and high technology exports are considerably more important for some of the NIEs than for others. For example, one can contrast the export structure in India, Brazil, Turkey and Indonesia, where high technology exports are less than 10% of total manufactured exports, with that in most of the East Asian NIE, where they normally exceed 25%, and where in some cases, principally Singapore and Malaysia, they provide a major part of all manufactured exports.

Overall growth has also been very uneven within the group. Since 1980 growth has been relatively slow in the three major Latin American economies of Brazil, Mexico and Argentina, with the latter experiencing a substantial absolute decline in the sector during the 1980s. In the East Asia economies, India and China growth has been much more rapid, with China demonstrating dramatic growth of nearly 15% annually over most of the 1990s and the others growing by at least 6% annually. However, these figures do not fully capture the effect of the East Asian financial crisis of 1997–98, which had a strongly negative impact, principally on Indonesia, Thailand and Korea, and from which recovery has been strongest in Korea and weakest in Indonesia.

Whether or not all of the NIEs should be considered to be genuinely industrialised is unclear, since there are no commonly agreed criteria for defining an industrialised economy. In very general terms it is an economy where the industrial sector, and manufacturing in particular, have come to play a 'critical' role, but what constitutes such as role is open to differing interpretations. Further, it could be argued that despite the structural change that has taken place, much of the industrialisation in the NIEs is premature, in the sense that in most of these countries the value of manufacturing output per head of population is still significantly below that in the developed economies. Therefore, whilst the share of manufacturing in national income in many of the NIEs may be close to or greater than that in developed economies, labour productivity in manufacturing remains much lower. Further allowing for differences in age structure and hours worked in manufacturing, output per worker in relation to that in developed economies is even lower. In addition, even in the fast growing East Asian NIEs total factor productivity growth, which should measure the increase in efficiency of resource use, was only modest in the period since 1960, averaging 2% or less annually in Korea, Taiwan and Singapore.[29]

De-industrialisation

At the other extreme, the question can be raised as to whether or not in some sense a significant number of developing countries have been experiencing a process of industrial regression or de-industrialisation. In its strongest sense this can be interpreted as an absolute fall in manufacturing (either output or employment) and in its weaker sense as a relative fall. Table 1.11 shows the position in all countries for which there is comparable data where the share of manufacturing in GDP has fallen since 1980.

It can be seen that in the majority of the twenty-five countries for which we show a relative fall in manufacturing, in all but four this is at a time of positive absolute growth. Hence what we are picking up is a reallocation of resources at a time of overall expansion, which may reflect a more efficient allocation of resources in response to the opportunities opened up by a more liberal international trading environment. The four countries where there was both an absolute and relative fall in manufacturing in the 1990s are Colombia, Jamaica, Zambia and Zimbabwe.[30]

The collapse of manufacturing has been most dramatic in the African economies of Zambia and Zimbabwe. In addition there are a number of other countries in Africa where there was a substantial fall in the absolute size of manufacturing during the 1990s at a time of general economic decline, so that the share of manufacturing in national income did not fall. These are Angola, Burundi, Cameroon, the Central African Republic, Congo and Mauritania. Hence de-industrialisation appears largely, but not entirely, an African issue. Neoclassical thinking, discussed in Chapter 3, would argue that much of the industrial sector in African was highly inefficient and would be expected to contract as these economies were opened up to international competition. However, whilst by definition closure of inefficient activities must be sensible in economic terms, it is clearly a cause for concern that little new investment has gone into the manufacturing sector in Africa in recent years to create more competitive new industries.[31]

Simple comparisons such as those in Table 1.11 take no account of the income level, size and natural resource endowments of particular economies, all of which can be expected to influence the share of manufacturing in total economic activity. To address this, a study by the author estimated a cross-country regression model that attempts to take account of these country characteristics. This shows that, as expected, for all developing countries the share of manufacturing in GDP rises with income per capita and population. However, controlling for these factors, there is a tendency for this share to fall across all countries in more recent periods (covering the late 1980s to early 1990s). Once one allows for other relevant variables, no specific regional effect for Africa is found, so that there is no evidence that this downward trend is more important in Africa than elsewhere. However, as expected, in the more recent period there is a strong tendency for a larger-than-expected industry share to be found in East Asia, suggesting a regional effect at work there. Within Africa, of the sixteen

Table 1.11 Candidates for de-industrialisation

Country	Manufacturing/GDP (%)		Annual growth of manufacturing 1990–98 (%)
	1980	*1998*	
Latin America and Caribbean			
Argentina	29	19	4.3
Brazil	33	23	2.5
Chile	21	15	5.7
Colombia	18	13	−1.1
Guatemala	17	14	2.8
Jamaica	17	15	−1.8
Mexico	21	20	3.6
Nicaragua	26	15	3.1
Panama	12	9	4.2
Paraguay	16	15	0.9
Uruguay	26	18	0.3
Venezuela	16	15	1.5
Asia and Pacific			
China	41	37	14.7
Hong Kong	24	7	n.a.
Myanmar	10	6	6.7
Philippines	26	22	3.1
Papua New Guinea	10	9	5.8
Singapore	29	23	6.7
Sri Lanka	18	17	8.5
Sub-Saharan Africa			
Angola	n.a.	6	−2.7
Burundi	7	8	−9.3
Cameroon	10	11	−1.0
Central African Republic	7	9	−0.7
Congo	7	8	−2.5
Ghana	8	2	3.2
Mauritania	n.a.	9	−1.7
Kenya	13	11	2.5
Rwanda	17	13	4.6
South Africa	22	19	1.1
Zambia	18	11	−14.5
Zimbabwe	22	17	−1.7

Source: World Bank (2000).

Note
n.a. is 'not available'.

countries included, half show evidence of de-industrialisation by the technical criteria used.[32]

Conclusion

Having noted the mixed record between developing economies, the general conclusion remains that, from the available data, it appears that a significant degree of industrialisation has taken place post-1960, although only a few previously developing countries can be seen as having graduated to the group of the industrialised. Nonetheless, success in industrialisation has not been enough to transform social and economic conditions within most countries. The most obvious exception is East Asia, and to a lesser extent China, where rapid income growth, driven by manufacturing expansion, has reduced very substantially the numbers living in poverty.[33] An important question is the cause of the uneven expansion of manufacturing. Naturally one should not expect all countries to grow at equal rates, since factors like natural resource endowments, current output levels, social systems, political and economic external links, and economic policies, will all influence the growth that can be achieved in a specific period. The explanation for this range of performance is clearly complex, and this chapter only sets out basic data. The links between different aspects of policy towards manufacturing and performance are examined in later chapters.

2 Are there different paths to industrialisation?

This chapter considers different aspects of industrial policy and examines the possibility of classifying developing countries by the policies they have pursued. It also discusses the link between these aspects of policy and economic performance.

Industrial policy can be approached from a variety of perspectives, since governments may attempt to control or influence different areas of economic activity relating to the industrial sector. Consequently, industrial policy can cover a broad range of questions, for example, relating to international trade in industrial goods, the allocation of finance between enterprises, the choice and development of technology, the competitive behaviour of producers, and the relative roles of large and small-scale firms. However, if one wishes to generalise about the policies pursued across a large group of countries it is necessary to narrow the discussion to specific aspects of policy. This can allow a classification of countries in terms of their policies in these areas. In the past literature on industrialisation in developing countries, four major aspects of policy have received particular attention:

- the treatment of foreign trade, particularly the use of various forms of import taxes and trade restrictions to protect domestic industry;
- the use of direct controls, such as investment licences and price controls, to influence the allocation of resources both within industry and between industry and other sectors;
- the degree to which foreign investment by transnational firms is relied upon to provide foreign exchange and technology for new industrial projects;
- the relative roles attributed to the public and private sectors in industrial programmes.

Different intellectual perspectives have focussed on different areas of policy with, for example, the Neoclassicals concentrating primarily on the first two, and the Radical literature on the last two. The conceptual basis for the approaches of alternative schools of thought is examined in later chapters. Here the aim is to consider attempts that have been made to classify the policies pursued by different countries in these broad areas. Such attempts normally work with simple dichotomies including:

- 'open' versus 'closed' trade policies;
- 'dependent' versus 'independent' policies, particularly in relation to foreign investors;
- 'capitalist' versus 'socialist' policies on industrial ownership.

Generally, such simple distinctions require major qualification but since they have been used widely in discussions of industrial policy, it is necessary to point to some of the ambiguities they involve. Furthermore it may be of interest to see how various countries have been classed in relation to different policies and to consider whether it is possible to link particular policies with good or bad economic performance, in general, and industrial performance in particular.

Open and closed trade policies

Although industrial policy can be considered from a number of different points of view, many discussions start from the side of foreign trade, not only on the grounds that the choice of trade strategy will be important in its own right, but that it will also have a major influence on other areas of policy; for example, the degree of competition in the domestic market, and the choice of technology for new investments. A distinction that was common in the literature of the 1970s and early 1980s was that between closed or inward-looking policies and open or outward-looking policies, where the former refers to policies aimed primarily at meeting the demands of the domestic market and the latter to those that do not discriminate against, and often encourage, export sales.[1] A major theme of this literature was the superior performance of countries that pursue the latter set of policies.

In general, inward-looking economies are those that have pursued policies of import-substitution industrialisation, defined as an explicit strategy in which government policies actively encourage domestic industry to supply markets previously served by imports. Trade policy measures often employed in such economies include relatively high import tariffs, quota restrictions on imports and controls on access to foreign exchange. In such economies, the export sector is generally penalised relative to the sector producing for the home market. A technical definition is that inward-looking economies are those where in aggregate sales in domestic markets receive a higher rate of incentive than do sales for exports. Therefore, on average, the proportionate rise in the domestic price of importables relative to their world prices will be greater than the proportionate rise for exportables.[2]

In contrast, following this approach, outward-looking economies are those where the bias against exports is removed, and in the aggregate net incentives to domestic sales and exports are equal. Industrial policies of this type do not necessarily imply free trade in industrial goods since domestic prices and world prices can still diverge. However economies generally classed as outward-looking tend to have lower rates of import tariffs, and to rely much less heavily on import and foreign exchange controls than the group of inward-looking economies.

Qualifications to simple distinctions

Whilst the simple distinction between inward- or outward-oriented economies and the related policy distinction between import-substitution and export promotion may be useful in focusing on the bias inherent in various incentives to production, it needs to be qualified in several ways.

First, it is important to stress that outward-looking industrial strategies need not imply that import protection is removed. For example, of the first tier NIEs, Hong Kong, Singapore, Taiwan and Korea during their formative periods in the 1960s and 1970s, only the first can be seen as a free-trade economy, since the others maintained varying degrees of import protection. This was generally low overall, but in the case of Korea, protection was relatively high for specific manufacturing branches, for example those producing transport equipment, machinery and consumer durables. Protection for these branches in Taiwan was lower than in Korea, but was still significant for transport equipment and consumer durables.[3] Furthermore it should not be thought that import-substitution – measured as a falling share of imports in total supply – did not take place in these economies in several branches of industry. Although the incentive structure may not bias incentives in favour of home market sales, import-substitution can still take place without high import protection as domestic producers gain in experience and efficiency, and thus are able to compete with imports in the home market. This can be seen as a 'natural' form of import-substitution, where no direct policy intervention is involved. There is evidence, for example, that during the 1960s and 1970s, in Korea and Taiwan, substantial import-substitution of this type took place, despite no overall bias in favour of the home market. Further, these protected industrial activities were able to break into export markets relatively quickly.

Second, a sharp distinction between inward- and outward-looking policies ignores the shifts in policy that took place in many countries. It is well known that some of the leading outward-looking economies – again, Korea and Taiwan are the clearest examples – pursued inward-looking protectionist policies prior to their shift towards a greater export orientation in the early 1960s. However it is also important to note that, even in many economies that remained predominantly inward-looking up to the early 1990s, some shift in policy in favour of exports took place, as the need to expand exports to overcome foreign exchange crises became increasingly apparent. This often involved exchange rate devaluations to boost exports and the widespread use of duty-drawback schemes so exporters could claim refunds of import tariffs on imports used as productive inputs in export production.

Third, it should be noted that the term 'outward-looking industrial strategy' may imply, somewhat misleadingly, that for all countries following such a strategy exports form a major proportion of manufacturing output. In general, exports of manufactures can be placed in four broad categories:

- exports of processed raw materials and primary products;
- exports of intermediates required as inputs into production processes located abroad;
- exports of industries established initially to substitute for imports in the local market;
- exports of final goods produced specifically for the international market.

In only the second and fourth of these categories is it inevitable that an outward-looking approach will involve a very high proportion of exports in total output. Empirical studies have demonstrated that, in general, exports play a much larger role in total demand in small as compared with large economies. This can be explained in that large economies are likely to have a much higher proportion of manufactured exports from industries established initially to serve the local market.[4]

Exports are important for economic growth. Although in many larger developing countries they may provide a relatively small share of the total demand for manufactures, export earnings may still make a key contribution to growth by relieving a foreign exchange constraint. Thus, if growth is held back by scarcities of imported inputs or by demand deflation used to remove excess demand for foreign exchange, additional exports can play a key role in allowing the expansion of economic activity. Nonetheless, it still remains the case that even for relatively outward looking economies, exports need not dominate sales of manufactures, so that a major proportion of output may still go to the home market.

To summarise, the inward- versus outward-looking distinction has a relevance in discussions of the biases arising from trade and other policies. However, it cannot be taken to imply that outward-looking economies necessarily pursue free trade nor that they are dependent on exports for their main source of demand. Furthermore, policy shifts can take place fairly rapidly so that country classifications based on this distinction can easily become out of date. We address issues of classification below.

Classification of countries by trade strategy

The classification of countries in terms of trade strategies has proceeded in various ways. The most theoretically satisfactory approach, in line with the definitions given above, is to examine the incentive structure for manufactures to establish the direction of bias in the incentive system. Studies of this type are time-consuming and have been carried out in detail for only a limited number of countries.[5] Given this lack of comprehensive coverage there is no definitive classification of countries into those that have followed outward- or inward-looking industrial strategies. There is broad agreement, however, on some of the main members of each group. The leading outward-oriented economies are normally seen as the four East Asian NIEs – Hong Kong, Singapore, Taiwan and Korea – that achieved an impressive growth of income and exports post-1960 (although as we note on page 184, n.7, that there is dispute concerning how Korea should be treated in a classification of trade policy). These are sometimes referred to as the 'Gang of Four', and in the Neoclassical literature their success is held out as a model for other developing countries to emulate. As we noted in Chapter 1, they have been followed by a group of second tier NIEs from the same region that include Malaysia, Thailand, Indonesia and, in some discussions the Philippines.

Prior to their relatively recent trade liberalisation, the major inward-looking economies were seen as India, China and some of the larger Latin American economies, such as Mexico, Argentina and Brazil. Egypt, Turkey and the Philippines were also linked with this group. However the on-going process of trade reform has reduced significantly the number of heavily protected economies, but even in the early twenty-first century, liberalisation has been carried further in some countries than others.

In analysing country trade policy over the period from 1960 to the 1990s, several alternative indicators are available. The index of Sachs and Warner (1995) is a well known example. The authors produced an openness index based on a combination of subjective and quantitative data. A country is classed 'closed to trade' if it has one or more of the following characteristics: a socialist economic system; a state monopoly on major exports; non-tariff barriers covering more than 40% of imports; average tariffs of above 40% or a black market exchange rate that is depreciated by 20% or more relative to the official rate.[6] Table 2.1 uses the definition of openness from this index to group countries into four categories; those who are classed as open in trade policy over the whole period, those where there were changes from open to closed or vice versa, those who opened their economies relatively late (that is, from the late 1980s or early 1990s) and those who remained closed over the whole period.

From Table 2.1, the size of the late-liberaliser group gives a simple indication of the shift that has taken place in many countries since the early 1980s. Trade reform has had a major impact in Latin America, with most economies in the region falling into this group. Similarly a number of sub-Saharan African countries have also liberalised sufficiently to fall into this category. The fully open economies over the whole period include the obvious cases of Hong Kong, and Singapore but also, less obviously, Taiwan, Indonesia and Thailand. Chile is the only Latin American economy in this category, whilst Botswana and Mauritius represent Africa. The fully closed group includes the large South Asian economies of India, Pakistan and Bangladesh, as well as Egypt, many countries from sub-Saharan Africa and China. Given the very high rate of manufacturing growth that has occurred in Korea and China, how they are classed in any comparison between open and closed groups will be important.[7]

Clearly since the early 1990s trade reform has continued at a relatively rapid pace in many developing economies. Table 2.2 lists countries that went furthest

Table 2.1 Country classification Sachs–Warner openness index

Fully open economies	Policy reversals	Late liberalisers	Fully closed economies 1960–92
Barbados 1967–92	Bolivia 1960–74, 1985–92	Argentina 1991–92	Algeria
Botswana 1979–92	Costa Rica 1960–61, 1985–92	Benin 1991–92	Bangladesh
Chile 1976–92	Ecuador 1960–82, 1991–92	Brazil 1991–92	Burkina Faso
Hong Kong 1960–92	El Salvador 1960–61, 1989–92	Colombia 1986–92	Burundi
Indonesia 1971–92	Guatemala 1961, 1989–92	Gambia 1985–92	Cameroon
Jordan 1965–92	Honduras 1960–61, 1991–92	Ghana 1985–92	Central African Republic
Malaysia 1963–92	Jamaica 1962–73, 1990–92	Guinea Bissau 1987–92	Chad
Mauritius 1968–92	Kenya 1963–67	Guinea 1986–92	China
Singapore 1965–92	Morocco 1960–64, 1984–92	Guyana 1988–92	Congo
Taiwan 1963–92	Peru 1960–67, 1991–92	Mali 1988–92	Dominican Republic
Thailand 1960–92	Sri Lanka 1977–83, 1991–92	Mauritania 1992	Egypt
Yemen 1960–92		Mexico 1986–92	Ethiopia
Korea 1969–92		Nepal 1991–92	Gabon
		Nicaragua 1991–92	Haiti
		Paraguay 1989–92	India
		Philippines 1988–92	Ivory Coast
		South Africa 1991–92	North Korea
		Tunisia 1989–92	Madagascar
		Turkey 1989–92	Malawi
		Uganda 1988–92	Mozambique
		Uruguay 1990–92	Myanmar
		Venezuela 1989–92	Niger
			Nigeria
			Pakistan
			Rwanda
			Senegal
			Sierra Leone
			Somalia
			Tanzania
			Togo
			Trinidad
			Zambia
			Zimbabwe

Source: Adapted from Sachs and Warner (1995).

Note
Years shown are periods during which countries are classed as open.

in tariff reform (defined as those with the largest fall in average rates of import tariff) between the mid-1980s and the late 1990s. This list therefore excludes the obviously open economies and early liberalisers. However, it includes some of the large closed economies from Table 2.1 such as Bangladesh, China, Egypt, India and Pakistan, as well as a number of African economies, in reflection of the tariff reforms that they have introduced.

Table 2.2 Tariff reforming economies post-1985

Country	Average import tariff mid-1980s (%)	Average import tariff late 1990s (%)
Argentina	27.5	11.0
Bangladesh	92.7	26.0
Benin	42.8	12.7
Brazil	45.8	11.5
Burkina Faso	60.8	28.5
Cameroon	32.0	18.1
Central African Republic	32.0	18.8
China	38.8	20.9
Colombia	29.4	12.2
Dominica	31.9	15.0
Ecuador	34.3	11.7
Egypt	39.7	28.3
Ethiopia	29.6	16.3
India	99.4	38.3
Indonesia	27.9	13.2
Kenya	39.4	13.5
Nicaragua	22.1	10.7
Pakistan	69.2	41.7
Peru	45.0	13.3
Thailand	41.0	23.1
Uganda	25.0	13.0
Uruguay	33.7	9.6
Venezuela	31.1	12.7
Zambia	29.9	17.0

Source: Dollar and Kraay (2001) Table 2.

A question of considerable importance is whether an economy's general stance on trade policy can be linked with economic performance in general and manufacturing performance in particular. Hence is it possible to assert that through various routes trade reform improves economic activity in the aggregate? The tests of this apparently simple proposition can be conducted at different levels. A relatively unsophisticated approach requires grouping countries by the stance of their trade policy and testing for differences in average performance. An influential use of this approach was in World Bank (1987), who attempted to assess the response of different economies to the shocks of the 1970s on the basis of a classification of their trade strategy.

The results in Table 2.3 are not wholly convincing as the basis for judgement on a particular strategy. Although a small number of outward-looking economies, principally Hong Kong, Singapore and Korea (which is treated as outward-looking here), performed well and equally a few inward-looking economies performed poorly, setting aside these extremes the performance of the two moderate groups was fairly similar and hence broad comparisons are sensitive to the way individual countries are classified. As an updating and extension of this exercise we use the groupings from Tables 2.1 and 2.2 to test

Table 2.3 Manufacturing performance by trade orientation

Orientation	Average annual growth of manufacturing value added (%)		Average annual growth manufactured exports (%)	
	1963–73	1973–85	1963–73	1973–85
Strongly outward	15.6	10.0	14.8	14.2
Moderately outward	9.4	4.0	16.1	14.5
Moderately inward	9.6	5.1	10.3	8.5
Strongly inward	5.3	3.1	5.7	3.7

Source: World Bank (1987: 83–87).

Table 2.4 Differences in manufacturing growth rates: average annual growth in value-added mid-1980s to late 1990s[a]

Groupings	% growth per annum
Fully open	14.2[b]
Policy reversals	4.3
Late liberalisers	4.4
Fully closed	3.1
Tariff reformers[c]	6.2

Source: Calculated from World Bank (2000).

Notes
a Period covered is 1984–86 to 1996–98.
b Significantly different from mean for all other groups.
c Countries covered in Table 2.2.

for differences in manufacturing growth rates. Table 2.4 shows clearly that for a period from the mid-1980s to the late-1990s the fully open economy group grew significantly more rapidly than all other groupings. The performance within the fully closed group was very mixed and the average growth of 3% annually is a mixture of a very high figure for China, some respectable growth rates for large economies like India, Pakistan and Bangladesh and several negative figures principally for economies in Africa.

A more rigorous approach in terms of econometric complexity involves large numbers of cross-country regressions to establish an average pattern and to identify deviations from it.[8] Recent developments in econometrics using panel data allow the specific characteristics of individual economies to be included in models that explain growth on the basis of a combination of factor inputs, an economy's starting point (as a proxy for its human capital development) and its policy environment, particularly its openness to trade. The basic model underlying such studies is summarised in Chapter 3. The major difference between studies of this type tends to be in the measure of trade openness that is applied, since there is often little relation between alternative measures.[9]

Despite minor difference of technique and data, a number of studies concur that openness to trade has a positive, although sometimes modest, impact on long-run income growth. For example, Dollar (1992) using a relative price index as the explanatory variable for trade policy finds that, allowing for other inputs, countries with a high level of the index, implying a high price distortion and an inward orientation, tend to have lower economic growth.[10] Similarly, Edwards (1992) uses as a measure of openness an index of trade orientation based on deviations from the expected pattern of foreign trade for a given set of country characteristics. It is assumed that the greater the deviation from the norm the more closed or restrictive will be trade policy. The index is statistically significant so that, allowing for other inputs, countries with a lower degree of deviation from the expected trade pattern have a higher rate of growth. Edwards (1998) extends the analysis to productivity growth rather than aggregate income growth. Harrison (1996b) tests the robustness of the relationship between economic growth and measures of trade policy by using seven different variants of the latter. For several openness measures there is a statistically significant association with economic growth. Similarly, Greenaway *et al.* (1998) find that, once one allows for a time lag, economic growth is positively associated with openness to trade. Sachs and Warner (1995) also find that their openness index is positively associated with economic growth.

All these studies use a measure of trade policy to explain growth. However, it has been pointed out that trade will be only one of a number of aspects of economic policy, all of which may be influential, and measures of these different aspects may also be closely correlated with whatever measure of trade policy is applied. Omission of variables to capture the other aspects of policy will lead to a biased result for the impact of the trade policy variable. To overcome this problem an alternative is to examine whether countries' geographic characteristics, like size and distance from trading partners, which will be unrelated to other aspects of economic policy, can explain growth of income across countries. In other words, if some trade can be explained purely in geographical, not policy, terms does this component have an impact of growth? This is the approach of Frankel and Romer (1999) who find that this purely geographical trade variable has a positive, if only modestly significant, effect on growth. Table 2.5 summarises the results of these various studies.

Whilst econometric results such as these, that rely heavily on imperfect proxies for the underlying variables, are rarely conclusive, the unanimity of results suggests that there is a real relationship between higher growth and a trade policy of relative openness. What is less clear, and should remain the subject of dispute, is the issue of causation. Does a liberal foreign trade policy stimulate higher growth or does higher growth allow the relaxation of trade controls and does poor growth lead to the re-imposition of trade restrictions? Harrison (1996b) tests explicitly for the direction of causation and concludes that both directions of causation are possible and that neither can be ruled out. However, the Neoclassical literature, for reasons examined in Chapter 3, is unanimous in arguing that the strongly expected causation runs from openness to higher growth, rather than vice versa.[11] Authors working from different perspectives are not so sure, for reasons we consider in Chapter 4.

Table 2.5 Studies on openness and growth

Author	Period	Measure of openness	Impact
Dollar (1992)	1976–85	Real exchange rate distortion.	Lower distortion, higher GDP growth.
Edwards (1992)	1970–82	Trade patterns index.	Lower is deviation from predicted trade pattern, higher is growth of GDP.
Harrison (1996b)	1960–87	Seven alternatives for trade protection.	For three out of seven, the lower is the measure of trade protection, the higher is growth of GDP.
Edwards (1998)	1960–90	Openness index.	The more open the economy, the higher is growth of TFP in thirteen out of seventeen cases.
Greenaway *et al.* (1998)	1979–91	Three alternative measures of trade reform.	The more open the economy, the higher is growth of GDP once lag is introduced.
Frankel and Romer (1999)	1985	Geographic measure of openness to trade.	The more open the economy, the higher is growth of GDP.

Further, the precise link between manufacturing performance and trade liberalisation also remains the subject of dispute. For example, whilst openness measures may explain aggregate economic growth, they do not always work well in explanations of manufacturing growth. Jalilian and Weiss (2000) find that there is no significant relationship between openness (as measured by the Sachs–Warner index noted on page 24) and growth in manufacturing. Studies that consider trade reform and changes within manufacturing, both at the sector and enterprise levels, are discussed in more detail in Chapter 3. However, it should be noted that whilst in the literature there is evidence of positive effects from a more open trade policy, it is clear that trade reform is only one of a number of influences at work in determining productivity gains within manufacturing.

Although there can be no doubt that some export-oriented economies have grown very rapidly post-1960, nor that countries that experience high export growth find it easier to maintain a high growth of national income, one cannot necessarily deduce from this evidence support for the generalisation that outward-looking trade strategies are inevitably the most effective policy for all developing countries at all times. The real issue is how best to stimulate the long-run growth of non-traditional, manufactured exports. Does one do it through a reform of the price system involving a competitive exchange rate and the removal of various incentive biases against exports, hoping that resources will move into export manufacturing in response to these incentives?

Alternatively, does one aim to first promote a domestic manufacturing sector, which over time can become sufficiently competitive to sell abroad, provided incentives and support facilities are adequate? These are two different policy scenarios; the first can be interpreted as a simple export promotion view where potential exporters emerge in response to perceived profit opportunities, whilst the latter involves a gradual shift from import-substitution to more balanced policies. The possibility that there is a close link between initial import-substitution and later export success is raised by interpretations of the East Asian miracle that stress the role of limited government protection and export targeting in the emergence of export success. We return to these questions in subsequent chapters.

Dependent or non-dependent industrial policy

Whilst the benefits offered by globalisation have been stressed by many observers in recent years within the Radical literature on economic development, there is a long tradition that argues that the major obstacle to the economic progress of developing countries is their dependent relationship with the rich developed countries. These views are examined in more detail in Chapters 4 and 7, and here the aim is to consider whether it is possible to identify countries that can be said to have followed dependent industrial policies. The concept of 'dependence' is itself both ambiguous and controversial, and can have both economic and non-economic dimensions. The economic characteristics of dependence in developing countries mentioned most commonly are probably:

- a heavy penetration by foreign investment in the major sectors of the economy;
- the use of capital-intensive imported technologies;
- consumption patterns of domestic elites copied from the rich countries;
- 'unequal exchange' in trade, defined in various ways;
- growing inequalities in income distribution.

The first of these characteristics relating to the role of foreign investment by transnational corporations (TNCs) is generally viewed as central to the creation and continuation of dependence, and therefore a major cause of the other characteristics associated with dependence. TNCs are the representatives of international capitalism and transfer capital, technology, management and marketing techniques between countries.[12] For the discussion here a dependent industrial policy is taken to be one where the government concerned invites or allows a heavy foreign involvement in industrialisation, through foreign direct investment (FDI) by transnationals.

Unfortunately, although the concept of dependence has been used widely in the Radical literature, it does not allow a comprehensive classification of countries, partly because of lack of accurate data on the magnitude of foreign involvement in many developing countries (which extends beyond simply ownership of assets), and partly also because of the difficulty of determining what size of foreign presence is sufficient to create a dependent industrial policy. Critics of this approach have pointed out that, by the criteria of the share of foreign firms in industrial activity, many of the developed economics would appear to qualify for the description 'dependent', which appears paradoxical given the role dependence plays in explaining economic backwardness. Nevertheless, given the attention that the role of transnationals has received in the literature on industrialisation, it is necessary to summarise the data available on their involvement, and to identify the countries that have relied most heavily on foreign investment in manufacturing.

Role of TNCs

In terms of motivation for FDI it is now conventional to distinguish four types:

- resource-seeking (to exploit natural or human resources in the host economy);
- market-seeking (to supply the host economy market by local production rather than by exports);
- efficiency-seeking (to rationalise production on a global basis by sourcing parts from the host economy);
- strategic asset-seeking (to acquire assets with particular advantages through the acquisition of local firms from a host economy).

Prior to 1970 the primary and extractive sectors were the main focus for FDI in developing countries. During the 1970s, however, there was a relative shift in foreign investment towards manufacturing and services. For manufacturing, much of this investment was market-seeking and reflected the aim of TNCs to establish local production in the markets of higher income and rapidly growing developing countries. In many cases, these domestic markets had been closed to imports due to the protection associated with import-substitution trade policies. Also some of this new foreign investment in manufacturing was efficiency-seeking and reflected a shift in location for some of the more labour-intensive aspects of the production carried out by transnationals. In this 'sourcing' investment TNCs established new production units with the explicit purpose of providing parts and components to sections of the corporation in other countries. Therefore, this type of investment could contribute directly to an export-oriented industrialisation programme. As noted in Chapter 1, sourcing investment has been carried furthest in electrical goods branches, particularly in the production of electronic components. Also, recent years have seen a significant growth in mergers and acquisition as industries are restructured globally in asset-seeking foreign investment. Some of this has occurred in developing countries, particularly in Latin America and East Asia. Within manufacturing the vast majority of foreign investment assets are now held in Asia, particularly in East

Table 2.6 Stock of foreign investment in manufacturing: by developing region (millions US$)

	1988	1997
Sub-Saharan Africa	940	862
Asia	42,192	555,587
Latin America and the Caribbean	26,518	32,549

Source: UNCTAD (1999b), Annex A.

Asia, as illustrated in Table 2.6. Africa still receives very little manufacturing FDI in absolute terms.

Most analyses explaining foreign investment flows stress the role of GDP levels, GDP growth, political stability and supporting infrastructure as key factors. Also in many branches of manufacturing wage cost advantages remain important. Hence, as with other indicators of industrialisation, the flow of FDI in manufacturing has been very unevenly distributed between countries with a clear tendency for those with a higher income to receive a disproportionate share. This tendency to polarisation was heightened during the 1990s. Within Asia the main recipients in the 1990s of total foreign direct investment were China, Malaysia and Indonesia and in Latin America they were Brazil, Mexico and Argentina.[13]

In so far as foreign firm involvement implies dependence, one can gauge overall dependence by the transnationality index developed by the United Nations Conference on Trade and Development (UNCTAD). Using data from the 1990s, this index is a simple average of four indicators on TNC involvement. These are the ratios of FDI inflows to gross capital formation, FDI inward stocks to GDP, value added by foreign affiliates to GDP and employment in foreign affiliates to total employment. Unfortunately all of these figures are totals and do not relate specifically to manufacturing. The ten most dependent developing economies of the thirty for which data are compiled are, in order of dependence, Trinidad and Tobago, Singapore, Malaysia, Hong Kong, Panama, Costa Rica, Chile, Honduras, Indonesia and Colombia. Four of these economies are part of the group of NIEs in Table 1.10. With the exception of Indonesia, all are relatively small in market size and four are shown as fully open economies in Table 2.1. Of these, Trinidad is classed as fully closed. On the other hand, the ten least dependent economies by this measure in order of lack of dependence are Korea, India, Turkey, Thailand, Saudi Arabia, Brazil, Barbados, Philippines, Peru and Guatemala. Five of these are shown as NIEs in Table 1.10. They include a mixture of large (Brazil, Korea, India) and small economies (Barbados, Guatemala). In terms of trade policy, two, Korea and Thailand, are shown as fully open in Table 2.1, and one, India, as fully closed. Most of the others appear as either late liberalisers or countries with policy reversals. Hence the transnationality index appears to bear little relationship to either the conventional grouping of NIEs nor to the openness classification noted earlier, page 25.

Table 2.7 Share of foreign-owned or affiliated enterprises in manufacturing in selected countries (various years)

	Employment (%)	*Gross value of production or sales (%)*
Brazil (1995)	13	–
China (1997)	4	–
Hong Kong (1994)	16	21
Indonesia (1996)	5	–
Malaysia (1994)	44	57
Mexico (1993)	18	–
Sri Lanka (1996)	54	–
Singapore (1996)	52	70
Taiwan (1995)	21	–
Turkey (1990)	3	8
Vietnam (1995)	15	–

Source: UNCTAD (1999b) Annex A.

Data on foreign investment in manufacturing alone is patchy, and Table 2.7 gives the share of foreign owned subsidiaries or affiliated firms in employment or sales in selected economies. A major drawback of this data is that it is not clear how foreign firms are defined, in terms of the share of equity needed to constitute a foreign firm in the different countries. Nonetheless, the figures show a striking degree of foreign involvement in several countries, so that the share of foreign firms in total sales is 70% in Singapore and nearly 60% in Malaysia. In Latin America only employment shares are available and, whilst substantial in both Brazil and Mexico, they do not approach the levels found in some of the smaller economies in the table, principally Sri Lanka and Singapore.

Foreign firms have also participated in the expansion of manufactured exports from developing countries, and in some countries have come to supply a major proportion of these exports.[14] This is particularly the case in some East Asian NIEs. Table 2.8 shows estimates of the share of foreign affiliates in

Table 2.8 Share of foreign affiliates in exports of manufactures: East Asia (various years)

Country	*Year*	*Share of manufactured exports (%)*
China	1996	48
Hong Kong	1984	17
Korea	1986	26
Taiwan	1989	18
Malaysia	1992	76
Singapore	1991	92
Philippines	1983	58
Thailand	1988	33

Source: Hill and Athukorala (1998).

manufactured exports in various years. The key role of such firms in Singapore, Malaysia, and now China, is clear, although the data for other countries are much less recent.

In terms of the distribution of foreign investments between different manufacturing branches, foreign investments in developing countries tend to be greatest in the chemicals, machinery, electrical machinery and electrical goods, transport equipment and food processing branches.[15] Not surprisingly, foreign firms often dominate production in recipient countries in the more sophisticated capital-intensive manufacturing branches. The pharmaceutical branch of chemicals is probably the clearest example of this, since in many developing countries foreign firms provide over 80% of output. Foreign firms also tend to have a high share of output in branches like electrical machinery, metal products, transport equipment – particularly automobiles – and chemicals in general. However, it is difficult to generalise about transnational involvement in manufacturing on the basis of simple dichotomies between light versus heavy industry, or new versus mature products. Whilst there is evidence that transnationals are particularly strongly represented in the technologically more complex branches, it is also clear that in some countries in the past they were important in some of the more traditional branches, like textiles, tobacco and paper. Furthermore it is by no means inevitable that all complex manufacturing activities need heavy direct foreign investment. For example, in India and Korea, two of the countries in which domestic production of capital goods has advanced furthest, until recent liberalisation government policy towards these branches limited significantly the involvement of transnationals. Firms in both countries relied heavily on technology transfer agreements and licensing rather than FDI as a means of obtaining foreign technology. Hence in these countries, direct transnational participation in capital goods production through either wholly-owned subsidiaries, or through joint ventures where they have a majority ownership, has been relatively low, in contrast, for example, with the situation in Brazil and Mexico.

Large domestic groups and TNCs from developing countries

In some countries post-1960, large nationally-owned manufacturing firms emerged, often as part of conglomerates with a variety of sectoral interests including banking. These domestic groups themselves later undertook direct investment overseas to become TNCs in a process, which appeared to run directly counter to the dependency argument. Table 2.9 summarises data on the fifty largest manufacturing enterprises in the higher income developing countries. The dominance of Korean groups is clear and the number of groups for the East Asian NIEs would be increased if data on Hong Kong and Singapore had been included. National private groups are less significant in Latin America, where both TNCs and state enterprises play a proportionately greater role in manufacturing.

The phenomenon of direct foreign investment by firms with a head office in

Table 2.9 Distribution of fifty largest manufacturing enterprises by type and country (1993)

Country[a]	Groups[b]	Specialised[c]	State owned	TNC affiliates	Total
Argentina	1				1
Brazil		1	2	4	7
India	1		2		3
Indonesia	1		1		2
Korea	26				26
Mexico	1		1	3	5
Taiwan	1	2	2		5
Thailand	1				1

Source: Amsden (2001) Tables 8.2a and 8.2b.

Notes
a Data on Hong Kong and Singapore are not given.
b Private sector groups with operations in more than one manufacturing branch.
c Private sector enterprises specialised in one branch.

Table 2.10 Top fifty TNCs from developing countries (1998)

	Share in total foreign assets
Asia	65.7
of which PRC	8.8
Hong Kong	22.0
India	0.8
Korea	16.7
Malaysia	6.3
Philippines	1.5
Singapore	7.2
Taiwan	2.4
Latin America	28.2
of which Argentina	4.1
Brazil	7.6
Chile	3.4
Mexico	5.9
Venezuela	7.3
Africa	6.3
Total	100.0[a]

Source: UNCTAD (2000) Table 3.15.

Note
a Slight rounding error.

a developing country is not new, but the numbers of such firms have grown rapidly since the 1970s, although their size is still small in relation to total FDI.[16] As is to be expected, almost all of the large international firms from developing countries come from the NIEs. Table 2.10 gives data on the fifty largest transnationals from developing countries.

Although much of this investment is outside manufacturing, in activities like trade, telecommunications and construction, nonetheless these activities can be interpreted as an important illustration of the depth of the industrialisation that is taking place in the higher income developing countries. The first wave of FDI from developing country firms commenced in the 1970s with investment by firms from relatively protected home markets. Their advantages were seen as lying principally in technological adaptation, that is the modification and application of standardised technologies in ways that suited production conditions in poor economies. The conventional view was that firms from developing countries could compete overseas using either smaller-scale, less modern and perhaps more labour-intensive technology to that in use in developed economies. This type of technology was seen as more appropriate for the market conditions of other developing countries. In addition, since some relatively large conglomerates or groups were involved, these new TNCs could obtain the benefits of scale economies in finance, managerial and technical resources. This early FDI was primarily market-seeking, in the sense that it aimed to supply goods for the domestic markets of the host economies and was often motivated by the need to avoid import barriers against direct exports from the home economy.

Whilst this interpretation may have been valid in the 1970s and early 1980s to explain advantages, for example of Indian firms in other South Asian or African markets, it is clearly inadequate to explain the second wave of FDI by firms from NIEs. Since the second half of the 1980s, firms from these economies have been investing heavily in a range of locations, both in lower-wage developing economies and in Europe and North America. The prime movers here have been firms from Hong Kong, Singapore, Korea and Taiwan – the original first tier NIEs – and this burst of FDI is no doubt related directly to their accumulation of economic competitiveness. The industries involved tend to be relatively sophisticated technologically and here FDI reflects the advantages derived from the growing technological capability these firms have achieved in these sectors. Overseas investment in developed country markets is both market-seeking to exploit this technical advantage through local production rather than foreign trade and to acquire strategic assets through the acquisition of firms from developed economies. For example, Samsung and Hyundai (Korea) and Acer (Taiwan) have made major acquisitions of electronics firms in many higher income economies. In addition, there has been a regional focus to much of this FDI with firms from the East Asian NIEs investing in other countries in the region, such as Vietnam or the Philippines, to take advantage of lower wage costs there. The interpretation is that TNCs from the NIEs have begun to behave very similarly to TNCs from developed economies.

The 1990s also saw the re-emergence of significant FDI by Latin American transnationals. This was primarily by local groups from Mexico, Argentina, Chile and Brazil, who aimed to internationalise their production in response to the highly liberalised trading and investment environment in the region. The advantages of such firms are said to lie more in management and finance than in technological upgrading, so they are active principally in the technologically more mature branches of manufacturing, for example transport equipment, engineering, food and drink, cement, steel and glass, which is a major contrast with firms from the East Asian NIEs. The bulk of this FDI is within Latin America and the motive is principally market-seeking to supply regional markets with local production rather than through foreign trade, although there are instances of acquisitions for the assets and expertise of the firm concerned. Here FDI to exploit low labour costs is also relatively rare.[17]

FDI and economic performance

In terms of trade classifications, as noted earlier (page 23), it appears that there is no direct link between dependence in industrial policy, as defined by the degree of transnational involvement, and inward- or outward-looking trade policies. For the 1970s and 1980s, several of the inward-looking economies, such as Brazil and Mexico, relied heavily on manufacturing foreign investments, whilst others, particularly India, did not. For the outward-looking group reliance on transnationals has varied; taking the 'Gang of Four', for example, transnationals have played a much more important role in Singapore than in the other three countries. It does not seem possible therefore to link dependent industrialisation, defined in this way, simplistically with a particular trade strategy. However, since the second half of the 1980s it has become increasingly common for manufacturing foreign investment to be aimed at export rather than national markets, in part in response to the trade liberalisation that has occurred in many countries.[18]

Many studies consider whether a link can be established between a measure of dependence and economic performance. As noted earlier, probably the most common quantitative indicator of dependence is some measure of transnational corporation involvement in an economy, such as the UNCTAD transnationality index. A large number of studies, for example, test for a statistical relationship between transnationals' penetration of an economy and growth in national income.[19] A common finding is that high foreign investment inflows are generally associated with high rates of economic growth, with the possibility of dual causation, both from foreign investment to growth and from growth to more investment inflows in response to profit opportunities in an expanding market. The evidence on causation is sufficiently ambiguous to allow for the possibility that under different country circumstances either direction is possible. However there is also evidence of a threshold effect at work, which implies that a country has to achieve a minimum level of absorptive capacity, for example in terms of human resources, technological capability or general macro economic competence, before it can benefit from foreign capital inflows.

For example, Blomstrom *et al.* (1994) test for a relation between FDI share in GDP and GDP growth per capita. They find a significant positive relationship across developed economies. When the developing country group is divided by income level it is only within the higher income half of the group that such a positive relationship is found. The importance of a minimum education level to benefit from FDI was highlighted by Borenzstein *et al.* (1998). Similarly, Lipsey

(2000) introduces lagged relations between FDI inflows and growth and finds that the FDI to GDP ratio in one year is positively and significantly related to GDP growth in the following year. However, the strength of this effect is related to country circumstances, since when the FDI inflow is combined with a measure of the level of schooling of the population, the overall explanatory power of the analysis is improved.

The importance of the policy environment for the impact of FDI on economic performance is demonstrated by Balasubramanyam and Sapsford (1996). Using a production function model with foreign capital as a separate factor of production, they show that when their sample of forty-six developing countries is split into those following closed (import substitute) and open (export promotion) trade policies that the coefficient on the foreign capital variable is both significant and positive for the latter group, but insignificant for the former. In other words, foreign capital appears to contribute positively to growth in the more open (and, by implication, more competitive) economies, whilst having no discernible impact on growth in the more closed (and, by implication, less efficient) economies.[20]

This evidence addresses the link between FDI and economic growth in general rather than between FDI and manufacturing performance. Nonetheless, given the normally close relation between growth of national income and manufacturing, reported in Chapter 1, the expectation is that similar relations apply and that FDI has been one of the driving forces of manufacturing growth in countries with a critical minimum level of absorptive capacity. Clearly not all developing countries have benefited significantly from FDI inflows, but a narrow dependency interpretation of poor countries drained of resources by large global corporations is now difficult to sustain. However, in the past, some countries have chosen to stress their independence from world market forces as part of a socialist (or nominally socialist) strategy of development, which involved significant restrictions on the access of TNCs to domestic markets. We consider this path to industrialisation below.

Socialist industrial policies

The data considered up to this point have not distinguished between countries on the basis of socioeconomic system, whether capitalist, socialist or a form of 'intermediate regime', and have been confined largely to capitalist developing countries. One might expect that policies in socialist economies would differ significantly from those in capitalist economies with a similar income level and resource endowment, and in the period from 1960 to the late 1980s there were a number of countries in which government rhetoric implied a socialist pattern of development as a central objective.

In considering which developing countries might qualify for the classification of socialist, it is clear that measures of the degree of public sector involvement in economic activity, for example in terms of its share in new investment or in manufacturing output, are inadequate on their own. For example, World Bank

(1993b) brings together such data for a number of developing countries, and in the period from the late 1970s to early 1990s, by this type of indicator, a relatively significant role for the public sector is identified in several, such as Algeria, Burundi, Congo, Egypt, Tunisia, and Turkey, that many would feel were far from socialist judged by the practice of their political regimes. In addition, the official statements of governments are also of little value in assessing the social base of their support and the overall direction of their policies. Most observers rely on judgement rather than on objective tests of socialism when attempting this type of classification. Table 2.11 summarises one attempt, based on policies and practice up to the early 1980s. This employs the concept of an 'intermediate regime' to cover a relatively large number of ambiguous cases. These can be seen as regimes where the power of large private capital had been weakened very substantially and where state officials, often with the support of lower middle-class groups, played a major role in directing the economy. Socialism in the sense of full public ownership and widespread working class or peasant involvement had not been attained.[21] This classification of countries was never acceptable to all, and is reproduced here as a reminder that up to relatively recently a number of developing countries were widely seen as socialist and their performance vis-à-vis capitalist economies of a similar type was contrasted in serious comparative studies.[22]

Table 2.11 Classification of socialist and socialist intermediate developing countries (early 1980s)

Socialist countries	Socialist intermediate regimes
Middle-income	Middle-income
Albania	Algeria
Angola	Iraq
Congo	Libya
Cuba	Nicaragua
North Korea	Yugoslavia
Mongolia	Zambia
Romania	Zimbabwe
Yemen P.D.R.	
Low-income	Low-income
Afghanistan	Burma
Benin	Guinea
China	Madagascar
Ethiopia	Somalia
Kampuchea	Tanzania
Laos	
Mozambique	
Vietnam	

Source: White (1984) Table 1.

Note
Countries on which White is doubtful – Syria, Tunisia and Sudan – have been omitted.

The list in Table 2.11 reveals a wide diversity, with some countries, particularly Benin, Ethiopia, Somalia, Tanzania, Burma and Mozambique where little industrialisation had taken place. In others, however, particularly Romania, Yugoslavia, China and North Korea, both socialism and industrial development have a longer history. However the collapse of the Soviet Union and the shifting political orientation of elites in these countries, combined with external pressure for policy change arising from the conditionality imposed by international agencies, has meant that the list in Table 2.11 no longer even loosely reflects the contemporary situation. Of the countries identified as either socialist or intermediate regimes in the 1970s and early 1980s, now probably only China, North Korea, Vietnam and Cuba would be classed by most observers as falling into this category. Further apart from North Korea, the economic policies in the other countries have changed significantly over this period with significant moves towards both greater use of markets as a means of resource allocation and divestiture and privatisation of state industrial enterprises.[23]

In terms of industrial policies, there was always a significant diversity within the grouping of socialist developing countries, although it is clear that industrialisation can be expected to have a key role in a socialist economic strategy. Industrialisation was seen not only as a means of raising material living standards, but in addition as a way of reducing dependence on foreign trade and a hostile external environment, and of extending the political base of a regime through the creation of an industrial proletariat. In the early post-1945 period, the Soviet model was highly influential, with the path to industrialisation viewed as that marked out there in the 1920s and 1930s. This inward-looking industrialisation, with a strong emphasis on the production of domestic capital goods, was a characteristic of the industrialisation programmes of the majority of socialist developing economies in the 1950s and 1960s. This pattern created high growth in some countries, most notably in China, but at the same time created costs and inefficiencies that received increasing attention during the 1970s. The list of alleged inefficiencies included lack of access to modern technology, high cost and low quality production by international standards, imbalances between consumer demands and domestic supplies, and a scarcity of foreign exchange. There is a similarity here with many of the arguments on the inefficiencies of import-substitution industrialisation in capitalist developing countries, and similar issues appear to have been debated in the context of socialist planning with some differences of emphasis and terminology. In China and Vietnam the policy response to these arguments has been moves towards trade liberalisation, a far more open policy on foreign technology and investment, and a shift towards greater use of markets as a means of allocating resources. Changes in North Korea have been far slower.

The small, poor socialist economies in Central America and Africa always relied heavily on traditional exports and concessional support from the Soviet bloc to provide foreign exchange. At various times this group included Cuba, Nicaragua, Angola, Mozambique and Ethiopia. Here the small size of the domestic market and the general poverty of the countries meant that large-scale industrialisation programmes to establish integrated industrial sectors in these economies were largely inapplicable. Scarcity of foreign exchange was a key constraint and the traditional export sector continued to play a major role to allow the imports of plant and equipment necessary to restructure the economy. Of these countries now Cuba remains alone in maintaining its nominal allegiance to socialist ideals, although again there have been moves to open the economy to foreign trade, foreign investment and in particular tourism. Whether such economic change is compatible with existing socialist political systems is open to much debate with many feeling that in countries like China, Cuba and Vietnam a move from socialism to a form of liberal political pluralism is, if not inevitable, then very likely.

However, it must be stressed that, despite past practice, there is nothing inherently contradictory between avowedly socialist regimes using the market as a means of resource allocation. It was the Stalinist command economy model of central planning that provided the blueprint for planning systems in several of the socialist developing economies. Other elements of the socialist tradition, such as the brief period of the New Economic Policy in the early 1920s in the Soviet Union and the theoretical academic literature of the 1930s associated with optimality under public ownership, allow for the functioning of market relationships between enterprises, consumers and workers. The qualifications necessary to maintain a socialist dimension are that markets are used to achieve democratically determined public goals, that any undesirable distributional changes created by this reliance on markets are compensated for by government interventions and that public ownership is retained in critical sectors (the so-called 'commanding heights' of an economy).

At one point it appeared that socialist industrialisation might have turned Marx on his head by succeeding in relatively backward and peripheral contexts and emerging as an historical substitute rather than as an historical successor to capitalism. This claim now appears hollow given the shift in direction in recent years.[24] On the contrary the weak performance of socialist industrialisation whether in Africa (Angola, Mozambique), Central Asia (in many ex-Soviet Republics), Central America (Cuba, Nicaragua) or East Asia (Vietnam, North Korea) is well known. There is strong evidence that closed economies tend to foster obsolete technology and high cost activities and the only successful socialist industrialisation in a development context has occurred in China after its reform initiatives commencing in the late 1970s, which led to decentralisation of many decisions to enterprises, the development of market relations and ultimately an opening to the world market. The socialist path as practised up to the mid-1980s has been abandoned virtually everywhere and, whilst unreformed political systems may remain in power in a few countries, economic reforms in those economies are generally seen as positive steps necessary for improvements in material wellbeing.

In the unambiguously non-socialist developing countries, state enterprises were used to channel public funds to the manufacturing sector, principally in the heavy branches of industry characterised by high levels of capital investment and hence relatively high levels of risk for the private sector. Public ownership in lighter consumer goods industries was most common in economies with only a small private sector, for example in parts of Africa, where the alternatives were seen as either public investment or investment by foreigners, often from minority, that is Asian, ethnic origins.[25] These initiatives were often not ideologically driven but reflected the need to boost industry where private investment was not forthcoming.

Even in the early 1990s, manufacturing state enterprises remained important in petroleum-based activities, iron and steel and some heavy machinery activity.[26] The efficiency of such enterprises and their alleged drain on public sector finances received very considerable attention in policy debates and most developing countries embarked on privatisation programmes in the 1990s, with manufacturing enterprises often the first candidates.[27] Hence in the vast majority of developing countries, state-owned manufacturing enterprises are becoming increasingly rare and industrial initiatives are seen primarily as the preserve of the private sector.

Conclusion

This chapter has considered different perspectives on industrial policy in developing countries, and discussed how individual countries may be classified on the basis of their policies. In the period since 1960 a relatively small number of developing countries have performed extremely well in terms of growth of both GNP and industry. Up to the early 1970s, it was not easy to distinguish between countries within this group on the basis of trade policy, but in the turmoil of the 1970s an outward-looking sub-group, whose performance was strongly influenced by the first-tier NIEs, appears to have done considerably better than the inward-looking economies. Since then a follower group of second-tier NIEs from the same region have also had significantly high rates of economic growth. Relatively closed, often highly distorted economies have not, in general, done well in growth terms. FDI has appeared to be an important engine for growth in some countries, principally those where the mix of policy and the education base is supportive. Socialist strategies of industrialisation have now largely been abandoned in favour of a more open, market-based alternative driven by private capital.

In terms of the title of the chapter, it appears that there is only limited scope for choosing different paths to industrialisation. The desirability of de-linking from the world market by restricting trade and capital flows and thus bypassing the process of globalisation was once advocated as a plausible option. Today this appears highly unrealistic given the need for both foreign finance and technology. Also whilst public ownership in a socialist path to industrialisation cannot be ruled out in principle, recent practice suggests that the state in developing countries lacks the capacity to provide the material base necessary for a socialist transformation of these societies. The implication is that the goal of sustained economic growth will require developing countries to participate in the process of globalisation that accelerated rapidly in the last quarter of the twentieth century. Nevertheless, despite this broad conclusion, legitimate areas of dispute remain in relation to specific policy issues. The purpose of the chapters that follow is to explore the theoretical arguments that underlie different analyses of industrial performance and policy.

3 Neoclassical orthodoxy dominant

In contrast with the early literature on industrialisation which we discuss in Chapter 4, a clearly defined and logically consistent alternative view became increasingly influential during the 1970s and became the dominant perspective by the early 1980s. This is what is conventionally termed the Neoclassical perspective or paradigm, which essentially brings the tools of conventional economic analysis to bear on the problem of development. Little (1982), one of the foremost authors of this school, defined its key characteristic as a belief in the importance of the price mechanism and of the role that market forces can play in development policy. Little's explanation of 'the Neoclassical vision of the world' is worth quoting, since it provides a clear statement of the Neoclassical position in the development context:

> a Neoclassical vision of the world is one of flexibility. In their own or their families' interests, people adapt readily to changing opportunities and prices, even if they do not like doing so, and even though they may take their time. Businesses pursue objectives roughly consistent with the assumption that they maximize risk and time discounted profits.... There is usually a wide variety of ways of making things such that production methods can be expected to shift when input prices change. Demand schedules are consequently curves, neither kinked nor vertical. Supply schedules are also smooth and rarely vertical. Although demand and supply always depend to a greater or lesser extent on expectations of an uncertain future, nevertheless most markets usually tend to achieve an equilibrium without wild price fluctuations. In short the price mechanism can be expected to work rather well.[1]

The paragraph that follows this quotation makes it clear that the possibility that markets may also fail to work effectively in some circumstances is not ruled out. However a focus on the effectiveness of the market mechanism as a means of allocating resources is a central tenet of this approach. Coupled with this is also an emphasis on the potential gains from participation in world trade, and the cost to developing countries of neglecting the trade option.

The Neoclassical approach to industrialisation has strongly influenced governments and international agencies and, in recent years, has come to be linked with the broader stabilisation and adjustment programmes applied in many developing countries. The reforms introduced as part of such programmes aim not only to allow markets to function freely, but also to control inflation, primarily by monetary policy and in general to reduce substantially the share of the state in economic activity.[2]

Here two issues are the primary focus of attention. The first is the argument that government intervention stifles the operation of markets and contributes to an economically inefficient form of industrialisation, hence the recommendation to leave as much as possible to the market, in a 'market-friendly' industrialisation strategy. The second is the view that, in relation to trade, past policies associated with import-substitution have reduced export growth, ignored specialisation on the basis of comparative advantage and created significant misuse of resources. Since the concept of economic efficiency underlies much of this analysis, it is necessary initially to clarify what is meant in this context.

Economic efficiency

Efficiency is an ambiguous concept, since it must be related to performance in the achievement of particular objectives. Theoretically the problem of multiple objectives must be overcome by placing weights on each objective, so that the total contribution of an activity to the overall set of objectives, termed the 'objective function', can be assessed. The Neoclassical literature focuses primarily, but not exclusively, on the objective of utilising existing resources so as to create the maximum possible national income; what is generally referred to as the 'objective of allocative efficiency'. Efficiency in this sense, therefore, refers to the effectiveness of given resources in creating output and thus income. Additional objectives such as the growth of income over time, or the distribution of the benefits of growth, often via additional employment, can be allowed for, at least in principle. However, the most common use of the term efficiency is in the allocative sense.

As has been stressed, the defining characteristic of Neoclassical analysis is its emphasis on markets as a means of allocating resources. The argument is that with a few well defined exceptions, if left to operate freely, markets will create a more efficient allocation of resources than would government interventions. The theory underlying Neoclassical policy discussions of industrialisation can be illustrated using a simple two commodity model of foreign trade.

We consider an economy producing two goods, A and B, both of which are internationally tradable. The combinations of A and B that can be produced from given domestic resources are shown in Figure 3.1 by the concave curve AB, termed the production possibility frontier, and drawn assuming increasing unit costs. Potentially, allocative efficiency can be achieved when production takes place at any point of this curve, since a given quantity of resources will be producing the maximum possible output. The economically efficient combination of A and B will depend upon the relative prices of these commodities. Relative domestic prices are shown in Figure 3.1 by the price line *DD*. It can be demonstrated that under perfectly competitive conditions, with given resources, domestic production will be at point P_1 where *DD* is a tangent to AB. At this point in technical terms the marginal rate of transformation in production, given by the slope of AB, equals the ratio of the two prices. In other words, the ratio of the cost of producing an extra unit of each commodity is equal to the ratio of the price of each commodity. This is allocatively efficient, in that production of one good cannot be increased without reducing that of the other. Costs in this case will be opportunity costs, that is output lost elsewhere. The cost per unit of A is therefore the output of B foregone by producing an extra unit of A.

The possibility raised by international trade is reflected in Figure 3.1 by the introduction of an international price line *II*, which will differ from the domestic one where there is non-uniform tariff or quota protection. In other words, where the ratio of domestic prices for A and B differs from the international ratio, the efficient exploitation of trade possibilities requires that domestic production shifts to P_2, where the marginal rate of transformation in

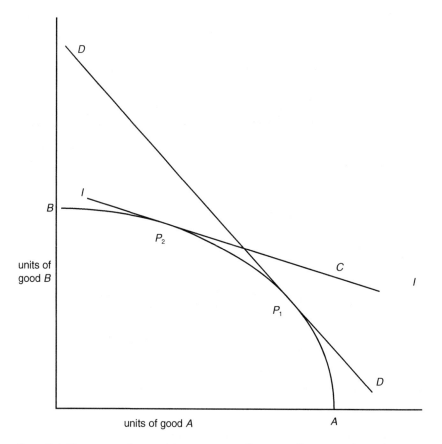

Figure 3.1 Two-commodity model representing allocative efficiency under trade.

production equals the international, rather than the domestic, price ratio. In this example, output of A is contracted whilst that of B is expanded, implying that the country's comparative advantage lies in the latter. Allocative efficiency is increased by this move, since the country, whilst producing at P_2, can trade along the international price line II, and obtain any combination of A and B along that line. The actual combination chosen will depend on demand conditions, but there is the potential to obtain more of A and B than would be possible before trade. For example at C, the levels of A and B consumed are higher than at P_1, where they are supplied from domestic production alone. For the given amount of domestic resources, therefore, trade has allowed more of one commodity to be obtained without less of the other.

This simple model has been used to support various important propositions, including the following:[3]

- that a perfectly competitive domestic market can achieve an efficient allocation of resources;
- that no trade is an inferior strategy to free trade;
- that once trade commences, decisions on what to produce can be divorced from decisions on what to consume;
- that relative international prices should be used to guide domestic production for traded or tradable commodities;
- that the relevant domestic costs for assessing efficiency are opportunity costs that can be defined in relation to international trading opportunities.

The criteria from the Neoclassical literature used to assess economic efficiency in production draw heavily on these propositions. In particular, it is argued that internationally traded goods should be valued at their world prices, and non-traded goods and labour at their opportunity costs. However, the model as stated here is clearly a major simplification of reality, and any applied criteria used to judge economic efficiency must attempt to overcome these simplifications. Several simplifying assumptions can be noted, since they have important implications for the use of efficiency criteria.

First, as stated here, the model makes the 'small country assumption' for the economy concerned. In other words, world prices are given exogenously and are not influenced by the economy's level of imports or exports. Where this assumption does not hold, the 'optimum tariff' case for protection becomes relevant, as a country improves its terms of trade by imposing taxes on imports or exports. As far as the logic of the model is concerned, economic efficiency requires the equality of the marginal rate of transformation in production with the marginal, and not the average, international price ratio. In this situation, therefore, it should be per unit marginal import costs and export revenues that allow for the impact of price changes on the quantities currently purchased or supplied, that should guide decisions on domestic production. However, relatively few developing countries will influence world prices and this qualification remains largely of theoretical interest.

Second, of considerably more practical consequence is the fact that, in probably the majority of markets in developing countries, conditions far removed from those of a perfectly competitive market will prevail. In addition to government interventions, domestic factors may be immobile, production may be dominated by a small number of oligopolistic firms, external effects may be important and information on market opportunities may be lacking. The existence of non-competitive market conditions implies that there will be two domestic cost structures; one for individual producers, often termed 'private costs', and another for the whole economy, what we term 'economic costs'. The domestic private marginal rate of transformation will differ, therefore, from the economic rate and efficiency requires that it is the latter that is equated with the international price ratio.[4]

The theoretical problems posed by these 'distortions' or deviations from perfect competition were considered at length in the international trade theory literature. The case had been argued that such deviations from competitive conditions provided a rationale for departures from free trade, in the form of tariff or quota protection. For example, if labour market distortions meant that the private cost of employing a worker exceeded their economic cost, it was argued that this provided a justification for raising the profitability of domestic industry through protection to offset its disadvantage in labour costs. However, the conclusion to emerge from these debates was that, theoretically, deviations from perfectly competitive conditions do not provide a justification for protection *per se*, since tax-subsidy measures are a more effective means of offsetting distortions. The logic of the argument is that, whilst tariffs or quotas might counter some of the effects of distortions arising from non-competitive domestic markets, they would introduce additional costs of their own, in terms of deviations between domestic and world prices for traded goods. The 'first-best' solution is a set of taxes and subsidies aimed as directly as possible at removing the distortion concerned.[5] However, whilst non-competitive domestic markets may not invalidate the theoretical conclusions of the model in terms of the superiority of free trade, they do mean that prevailing domestic prices in these markets are no guide to economic costs. This provides the rationale for estimating economic or 'shadow' prices for commodities and factors as a guide to the economic efficiency of new activities.[6] Economic prices must be applied to estimate the economic costs of domestic production, and efficiency requires that it is relative economic costs that are equated with world prices.

The third area of simplification relates to the omission of non-traded goods. Non-traded goods can be interpreted as commodities which an economy does not trade internationally, and whose prices are unaffected by world market trends. The introduction of non-traded items raises both theoretical and practical difficulties. For these goods decisions on what to produce cannot be divorced from those on what to consume. Furthermore production decisions cannot be guided by world prices, since there is no relevant world price for these items. The economic valuation of these goods requires reference to domestic market conditions, either in production or consumption, which is often the most difficult aspect of the application of economic efficiency criteria.

Finally, and perhaps most significantly, there are a range of dynamic arguments not allowed for in the simple static formulation of this trade model. The most important of these relate to learning and technical change over time. There is no guarantee that the activities in which a country has a current comparative advantage (B in this case) will be those where these dynamic effects are most significant, so that a policy that focuses only on short-term cost considerations need not be in the longer-term interests of the economy. The Neoclassical approach treats these dynamic arguments as further instances of market failure or non-competitive conditions; if producers do not move into dynamic activities this may be due to the fact that they do capture all of the gains, an example of externalities in production arising over time, or due to their lack of foresight, an example of information failure. The first-best policy recommendation is therefore that these should be handled like all other distortions by tax-subsidy measures. This would imply either using a subsidy to encourage firms to shift into activities with greatest dynamic potential or improving information dissemination on market opportunities.

Trade liberalisation and Neoclassical theory

Given its emphasis on the benefits of freeing trade from various tariff or quota restrictions, it is not surprising that Neoclassical theory provides the rationale for the trade liberalisation in most developing countries discussed in Chapter 2. Barriers to trade in the form of quotas or tariffs will create a divergence between domestic and world prices. This means that, under protection, domestic producers and consumers will be responding to the 'wrong' or distorted set of relative prices for different items. In the logic of the model this means that gains generated by the possibility of specialisation following comparative advantage are lost and real income is lower than it otherwise would be. Trade liberalisation in the sense of moving relative domestic prices closer to relative world prices will improve real income as resources shift in the 'right' direction to more efficient uses. This is illustrated in Figure 3.1 by a movement along the production possibility frontier in response to a change in relative prices induced by trade reform. If an economy starts with protection it will be at point P_1 and full trade liberalisation will result in a move to P_2. Alternatively if trade reform is partial, so some tariffs or quotas remain, welfare can still be improved if the domestic relative price line is moved closer to the world price ratio than in the pre-reform case. The gain arises from the fact that, whilst prior to reform production was at point P_1, with partial reform it shifts to a point which is closer to P_2 than was the original production point P_1 and this shift implies greater specialisation in the comparatively more efficient product B.

This conventional resource re-allocation gain from liberalising trade requires the assumption of perfect resource mobility so that producers can shift effortlessly between alternative activities. In practice instant adjustment is extremely unlikely and there will be adjustment costs, for example if resources shifting out of A cannot be absorbed immediately in B. Further, allocative gains arising from resource reallocation will be once-for-all and will cease once domestic relative prices accurately reflect trade opportunities. Empirical estimates of the allocative efficiency gains of this type have typically been only a small proportion of national income. Figure 3.2 illustrates the so-called 'welfare triangles' that are the costs at a micro level associated with the allocative losses arising from protection. The figure refers to a protected domestic market with a tariff of t which creates a domestic price Pd, of $Pw + t$, where Pw is the equivalent world price and t is the effect of the import tariff. At this price in the domestic market, domestic supply is OQ_1 and imports are Q_1D_1. The gross economic cost of the tariff is $PdABPw$, since domestic use of the protected good falls by DD_1. However of this, the rectangle $EACF$ is revenue to the government from the import tariff and $PdEGPw$ is surplus income to protected domestic suppliers. Hence the net cost is the two relatively small triangles EFG and ABC.

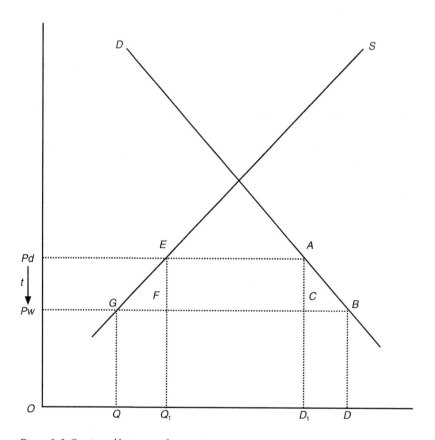

Figure 3.2 Static welfare cost of protection.

The more interesting question relates to the dynamic or long-run cost of protection. In other words, can we state with confidence that due to protection an economy will have a lower growth of productivity and hence income over time? This is more controversial since the theory as set out here is essentially short run and the gains from freer trade set out above are once-for-all rather than cumulative. However the more recent Neoclassical perspective on economic growth incorporates technical change and the impact of the policy environment on technical change. In other words, the negative link between protection and economic growth is that, in a relatively closed or protected economy, enterprises will be both less aware of technical change internationally and will have less incentive to adopt best practice innovation. This argument is set out more formally below.

Endogenous growth models

A specific strand of Neoclassical analysis relates to the study of growth. In the conventional Neoclassical growth model economic growth is determined by the growth of labour and capital inputs plus the impact of technical change.[7] Formally, in its simplest version the standard Neoclassical growth equation can be written as:

$$Y = A(t).(K^{1-a}, L^a) \tag{3.1}$$

where Y is national income,
K is the stock of capital
L is the labour supply
and A denotes the stock of public knowledge on technology,
with (t) signalling A is a function of time.

Equation (3.1) is based on assumptions of perfect competition and a reflects the share of wages in national income, so that $(1 - a)$ is the share of capital. Technical change is given exogenously, unexplained by the model itself.

Equation (3.1) can be rewritten in per worker terms, where L is number of workers and:

$y = Y/L$ (or income per worker)
$k = K/L$ (or capital stock per worker).

Using growth rates denoted by d we can express the growth of income per worker as:

$$dy = (1 - a)dk + dA \tag{3.2}$$

Equation (3.2) states that income per worker grows at a rate equal to the growth of the capital–labour ratio (k) multiplied by the share of profits in national income $(1 - a)$ plus the rate of technical change (dA). Hence the income growth due to technical change can be defined as the growth of income per worker minus the term $(1 - a)dk$. This forms the basis for analyses of total factor productivity growth (that we discuss later in this chapter), where the latter is treated as the unexplained residual growth that cannot be accounted for by growth of labour and capital inputs, which are reflected in dk. Hence, by rearranging equation (3.2), total factor productivity growth is:

$$dA = dy - (1 - a)dk$$

'New' or endogenous growth theory modifies the conventional Neoclassical analysis by treating technical change as a variable to be explained within the model rather than given exogenously. Once one allows for this, technology will not be freely available to all economies, but more realistically its level will differ between economies and will be a function of variables such as past investment either in physical capital or human capital, research and development activity, or economic policy. As a simple illustration in the spirit of endogenous growth, we can modify equation (3.2) so that

$$Yj = A(R).(Rj, Kj, Lj) \tag{3.3}$$

Where, as before, Y, A, K and L are income, technical change, capital and labour inputs, and the subscript refers to individual firm j. R is total research and development activity in the economy and Rj is research and development activity by firm j.

In equation (3.3) output in firm j is a function of research, capital and labour inputs from the firm itself (signified with subscript j) and the stock of public knowledge A, which depends on the collective research and development activity of all firms R. National output Y is now an aggregation of the output of all firms. Research expenditure by individual firms creates an external benefit for other firms via knowledge creation through the term A. The existence of such externalities is the theoretical means of justifying continued growth in the face of diminishing returns to individual factors.

This discussion may appear highly abstract, but it has an important policy dimension, since it gives a theoretical basis for the key dynamic element of the Neoclassical analysis. This is the argument that, in a competitive market environment that is open to international trade, the incentive to invest in knowledge creation and to innovate will be maximised. In this view, the main costs of import tariffs and controls are not in terms of inefficiency in the allocation of existing resources (the triangles in Figure 3.2), but in the barriers to innovation and the development of new products that they create. In terms of Figure 3.1, by this argument, the true costs of distortions are not to be found in the comparison between the combination of existing or 'old' goods A and B, but rather between the actual combination of A produced under protection and the combination of 'new' goods arising from product innovation not shown in the diagram that would be available in the long-run under a liberalised trading policy.[8]

The argument can be extended by incorporating foreign trade into equation (3.3). Now A, the stock of public knowledge, depends not just on national research expenditure, but also on the speed of technological 'catch-up' by a particular economy relative to international best-practice. Openness to foreign trade and markets then becomes a determinant of the inflow of knowledge and hence provides a dynamic link between trade reform and economic performance via technical change. Following this reasoning, we can write:

$$Yj = A(R,C).(Rj,Kj,Lj) \tag{3.4}$$

Where all items are as before, whilst C is catch-up for the economy relative to international best-practice technology. The speed of catch up is taken to be a function of trade policy and the assumption is that more open economies catch up more rapidly, so there is a negative relation between C and the height of trade barriers.[9]

Neoclassical theory has been criticised in the past for a neglect of the institutional dimension of development and a focus on narrow economistic market relationships. To some extent this charge has been answered with the development of the New Institutional Economics as an offshoot of mainstream Neoclassical theory.[10] The insight here is that institutions (seen as rules of the game or codes of conduct, as well as formal organisations) develop in response to particular market situations and, hence, one would expect significant differences in institutional patterns of evolution, which in turn will influence prospects for economic development. A central element in the New Institutional Economics is the acceptance of market imperfections and the assumption that actors in markets form the institutions they do as a means of minimising the transactions costs (defined broadly as the costs of acquiring information, reducing uncertainty and conducting exchange) of particular market imperfections. Changes in institutional form can be rationalised in this approach by changes in transactions costs; thus, for example, removal of tariff protection for an industry might be needed due to the transactions costs of an exporter using the output of that industry as one of its inputs. An efficient institution from this perspective is one that is most successful in reducing the costs of market failure. Formal econometric models of the type discussed above have been extended by including an explanatory variable as a proxy for the level of institutional development, however finding acceptable cross-country measures of institutional quality is not straightforward.[11] The more general point, which has been accepted by international agencies, is that any successful policy reform package must have a distinct component for institution building, however this is specified.

Patterns of trade

In more specific policy terms, the Neoclassical interpretation of trade possibilities requires that production specialisation should be on the basis of an economy's comparative advantage, which requires concentrating resources where activities are internationally competitive, with domestic costs defined in terms of the opportunity cost of the commodities and resources that go into production. There is said to be a comparative advantage in a particular line of production, therefore, if domestic costs, that reflect the alternative uses of the input involved, are below the world price of competing production abroad.[12] The Neoclassical literature lays great stress on the importance of export markets for new industries. Apart from the technical change argument summarised earlier (page 51), other expected benefits from exporting include:

- greater competition with resulting productivity gains as producers are forced to compete internationally;
- greater awareness of international standards;
- greater equality in income distribution, if export growth is concentrated in labour-intensive activities;
- removal of market bottlenecks, where economies of scale are important and the domestic market is too small to allow these to be attained;
- alleviation of a foreign exchange constraint on growth.

Stages of comparative advantage

In relation to the development of new exports, it is recognised that comparative advantages change over time, and this is incorporated in the so-called 'dynamic stages of comparative advantage'. This recognises that, as economies evolve, relative resource endowments will change as jobs are created and natural resources are used up. Hence, whilst initially developing countries' cost advantages may be based on their inherited resources, either natural resources or unskilled labour, this will change over time. Initial export success in manufactured products may be achieved in the processing of natural resources or in simple labour-intensive goods, since the opportunity costs of such goods will be low. These are the natural resource based and low technology exports identified in Chapter 1. Over time as labour surpluses are removed, real wages will rise and natural resources will be used up, so that the comparative advantage of such countries may move to more sophisticated commodities embodying first more physical capital inputs and latterly more skill-based human capital inputs; these are broadly the medium and high technology products referred to in Chapter 1. In other words, the opportunity costs of producing different types of commodity will shift over time.[13]

As an elaboration of this stages approach, further schematic sequences for trade strategy were noted. In the early Neoclassical discussion of trade special-isation, a strategy of export-substitution was recommended in contrast with the more familiar import-substitution strategy. Export-substitution refers to a shift in the composition of exports, so that new manufactured exports rise as a share of total exports and substitute for more traditional primary/products. A simple descriptive sequence of stages was used to illustrate alternative trade strategies. The stages are as follows:

- primary import-substitution;
- primary export-substitution;
- secondary import-substitution;
- secondary export-substitution.

The adjectives 'primary' and 'secondary' refer to the technological complexity and capital intensity of commodities; commodities that are primary are there-fore relatively unsophisticated, labour-intensive goods, the most obvious examples for manufacturers being textiles, clothing and toys. These are broadly the low technology exports of Chapter 1. Commodities covered under the heading 'secondary' are technologically more advanced, skill- and capital-intensive; both consumer durables, such as electrical domestic appliances, and intermediates and capital goods, like iron and steel and machinery of various types. These approximate to the medium technology and some of the high technology exports of Chapter 1. The argument is that new industries will generally commence production with sales to the home market of primary goods that were previously imported. This primary import-substitution can be 'natural' in the sense that it occurs as a result of transport and other cost advantages. Alternatively, it can be policy-induced, as new industries are protected and encouraged by governments.

The Neoclassical view is that there is nothing intrinsically wrong with import-substitution provided it arises from market-based decisions. However, primary import-substitution, if it arises from substantial protection, will create biases and distortions that are discussed further (page 57). In addition, once the 'easy' stage is passed and all previous imports have been replaced, its growth will be limited by the expansion of the domestic market, which will be a constrain-ing factor in small economies. An economically more efficient alternative for most developing countries is seen as a shift to a strategy of primary export-substitution. This involves the export of the goods intensive in an economy's abundant resources. These may be simple labour-intensive goods, produced ini-tially for the home market, exports of parts and components for production located overseas or processed natural resource based goods. The balance between these types of goods will be determined in large part by the resource endowment of economies, so that where natural resources and land are abun-dant relative to labour (as is often suggested for much of Africa), the expecta-tion will be that primary stage exports will have a relatively high natural resource component. A shift to a strategy of primary export-substitution involves at least the removal of the anti-export bias normally associated with protectionist trade policies.

Primary export-substitution will be relevant as long as wage costs remain sufficiently low for a country to maintain a comparative cost advantage in labour-intensive commodities. After a time, however, as real wages rise in response to growing demands for labour, it will become economically efficient to shift into the production of secondary commodities, and establish a more sophisticated industrial structure. This may necessitate some encouragement for these new industries, either through modest protection, but preferably in this view through promotion via subsidies. Secondary import-substitution of these goods occurs as their local production supplants imports. However any anti-export bias at this stage should be short-lived and it is recommended that adequate incentives be given to encourage producers of secondary commodities to break into export markets. When this is achieved the stage of secondary export-substitution will be reached. The time lag between secondary import and export-substitution will be determined not only by level of incentives offered for domestic and export sales, but also by the size of the domestic market and the importance of economies of scale in production in individual branches of activity. For example, the more important are scale economies relative to the size of the domestic market for a commodity, the greater will be the pressure to enter export markets to remain competitive. As economies develop successfully, new technology exports based on modern best-practice technologies, usually provided by TNCs, may also emerge, as illustrated in Chapter 1. Such goods can be seen as embodying qualitatively different technologies from that associated with import-substitution goods.

It must be recognised that this schematic sequence is an over-simplification of a complex sequence of shifts in industrial specialisation and orientation. The speed at which countries can and should move through these stages will vary with factors like national resource endowments, domestic market size and export market prospects. At any one time the strategy of an economy might be considered a hybrid of at least two stages. Nonetheless, this sequence has been considered sufficiently useful to be applied in a normative sense to suggest how developing countries could organise their trade strategies.

For example, a common interpretation of the performance of the NIEs, and in particular Korea and Taiwan, in comparison with many of the larger Latin American economies, argues that there have been two key differences in trade strategy between the two groups. First, the primary import-substitution phase in the two East Asian economies was both mild in terms of levels of protection and short-lived, ten to fifteen years. In Latin America, however, protection was higher and the strategy of primary import-substitution was continued for much longer, thus creating more distortions and vested interests committed to the continuation of the system. Second, whilst Korea and Taiwan shifted fairly rapidly to the primary export-substitution phase, and gained the benefits associated with rapidly rising exports, the Latin American economies moved to a further stage of protection, in the form of secondary import-substitution. Since the commodities produced at this stage were capital and skill-intensive, they were often high cost in international terms and thus required higher levels of protection than simpler primary goods. Hence, the distortions and biases of primary import-substitution were magnified at the secondary stage.[14]

Whilst Korea and Taiwan are seen as passing through all four stages relatively quickly from the late 1960s to the late 1970s, in Latin America import-substitution dominated trade strategy until industrial exports began to emerge gradually from secondary import-substitute industries. In this view, however, many of these exports arose not from the emerging competitiveness of domestic producers but from government willingness to subsidise high cost exports. Thus the Latin America sequence before the liberalisation of the 1980s and 1990s is seen as inefficient since selective export promotion, often of high cost industries, was grafted onto an unreformed secondary import-substitution strategy. The consequence of missing the primary export-substitution stage was not only that many distortions and biases remained, but also that the possibility of raising industrial employment through an expansion of labour-intensive exports was also lost. Currently, as Chapter 7 shows, the emergence of significant high technology exports has been much slower in Latin America than in East Asia.

As an interpretation of Latin American experience, this view is controversial, since it neglects the significant exports of apparently competitive manufactures that emerged in a number of countries in the 1980s from previously protected industries.[15] However, the argument clearly illustrates the Neoclassical view of trade strategy. It is not that developing countries should remain as permanent exporters of labour-intensive goods, but that it will be economically beneficial at a certain stage of their development to focus trade strategy on these exports. At a later stage industrial diversification can and should take place. Where an economy is only at the stage of primary import-substitution, the chief objective is to remove anti-export bias, and shift to primary export-substitution. Where a more sophisticated industrial base has been created at the secondary import-substitution stage, reforms will aim to encourage greater export, probably of both the primary and secondary type. As industrial sophistication develops, further export of higher technology goods may be possible. Export diversification can be accepted by all as essential for industrial success. The key issue for debate is how far governments should attempt to encourage and influence this process. In the Neoclassical view the answer is not very much.

Government intervention and distortions

As we have seen, the central tenet of Neoclassical theory is that, in general, market distortions caused by government intervention are to be avoided. This view has been linked particularly with strong critiques of past import-substitution trade policies, but the argument is considerably more general. Governments may intervene in markets for a variety of reasons; for example to conserve foreign exchange, to protect local producers from foreign competition, to guarantee a minimum wage, to encourage investment and to raise government revenue. These interventions will involve a range of policy instruments – including quantitative import restrictions, tariffs, minimum wage legislation, credit subsidies via controlled interest rates and indirect taxes. The argument is that intervention in the operation of markets will force prices away from economic values that reflect the scarcity of commodities or resources. Thus significant losses in economic efficiency will be created if producers and consumers respond to distorted rather than 'efficient' prices.

A large number of empirical studies within the Neoclassical tradition have identified significant divergences between market prices, and economic values.[16] In addition work on the systems of protection in developing countries under import-substitution policy regimes has focussed more narrowly upon the relative incentives, which have been created by various forms of protection, and the implications of these incentives for economic efficiency.

Import-substitution and economic efficiency

The extent to which many developing countries have used these trade interventions in the past is now well documented, and the undesirable consequences for economic efficiency of many protective measures have been stressed frequently. Three separate strands of the argument can be distinguished.

- The varied and often unanticipated effect of protective measures in terms of the incentives created for different branches of manufacturing; in other words, not all branches will benefit equally and the relative levels of incentive may be unplanned and, in some cases, undesired.
- The general encouragement protection from import competition gives to high cost domestic production, and the lack of stimulus it provides to reduce costs to international levels.
- The harmful impact of manufacturing protection on other parts of the economy, particularly agriculture and exports in general.

Variations in incentives

Considering the relative impact of protection on different industrial branches, the essential point is that the final degree of incentive will generally not be known in advance, when the protective measures involved are being planned. This may be either because of the uncertain impact of quotas, or because of the effect of imposing different rates of tariffs, taxes or subsidies on inputs as compared with outputs.[17] The observed or Nominal Rate of Protection (NRP) is given by the ratio of the domestic price to the world price for a comparable commodity. However the full effect of a protective system can only be estimated by comparing the tariff or tariff equivalents on the output of a producer, with those on the inputs it must purchase. The logic of this is that if a producer's input prices are raised above international levels, by more than their output prices, it is being penalised rather than encouraged by the protective system, even though its own output may have a positive tariff. A comparison of the output tariff of a producer with a weighted average of the tariffs on their inputs, with the weights determined by the share of inputs in the value of the output gives the effective rate of protection (ERP). This measures the extent to which value-added of a producer, or the aggregate of all producers in a branch, at domestic, that is protected, prices exceeds what it would be in a free-trade situation, where world and domestic prices for traded goods are assumed to be equal.

Formally ERP for activity i can be given in two alternative but equivalent definitions:

$$ERP_i = \frac{VADP_i - VAWP_i}{VAWP_i} \tag{3.5}$$

where $VADP_i$ is value-added at domestic prices in i and $VAWP_i$ is value-added at world prices in i, under free trade.

$$ERP_i = \frac{t_i - \sum_j a_{ji} t_j}{1 - \sum_j a_{ji}} \tag{3.6}$$

where t_i and t_j are the tariffs, or tariff equivalents, for output i and input j respectively, and a_{ji} is the number of units of j required per unit of i under free trade.[18]

The argument is that those activities with the highest ERP will have the greatest incentive for expansion arising from the price effects created by protection. The degree to which resources will actually move in response to these incentives will depend upon supply elasticities; however, other things being equal, a relatively high ERP will mean an activity will have a relatively high output as compared with what its output would be in the absence of protection.

ERP measures have been used extensively in applied work on industrial development in developing countries, although they are not without both empirical and conceptual problems. For example, empirically there are difficulties in obtaining comparable world and domestic price data, and in achieving a sufficient degree of disaggregation to estimate separate ERPs for a large number of branches. Conceptually there are also difficulties in the treatment of non-traded goods, in the need to use fixed input coefficients, and with the appropriate exchange rate to use in the calculations. Nonetheless, despite these limitations, it is generally felt that the ERP measure is useful for analysing the extent to which protectionist policies create incentives for resources to shift in different directions.

From the peak of the import-substitution period in the 1960s and 1970s, there is a substantial body of evidence on the wide range of ERP for different sectors and manufacturing branches in different economies.[19] Even in the 1990s, significantly high levels of protection persisted in some economies, although in others there is evidence of declining protection. Table 3.1 gives aggregate ERP estimates for manufacturing and agriculture in a sample of

Table 3.1 Aggregate ERP manufacturing and agriculture: selected developing countries (various years)

	Manufacturing		Agriculture	
	Year	(%)	Year	(%)
Kenya	1967	92	1974–5	−19
Tanzania	1966	116	1979	−45
Ghana	1972	105	1979	−90
Ivory Coast	1970–72	62	1970–72	−28
Senegal	1972	70	n.a.	−32
South Korea	1978	32	1978	57
Malaysia	1971	38	1973	20
Philippines	1978	44	1974	18
Thailand	1978	70	1973–74	−7
Pakistan	1970–71	181	1975–76	−30
Sri Lanka	1979	38	1979–80	−10
Egypt	1966–67	42	1976	11
Turkey	1981	181[b]	1978	40
Yugoslavia	1974	9	1975–80	5
Argentina	1977	38	1969	−13
Chile	1967	217	1967	−5
Colombia	1980	37	1979	29
Mexico	1979	11	1979	−2
Bolivia	1980	24	1980	14
Peru	1980	52	1980	46
Taiwan	1969	14[a]	1969	−4
Israel	1968	76[a]	1968	48

Sources: Data come from Agarwala (1983) except where a and b are shown.

Notes
a Refers to Balassa (1982).
b Refers to Yagci (1984).
n.a. is 'not available'.

economies in the import-substitution era up to the beginning of the 1980s. Since the data come from different sources exact comparability is not possible, so the figures can only be taken as suggestive. In most cases shown, manufacturing has a high ERP relative to agriculture, which in some cases has negative protection (in other words actual value-added was below the free-trade level).

Within manufacturing, the possibility of a wide range of ERP estimates for individual branches can be illustrated with data for a single country, Malawi. Table 3.2 gives ERP by manufacturing sub-sector in 1991. The full range of ERP is from −30% for tea to 125% for leather and footwear. The ERP estimates are derived from an analysis of firm-level data, but the overall weighted average

Table 3.2 Effective protection by manufacturing sub-sector: Malawi

Sub-sector	1991 (%)
Food products	−1.4
Tea manufactures	−30.5
Beverages	109.6
Tobacco products	7.4
Textiles	101.0
Leather/footwear	125.3
Wood/paper	52.2
Chemical products	71.1
Plastic products	28.6
Metal products	19.1
All manufacturing	48.9

Source: Mulaga and Weiss (1996).

protection of nearly 50% masks the fact that nearly one quarter of the firms in the sample had negative protection, either because they were exporters or because they used highly protected inputs.[20]

The important point about this wide variance in levels of protection is that activities, which are given a relatively low priority in government policy statements may, nonetheless, receive above average protection and thus resources may be encouraged to shift into these non-priority areas. Such a situation can arise because ERP estimates are not readily available in many countries, and where they are available are rarely up to date. Governments are therefore often not fully aware of the consequences for incentives of the structure of protection.[21]

Lack of stimulus to cost reduction

The second strand in the attack on the use of tariffs and quotas in developing countries is that they provide a shelter for inefficient domestic producers who have no incentive to lower their costs to international levels. Local production at costs above world levels imposes economic losses, it is argued, since, with the abolition of protection, resources would be reallocated to more internationally competitive activities. The ERP measure discussed above must be seen primarily as an indicator of the relative degree of incentive received by producers in particular activities from the protective system. It is not strictly a measure of the efficiency with which resources are employed.

Two related measures of economic efficiency that have been used frequently are cost–benefit (CB) returns at economic prices and domestic resource cost ratios (DRC). The former compares the present value of economic costs with the present value of economic benefits; the test of economic efficiency is whether, at economic prices, there is a positive net present value, or an internal rate of return above the economic discount rate. Application of this criteria requires both identification of all benefits and costs and their valuation at an appropriate set of economic prices.[22]

Where output is a traded good, as will be the case with many manufacturing investments, and there are no additional external benefits, one will be comparing the world price of output with the per unit domestic costs of production. Using the CB criteria, domestic production of a traded good will not be shown as economically justified unless either domestic costs at economic prices are below the world price of the good, or there are strong additional external benefits generated by domestic production.

The domestic resource cost measure can be shown to be formally equivalent to the cost–benefit criteria, although it expresses the same information in a different way. The DRC ratio gives the domestic resources required to earn or save an additional unit of foreign exchange and is therefore an exchange rate for a particular investment or activity. Economic efficiency requires that a DRC is below the economic value of an additional unit of foreign exchange, so that a DRC must be compared with either the official exchange rate, or where this is felt to be an inaccurate guide to the scarcity value of foreign exchange, with an estimate of the shadow exchange rate.[23]

A number of CB and DRC studies on developing countries have indicated substantial economic inefficiency, particularly amongst import-substitute industries. The argument is that high cost sheltered producers can continue to make commercial profits only because of the protection they receive, and that in economic terms their costs of production are un-competitive internationally.[24] Table 3.3 brings together DRC estimates for industrial activities from different sources for five developing countries from the height of the import-substitution period. These indicate a wide range of DRC estimates for activities in the same economy. The number of inefficient branches is shown to give a rough indication of the extent of inefficiency, by comparing DRCs with either the shadow exchange rate referred to in the original study, or the official rate where this is judged to be appropriate. Negative DRCs imply a loss of foreign exchange, where the value of traded inputs exceed that of output.

The wide variation between DRCs for different activities is often interpreted as evidence of resource misallocation, so that it is argued that efficiency in resource use would be improved by expanding activities with low DRCs, at the expense of those with high DRCs. The common sense of this is that if it costs $x\%$ more to save foreign exchange in activity i as compared with activity j, it will be desirable to expand j relative to i. Theoretically the case is not as clear as this, since one needs to assume constant costs of production and given world prices, but in general wide variations in DRC between different activities can be taken as evidence of a misallocation of resources, which is likely to have been made possible by the differential set of incentives created by the import protection system.[25] Protection therefore allows firms with high costs in both economic and financial terms to survive, and in the absence of reforms to the protective system they will have little incentive to lower these costs. The

Table 3.3 Summary of DRC results: selected developing countries

Country	Year	Range of DRCs[a]	Number of branches studied	Number of branches with negative DRC[b]	Number of efficient branches[c]
India	1963–65	Rs 2.7/US$ to Rs 1049/US$	75	6	n.a.
	1968–69	Rs 5.9/US$ to Rs 259/US$	75	4	17
Chile	1961	28% to 1255%	21	0	6
Turkey	1965–69	TL 10.2/US$ to TL 93.9/US$	16	n.a.	10
	1981	50% to 1015%	14	1	4
Ghana	1967–68	19% to 2037%	39	8	9
Tanzania	early 1970s	2.9 shillings/US$ to 12.2 shillings/US$	24	0	17

Sources:
  i India: Bhagwati and Srinivasan (1975), pp. 177–83. For India data on the shadow exchange rate is taken from Beyer (1975) and Weiss (1975).
  ii Chile: Behrman (1976), pp. 137–46.
  iii Turkey: Krueger (1974), pp. 215–26 and Yagci (1984), pp. 85–96. For Turkey firms with negative DRCs are excluded from branch averages.
  iv Ghana: Steel (1972), pp. 223–39.
  v Tanzania: Roemer et al. (1976), pp. 257–75.

Notes
a DRCs are either given as exchange rates, or as percentages. Where the latter are used they refer to the ratio of domestic resources in local currency to net foreign exchange earned or saved expressed in local currency at the shadow exchange rate, where this ratio is expressed as a percentage.
b Negative DRC implies a loss of foreign exchange.
c An efficient activity is defined as one where either DRC is equal to or below the shadow exchange rate or the DRC percentage is equal to or below 100%. Shadow exchange rates are taken from the original source, except for India where it is estimated to be Rs 12/US$ for the late 1960s.
n.a. = not identifiable from the original source.

expectation is that trade reform by loosening import restrictions will expose high cost firms to foreign competition and either force such firms to lower costs or to go out of business altogether.[26]

Effects on other sectors

Turning to the effect of trade controls on sectors of the economy other than import-substitute manufacturing, two important biases may be created by a protective system; one relating to exports, and the other to agriculture. As we have seen, the Neoclassical literature lays great stress on the importance of expanding manufactured exports. However, it is argued that by restricting the demand for imports, tariffs and quotas allow the maintenance of an exchange rate well above that which would obtain in the absence of such controls. This means that exporters receive less local currency for every unit of foreign exchange earned than in a free-trade situation, where a lower exchange rate would prevail. In addition, further biases against exports can arise from the effect of import controls in raising the price of goods sold in the home market, relative to those sold abroad, and in requiring exporters to use domestically produced inputs more expensive than, and often inferior to, the alternatives available on the world market. It is recognised that subsidies to exporters, for example, in the form of access to low cost credit, or reductions in tax, can be used to offset this bias, and in theory there will be a rate of uniform import tariffs and export subsidies, which can create the same incentive effect as any level of the exchange rate. The argument is, however, that in many of the countries, which adopted inward-looking industrialisation strategies in the 1960s and 1970s, export subsidies were no more than a partial offset to the biases against exports created by the protective system. Empirical attempts to substantiate this view have used an extension of the ERP measure – what is termed the effective rate of subsidy (ERS). The ERS allows for the fact that profitability can be affected by subsidies, as well as tariffs and quotas, and incorporates their impact on domestic value-added. A bias against exports can be said to exist when either effective protection or subsidy on domestic sales exceeds that on exports. This is an alternative measure of anti-export bias to that discussed in Chapter 2, so that anti-export bias exists where either

$$\frac{\text{ERP}_D}{\text{ERP}_x} > 1 \quad \text{or} \quad \frac{\text{ERS}_D}{\text{ERS}_x} > 1$$

where, D and x refer to domestic and export sales, respectively; where subsidies are significant, it is the latter measure that is more accurate.[27]

However, it is important to note that even in economies with little or no aggregate anti-export bias by this measure there can still be variations between branches, so that even in generally outward-looking economies discrimination against exports can still arise for some activities.[28]

Table 3.4 Nominal and true protection in some African economies

	Nominal protection		True protection	
	Importables	*Exportables*	*Importables*	*Exportables*
Côte d'Ivoire (1989)	33.0	0	12.6	−15.4
Madagascar (1990)	36.0	0	8.9	−19.9
Nigeria (1990)	33.0	0	12.6	−15.4

Source: Milner and Morrissey (1997) Table 3.

An alternative measure of anti-export bias follows what is termed 'shift analysis'. This is based on a comparison between domestic prices for importable goods, exportable goods and non-traded goods. Anti-export bias can arise not just because the price of import-competing goods are raised relative to exportables, but because as a result of protection, prices of non-traded goods also rise relative to exportables. This price impact on non-traded activities, like power or transport, that will be inputs into the export sector, is a form of hidden export tax that reduces exporters value-added relative to what it would be under free trade. Shift analysis estimates what it terms 'true protection', which is in effect the conventional nominal protection adjusted for the price rise for non-traded goods resulting from protection. Since the export sector will always have zero nominal protection, unless export subsidies are used, it will have negative true protection provided there is some feedback from price rises due to import tariffs (or quota tariff equivalents) to the domestic price of non-traded activities.[29]

Table 3.4 sets out estimates of anti-export bias following this methodology giving true protection estimates for importables and exportables for three African economies in 1989–90. For comparison nominal protection figures are also given. In each case, because of the impact on non-traded prices, which reduces value-added in all traded activities, nominal protection estimates are always above true protection and exporters are found to have their value-added reduced by 15% to 20% due to price rises for their non-traded inputs.

Considering the case of a bias against agriculture, this may arise where agriculture is still the major export sector, so that it naturally suffers most from any anti-export bias. However, this anti-agriculture bias can also stem from the lack of protection afforded agriculture relative to other sectors. Cases of negative ERP for agriculture can arise if domestic prices for crops and livestock are broadly comparable with world levels, whilst the locally produced or imported inputs in agriculture are protected or taxed, and thus have domestic prices above world levels. Alternatively if prices paid to farmers by marketing boards are controlled at levels below the border parity price (defined as the export price minus the necessary transport and distribution costs from the farm to the border) this will be a form of export tax and will create negative ERP regardless of whether input prices are above world levels. In some instances this discrimination against agriculture may have been the unanticipated result of the separate policies of keeping down food prices for urban consumers, whilst at the same time protecting local manufacturing.

The significantly greater incentive granted to manufacturing as compared with agriculture-based activities in the import-substitution era, can be seen in Table 3.1 by comparing the ERP estimates for agriculture with those for manufacturing. It is clear that, in many countries, particularly in Africa, agriculture was penalised quite strongly through a relatively high negative ERP. In fifteen of the twenty-five estimates covered in Table 3.1, ERP for agriculture was negative at some point during the period covered. Furthermore, in only one country, Korea, was the ERP for agriculture above that for manufacturing in general. Even in countries like Taiwan and Mexico, where the negative protection experienced by agriculture was low, it still suffered relative discrimination in comparison with the positive protection received by manufacturing. However, in more recent years with the move to much greater trade liberalisation, the expectation must be that the general anti-export and more specifically the anti-agriculture biases have been much reduced. In fact currently in WTO negotiations with many countries, it is often agricultural protection which is the more sensitive issue than protection of manufacturing.

To summarise, therefore, in many countries where interventions in the markets for traded commodities were widespread, it is frequently suggested that a number of harmful side-effects were created; these included unanticipated effective levels of protection and profit incentives to particular sectors, a shelter to high cost producers, a bias against exporting in general, and in many cases, a bias against agriculture in particular. Therefore even if there may be a case for protection of manufacturing in developing countries, along the lines discussed in Chapter 4, there is a substantial amount of evidence from a range of countries, that in practice the way in which protection was implemented in the past created a number of significant negative effects both within manufacturing itself and in other parts of the economy.[30]

Trade liberalisation and manufacturing performance: empirical evidence

Given the evidence on past economic inefficiencies and the substantial loosening of trade controls that has occurred in recent years, and the consequent opening of economies to the international market, it is highly pertinent to enquire how this has affected performance in manufacturing in liberalising economies. The macro link between reform and growth has already been considered in Chapter 2, but here we discuss evidence relating specifically to manufacturing. In general, as befits a complex area, the evidence is perhaps less clear than the competing interpretations might suggest; where positive effects can be found, and they are for a number of countries, they are less dramatic than some simple Neoclassical expositions would suggest. Conversely, the more apocalyptic predictions of critics of trade reform regarding the collapse of previously protected activities have rarely proved justified.

Employment

If liberalisation succeeds in reallocating resources quickly from inefficient to efficient activities, the net unemployment effect may be slight in the short run. In the long run it may be strongly positive, if sustained export growth can be achieved. On the other hand, if labour cannot be reallocated quickly, either because of wage rigidities or lack of demand, employment in industry may fall. It is not clear that major reallocation of labour has been caused by trade reform, although industrial employment has fallen in some countries, particularly in Latin America in the 1990s.

In general there is evidence that the industries which experienced the fastest employment growth in the 1970s (and by implication were at the centre of the import-substitution drive of that decade) also experienced above-average employment growth in the 1980s, implying relatively little industrial restructuring away from previously protected activities.[31] A similar story of relatively little employment impact from liberalisation is depicted by a large volume of country studies based largely on experiences in the 1970s and 1980s.[32] Out of eighteen trade liberalisation episodes in twelve countries, in only two cases, Chile and Spain in the 1970s, do we see a substantial rise in unemployment (defined as a five percentage point or more rise in the unemployment rate) comparing the last year before liberalisation with the first year after the liberalisation programme ends. On this comparison more modest rises in unemployment are recorded in Colombia, the Philippines and Yugoslavia in the 1960s. Naturally, simple before and after comparisons do not disentangle all the factors at work and cannot isolate the impact of trade liberalisation.[33] The authors suggest, however, that where the unemployment increase was significant, this was due to factors other than liberalisation; specifically to exchange rate overvaluation in Chile and wage rigidity in Spain.

Other evidence of modest employment consequences of trade reform are reported in studies on Mexico and Morocco, countries which introduced substantial trade reform in the 1980s. In both instances, there is little association between changes in protection and changes in employment, primarily it seems because output response was also weak.[34] In addition in one African economy – Mauritius – trade liberalisation appears to have been associated with rising wages and falling poverty levels.[35] Elsewhere, particularly in Asia, the links between manufactured export expansion and employment growth have been well documented.[36]

Counter examples can be found, of course, particularly from Latin America, where manufacturing employment fell in absolute terms during the first half of the 1990s, with a shift of labour out of manufacturing and into services.[37] Some studies of the experience in the 1980s have also concluded that in some Latin American economies trade liberalisation displaced rather than created manufacturing jobs.[38] An initial expectation of many was that it would be the smaller firms who would be more vulnerable to the competitive pressure created by liberalisation. However, as yet, there is little evidence that employment has been more adversely affected in smaller firms. One of the few detailed studies of industrial structure after liberalisation, on Indonesia, finds stability in employment shares by firm size.[39] Even in Latin America, where the employment position in manufacturing has been disappointing in recent years, there is little evidence that small firms have been the main source of job losses.[40]

Exports

Advocates of trade reform argue that exports will benefit from liberalisation through several mechanisms – access to imported inputs at free trade prices, access to foreign technology and capital, and a more competitive exchange rate. Numerous studies have shown export growth to be correlated with real exchange rate movements, but the real exchange rate as a ratio of traded to non-traded good prices is only indirectly linked with trade policy and changes in the real exchange rate will be influenced by a number of factors, of which trade policy will be only one.[41] Hence, such works shed little light on this problem. However there is evidence that, in general, country effects matter for export growth with some countries doing consistently well by this indicator, either because of their good export infrastructure or their macro and trade policies.[42] Evidence from East Asia, particularly from Korea, suggests that at the firm level early exposure to export markets for protected firms greatly speeded up their move to international competitiveness. This led to a reinterpretation of the infant industry argument (noted in Chapter 4), which in effect reversed conventional causation with learning in export markets leading to the achievement of international competitiveness.[43]

In general, one would expect a more open trading environment to be associated with higher export levels, so what is perhaps of greater significance for a discussion of the impact of trade reform on industrial performance is whether exporting as an activity is associated with higher productivity gains, and therefore efficiency improvements, than is production for the home market. The answer to this question in most empirical studies is predominantly yes. The logic here is that a combination of exposure to technical knowledge via foreign buyers or the more intense competitive pressure of export markets will create an environment of higher than average productivity growth. The alternative explanation, that export expansion leads to falling unit costs due to scale economies is less convincing, since such economies can also be achieved through expanding domestic sales.

The result linking higher exports and higher productivity growth is obtained from both cross-country international comparisons and from detailed plant or firm level analysis for one country.[44] The latter studies that show exporting firms to have a superior productivity performance to non-exporters are the more convincing since they are based on more detailed and consistent data. This relation is clearly documented in studies on Taiwan, Indonesia and Thailand, for example. For Taiwan, in the electronics sector, for three out of the four products examined there is a substantial difference in productivity levels between exporters and non-exporters. Similarly exporters are larger, older and more capital-intensive. For Indonesia, a study of detailed firm data shows that productivity growth is positively and significantly related to the share of output exported, so that the more export-oriented the firm, other things being equal, the higher will be productivity growth.[45] Also in Thailand a study using census data shows a substantially higher growth of TFP in exporting rather than import competing industries.[46] However, such results say nothing about causation and rather than export activity causing productivity growth, it is equally plausible that it is the more dynamic firms that exhibit strong productivity growth, which allows them to sell in export markets. Hence, causation may be reversed with productivity growth causing export success.

Few of the many studies on the link between exports and productivity actually test for causation. A notable and important exception is a very detailed study using plant-level data on Colombia, Mexico and Morocco. Productivity growth arising from exports, or 'learning by exporting' is tested by including a variable for past export experience in a model to explain productivity growth. The variable is rarely significant when other factors are allowed for. Hence, if export history has no significant impact on productivity, the alternative interpretation is that there is a process of self-selection at work, so that more efficient firms choose to become exporters.[47]

Total factor productivity (TFP) and related measures

If the evidence on the positive impact of liberalisation on exports is unclear, what of the much heralded productivity gains that are anticipated when resource reallocation occurs in response to the competitive pressure of import penetration in the domestic market? Further, the dynamic arguments discussed above suggest that, through more rapid technical change associated with an open competitive environment, long-run TFP growth may accelerate. Most detailed productivity studies for individual countries find dramatic differences between branches of industry in terms of TFP growth, with often substantial changes between different time periods. This is interpreted as part of the wider process of 'creative destruction' in a competitive economy.[48] The issue here is whether for any individual economy the disparity in TFP growth within the manufacturing sector can be shown to be linked to increased exposure to foreign competition through trade liberalisation. Based on data from the 1980s, two widely cited surveys of this issue concluded that it is, in fact, very difficult to link trade regime with productivity growth.[49] The more recent literature is not unambiguous, but there are an increasing number of studies that do detect a positive, if sometimes weak relation, between changes in trade policy and TFP or alternative measures of productivity. Comparability between studies is rendered difficult due to differences in measurement of trade reform. However, if we take changes in rates of protection, either nominal or effective, then a significant, if sometimes weak, relation between a fall in protection for a branch or firm and its productivity performance tends to be found. This relation has been identified in economies as diverse as Mexico, Malawi, Chile and Korea.[50] Precisely how this works is unclear, but from plant and firm level studies it does not appear that there is a systematic tendency for trade liberalisation to be associated with larger scales of production at the plant level. In the short run, at least, the relation appears to be between greater import competition and smaller plant size, so that internal economies of scale cannot be a factor. Other possible explanations include elimination of managerial slack, or X-inefficiency, easier access to foreign technology and capital equipment and improved incentives for technological investment. As yet there are few clues as to which of these candidates really matter.[51]

In addition there is evidence that during liberalisation episodes, price–cost margins fall. These are defined simply as the ratio of net profits to costs on a per unit basis and hence are a crude measure of monopoly pricing. A fall in such margins will imply lower profits and may also reflect improved productivity, part of which is passed on to consumers. As part of trade liberalisation, falling margins have been found in a number of countries. The standard interpretation here is that imports have 'disciplined' domestic producers and weakened their market power.[52]

These results indeed imply that trade reform has brought positive benefits, but theory suggests that trade reform will be only one of a number of factors at work in influencing performance and its precise impact in any given situation will vary with factors such as, the general macro economic environment, market structure, the way in which reform is implemented and its overall credibility. Given these qualifications, it is no surprise that some studies generate results that find no support for the trade reform–productivity link.[53]

Conclusion

This chapter examines the Neoclassical arguments and evidence on the inefficiency of past industrialisation policies pursued in many developing countries. Two aspects of the Neoclassical case are most critical – the impact of government on the operation of markets, and the neglect of trade opportunities through the implementation of policies that discriminated against exports. An economically rational industrial policy, it is argued, is one that removes both of these sources of inefficiency. Our survey of the evidence on the impact of trade policy reform shows some positive effects on performance, but perhaps not as dramatic as Neoclassical reasoning might suggest. We return to issues of industrial policy and the influence of these arguments on policy thinking in later chapters. However, prior to that, we consider how far this apparent orthodoxy remains challenged by dissenting voices.

4 What remains of the challenges to orthodoxy?

Early development economists in the late-1940s and 1950s were almost unanimous in stressing the importance of industrialisation. However their perspective differed significantly from what has become the current Neoclassical orthodoxy. Starting from the proposition that 'certain special features of the economic structure of the underdeveloped countries make an important portion of orthodox analysis inapplicable and misleading', their approach has been labelled Structuralist.[1]

Although conventionally a large number of authors are covered by this categorisation, their work can be seen as possessing several key characteristics:

- a belief that development is a process of major structural transformation with industry, and manufacturing in particular, having a major role: from this it follows that national income figures alone cannot be used to assess the level of development, since reference must be made to the production structure that generates this income, and its capacity for creating future growth;
- a scepticism regarding the role of the price mechanism as a means of allocating resources in developing countries, due primarily to the assumed low price elasticities of both supply and demand;[2]
- following from this, a belief in the importance of government intervention of various types as a means of allocating resources and achieving the structural shifts necessary for development;
- an emphasis on the need to change the pattern of trade, and in particular to reduce the importance of primary exports. This implies the need to protect new industries in developing countries until they are able to compete on equal terms with producers overseas.

The Structuralist approach has diverse origins. In one sense it can be seen in the tradition of the Classical economists and Marx, who saw industry in general, and manufacturing in particular, as having a key role as an engine of growth. More recent antecedents can also be identified, however. There seems little doubt that the Keynesian system of macro-economics, developed to explain mass unemployment in the capitalist economies, greatly influenced writers like Nurkse (1958) and Rosenstein-Rodan (1943). For the developing economies, these authors stressed the existence of underemployment rather than open unemployment; however, underemployment could also be identified with the failure of the labour market to generate adequate employment and could thus be used to justify active state intervention to raise investment and mobilise the underemployed.

Emphasis on the failure of the price mechanism to clear markets effectively has also been traced to both academic research and government planning in the UK in the 1930s and 1940s. Some of the individuals involved later visited developing countries, and in particular, it has been suggested that the Latin American authors who worked in the 1950s on the 'Structuralist theory of inflation' for their own continent may have been influenced by these contacts.[3]

However, despite representing the mainstream of thinking on development problems during the 1950s and 1960s, Structuralist analysis and the policies derived from it came under increasing criticism from the late 1960s onwards. A key line of attack, as discussed in Chapter 3, was associated with the Neoclassical school, who stressed the neglect in much of the early development economics of some of the fundamental precepts of conventional economic theory, such as the importance of prices for resource allocation and the role of comparative advantage in assessing trade possibilities. On the other hand, Structuralist analysis also came under attack from what can loosely be termed the Radical perspective, chiefly for its inability to analyse class formations in developing countries, and for its insufficient emphasis on the constraints to development posed by the external economic environment. Radical analysis has been described as 'that which is highly critical of capitalism, favours socialism, and often employs Marxian analysis'.[4] What we term here a Radical perspective encompasses a broad grouping covering conventional Marxist analysis, modifications to classical Marxism and authors writing from the Latin American Dependency perspective. From a different position, Radical authors often raised similar points to Structuralists on the obstacles to and limitations of industrialisation in developing countries under existing international and domestic conditions. For ease of exposition in this chapter, we discuss together both versions of the challenge to orthodoxy, without wishing to imply that we are surveying a comprehensive system of thought or critique of Neoclassical prescriptions. In organising the discussion we focus on three broad themes:

- the role of the state in fostering a process of industrialisation;
- the case for manufacturing having a special role in development policy;
- the possibilities offered by participation in world trade and investment.

The 'technological capability' critique of Neoclassical positions and policy prescriptions, which to some extent can be seen as an offshoot of Structuralist analysis, is discussed separately in Chapter 6. Further arguments on globalisation and the world economy that extend earlier Radical work on the global economy are considered in Chapter 7.

The state and industrialisation

The question of the state versus the market as a means of resource allocation is one of the central issues of debate in development studies.[5] As we have seen, drawing on a combination of empirical evidence and a priori theorising, the Neoclassical literature stresses what it terms 'government failure' and the inefficiency associated with attempts to block or restrain the functioning of markets. In contrast, critics argue that markets do not conform to simple precepts of Neoclassical theory. Structuralists stress the existence of real world conditions that depart from the world of perfect competition – the 'market failures' like external effects and lack of information – and point to alternative empirical evidence deriving primarily from the experience of Japan and the East Asian NIEs, where state intervention was generally felt to have positive effects. From this alternative perspective, for some the case for governments to steer and in some instances override markets appears self-evident on technical economic grounds, since the poorer an economy the more important structural rigidities and market failures are likely to be. Hence, state intervention becomes a means for correcting deficiencies in the operation of markets.

However, a wider critique is found in the Radical literature, which has devoted considerable effort to the study of class formation in developing economies. From this perspective it is essential to look beyond superficial market forms and to question what are the underlying factors that explain market behaviour. In other words, if supply response is weak, one should explain this in broader socio-economic terms. This is why much of the early development literature laid great stress on the weakness of the domestic bourgeoisie or capital accumulating class in such countries.[6] A natural concomitant to an emphasis on the weakness of the national bourgeoisie in developing countries is a stress on the importance of the state and the state bureaucracy. In terms of industrialisation strategy this implies that, where private capitalists have not emerged to undertake new investment, the state, through public sector enterprises managed by public officials, must play a major role in industrialisation, if total reliance is not to be placed on foreign investment.

Marxist, or Marxist-inspired, analyses of the state acknowledge that it cannot be seen as separate from the class organisation of a society; in other words, its organisation and operation must reflect the balance of class forces. However, crude interpretations that view the state and all state activity as simple reflections of underlying economic struggles are no longer accepted and it is commonly argued that the state has a degree of 'relative autonomy' from the control of dominant classes, although the extent of such autonomy will vary from case to case.[7]

An example of relative autonomy often referred to is the possibility that domestic classes may be divided or weak, and that the balance of class forces is not clearly defined. Here the state has much greater scope for autonomy and the consequence can be an authoritarian, military or quasi-military regime that lacks a clear social base.[8] As noted in Chapter 2, the concept of intermediate regime has been used to analyse this type of situation. This category, as its name implies, refers to a state neither wholly capitalist nor socialist, where the dominant alliance is between the lower-middle-class, including in this group state functionaries and small domestic capitalists, and the rich peasantry. The weakness of the domestic bourgeoisie and the nationalist orientation of such regimes mean that the state sector assumes a major role in the economy, creating what was often termed a system of 'state capitalism'. This may involve nationalisation of the assets of both domestic and foreign capitalists, and a heavy reliance on the state sector to carry out strategic new investments. However, given the class alliance on which the regime is based, it is not seen as a form of socialism, although the intermediate regime could be hostile to big business, both in the form of foreign capital and its local allies.

It was pointed out that such regimes could be merely transitory, reflecting the weakness and division of existing classes. If they are successful in generating economic growth they may at the same time create a national capitalist class that, in alliance with state functionaries, will change the nature of the regime. In other words, with the growth of a private sector, capitalism may emerge to replace state capitalism. On the other hand, if growth does not take place and the mass of the population remains excluded from participation in the political system, the regime may be pushed to a more radical position that perhaps leads to a form of socialism. Nonetheless, as discussed in Chapter 2, whilst the demise of many nominally socialist regimes is perhaps evidence that intermediate regimes are in fact transitory, it is clear that today nowhere are they in transition to socialism.

Developmental state

Interventionist states do not have to be socialist in political intent and the concept of the developmental state, implying an activist bureaucracy and set of institutions capable of stimulating and accelerating a process of economic growth, is at the heart of the Structuralist–Radical critique of orthodoxy. In terms of its class base, such a state is now likely to be far closer to that of capitalism than the older concept of an intermediate regime. A developmental state is one where the state, in alliance with private national and foreign capital, plays such an active role in promoting capital accumulation in general, whilst establishing a degree of independence from elements of capital, whether foreign or national. Therefore, where the objectives of foreign capital conflict with the requirements of accumulation in general, the state is able to represent these wider interests in opposition to transnationals and their local representatives.

The role of such a developmental state can be rationalised by drawing on several important functions that markets in the abstract cannot perform.[9] One of these is the provision of a vision for the economy; this vision can be seen as a broad form of public entrepreneurship by which the state on behalf of society drives or guides private agents into a particular direction that they might not otherwise have taken due to difficulties in information gathering or political bargaining. The Japanese government's encouragement to the private sector to shift into knowledge-based activities in the 1980s or the Korean government's encouragement of heavy industry in the late 1970s are commonly cited as illustrations of this process. As new areas are likely to be inherently more risky than established ones, industrial policy also plays a role in minimising the risk to private investors; for example, by providing subsidised credit or extra-normal profits through protection from foreign competition.[10] Management of conflict between economic groups is the other critical role. Development is, by definition, a process of structural change involving winners and losers. Management of this process is needed not just for social reasons, but also narrower economic ones relating to the incentive to invest and to take risks. Short-term market outcomes, for example relating to job losses or bankruptcies, may not be economically desirable and it can only be the state that overrides such outcomes. Such general propositions cannot imply that states inevitably get things right; rather, they simply serve to contradict orthodox suggestions that states have no obvious role beyond setting the boundaries for private sector development.

However the abstract case for the developmental state is usually reinforced by reference to experience in the NIEs, which can be interpreted as providing strong evidence of the usefulness of providing a vision and balancing conflicting social interests. Studies on the experiences of Japan, Korea and Taiwan have provided the empirical basis for the concept of a developmental state, which is capable of guiding a society on a successful process of industrialisation.[11]

Successful developmental states in East Asia, it is argued, were able to manage effectively the tension between national and foreign firms drawing on foreign technology in some cases and in others on foreign finance and management skills. Their interventions are seen as marking out the framework for an activist industrial policy for others to follow. For example, following a detailed analysis of the functioning of the developmental state in Korea and Taiwan, Wade (1990: 350–70) puts forward a series of guidelines for other economies in the form of simple propositions. Paraphrasing, these amount to:

- promotion by the state of industrial investment in activities with growth potential;
- use of protection to create successful infant industries;
- high priority within trade policy to export promotion;
- welcome for transnational firms that can export;
- promotion of a bank-based financial system under close government control;
- only gradual liberalisation of foreign trade and the domestic financial sector.

Whilst the Neoclassical concern with markets is not totally forgotten, the implication is that markets must be guided and if necessary 'distorted' to meet growth objectives.[12]

The theory of late industrialisation

These arguments have been generalised by Amsden (2001) into a broad interpretation of development since 1945. Discussing the experiences of the more successful developing economies over this period, she formulates a theory that gives the developmental state a central role in explaining successful industrialisation. The starting point is the insight that the process of industrialisation must differ in follower or latecomer economies from that experienced by the earlier industrialisers in Europe and North America. Of critical importance is technology and the creation of knowledge-based assets. Knowledge and the technology in which it is embodied create extra profits or technological rents for the enterprises that possess it and through reinvestment in equipment and adaptations to technology, these incomes can drive the process of industrialisation. A late start gave economies the opportunity post-1945 to develop industry on the basis of imported technology from Europe and North America. This was critical since developing countries could not industrialise on the basis of low wages alone, since low wages in any line of activity in a poor country can always be offset by higher productivity in a more advanced economy (see Table 7.2, page 157, for evidence on this). Foreign technology, at times adapted and modified, provided the opportunity for industrialisation. However, where the developmental state enters the picture, is that new industrial activities based on adaptations to foreign technology cannot compete with established firms abroad that can draw on their own specific knowledge of production built up over years of experience. The imbalance in knowledge-based assets is too great, so that successful late industrialisation requires state support and initiative to create the possibility of overcoming the disadvantage of firms in latecomer economies.

This broad interpretation is then generalised to cover the experiences of a diverse set of economies (termed 'the rest') largely corresponding to the list of NIEs in Chapter 1. Countries in East Asia, South Asia, Latin America and Southern Europe (Turkey) are linked in a general pattern characterised by historical differences, but also it is suggested broad similarities, where government support built up successful industries. The mechanisms varied in their detail between economies, but included the channelling of public funds through development banks, established specifically to meet developmental not commercial objectives, direct public ownership, principally in heavy industry, and control over investment and technology licensing, as well as more indirect measures of import tariff protection and subsidies. The whole purpose was to make manufacturing more profitable than it would have been at free trade or uncontrolled prices. These favours were granted in return for an understanding of reciprocity and, in general, monitorable performance standards were imposed. Again these standards varied, but included checks on levels of exports, use of local inputs, employment creation and development of new products. In the exceptional case where competitive assets were not lacking, that is Hong Kong, the government did not intervene, because it did not need to.

Differences in the evolution of industry and industrial policy in these economies are recognised, but these are essentially reduced to two broad patterns. In one, support by the state created large enterprises seen as national industrial champions, usually organised as groups with a diverse set of industrial interests (see Table 2.9); with state support these tended to invest heavily in the development of a national technological capacity. In general, this was the Asian model. In the other pattern, state support was more diffuse as between enterprises and the large national champion enterprise was less evident. Here national firms, whilst large by local standards, were smaller by global ones and TNC involvement in their national markets was much more significant. In terms of technology, firms in these economies tended to invest much less and to rely more on imports of foreign technology. In general, this was the Latin American model with Turkey included. The pressures and opportunities posed by globalisation are seen as contributing to a distinct parting of the ways for these two groups in the 1980s, with a significant number of countries in the first group (such as Korea, Taiwan, China and India) moving on an 'independent' path based on national knowledge-based firms and countries from the second group (such as Mexico and Brazil) moving further along an 'integrationist' route of heavy reliance on TNC investment and foreign-driven technological development. The position in Malaysia, Thailand and Indonesia is treated as unclear and they are placed in neither group. However, these are ideal types and 'independent' in this context does not mean closed to foreign technology, investment or trade, so that even the independent countries will continue to import and adapt foreign technology. The issue is the extent to which they attempt to establish a national set of knowledge-based assets by investment in education and R and D driven by national firms. From the perspective of knowledge creation, which is a focal point of much of this analysis, firm nationality does matter, so that other things being equal, a pattern of industrialisation with a higher proportion of domestically owned firms is taken to imply a more active national R and D effort and, by implication, a greater national technological capability. Nonetheless, whatever route is taken in future in these economies, given the strength of domestic private firms, as a result of its past interventions, it is suggested that the developmental state will be needed much less in the future than it was at earlier points in the post-1945 period.

The key factors explaining which countries followed which path are taken to be their pre-1945 history and their degree of income inequality. Historical industrial experience based on pre-war colonial industries encouraged the pattern of large national firms, since in the early post-independence years, foreign-owned firms were nationalised and replaced by locally owned firms that dominated the domestic market. On the other hand, in Latin America pre-1945, manufacturing experience was already based on foreign firms, who remained important in the domestic market after 1945. The role hypothesised for income distribution is more subtle. It is argued that countries where the state invested heavily in creating large national firms were those characterised by low levels of inequality since, in an egalitarian environment, it will be easier to mobilise resources and concentrate them for what is perceived as the greater national good. Conversely in unequal societies, it is suggested governments were more reluctant to be seen transferring resources in favour of a small number of firms or groups.

Some qualifications

These are stimulating generalisations, although it is not clear that all recent economic history in these countries can be explained in these simple terms. For the present purpose, however, it is important to draw out a few distinct points. First, implicit in this discussion is a direct challenge to the Neoclassical story on import substitute industrialisation. In the late industrialisation theory the impact of the developmental state was basically successful in that a substantial expansion of industry and knowledge-based assets, absent pre-1945, occurred in the countries surveyed. The technical measures of inefficiency from Chapter 3 are judged to be largely irrelevant since new industries could not be expected to be efficient at world prices and the whole thrust of policy was to generate rents for manufacturing firms that could be reinvested for future growth. Where this issue is addressed by Amsden (2001: 260–68) reference is made to the fact that, after the trade reforms of the late 1980s and 1990s, industrial structure in most of the economies covered changed relatively little. Had inefficiency been wide-spread, it is argued, there would have been substantial reallocations as ineffi-cient producers contracted and more efficient ones expanded. Further it is pointed out that, as we have seen in Chapter 1, some countries increased significantly their shares in world trade and production of relatively knowledge-intensive industries and that some of the export success came from firms ini-tially established as part of import-substitute activity. What matters is thus the incentive to invest in knowledge creation. Government failures, in the sense of support for enterprises that failed technologically and in terms of cost competi-tiveness, are acknowledged, principally where an adequate system of checks and controls was not put in place. However, the general picture is one of a successful development state that partially withered away as private firms strengthened their position. Hence in most of 'the rest' by the 1990s the types of intervention practised earlier were being withdrawn. In the Neoclassical view this was because of their failure, whilst on the contrary in the late industrialisation theory it was because of their success.

We discuss more details of an active industrial policy in Chapter 8, but given the range of interventions practised there is no simple blueprint for other fol-lower lower-income economies that Amsden calls 'the remainder'. Differing historical circumstances, particularly the global economic environment, will always have an impact on outcomes and the capacity of different states to inter-vene effectively will always vary. One explanation as to why developmental states appeared to function so effectively in Korea and Taiwan in the period from 1960 to the late-1980s is the combination of an authoritarian and corporatist political system; the former characteristic frees rulers from the need to seek popular consent and the latter means that interest groups are effectively dependent on the state.[13] How far this type of interventionism is compatible with a more democratic political system remains an open question, but at the very least a strong central authority is required. Developmental states must be 'hard' in the sense of being able to impose their policies, where the soft state is unable to, and have a committed and capable bureaucracy.

However 'Crony Capitalism', where state functionaries intervene for their own benefit or for the benefit of a narrow range of interests, is the other side of the developmental state. The experience of the East Asian crisis in the late 1990s provides a salutary warning that apparently highly successful economic regimes may not be what they seem and that the governed or guided-market model can be easily exploited for sectional interests. This seems particularly true where the financial sector is closely linked with the state bureaucracy through a directed credit policy that channels loans to particular sectors regardless of financial ability to repay. A poorly regulated financial sector, exposed to international capital flows arising from balance of payments liberalisation, is highly vulnerable to movement of short-run capital and this appears to have happened in the Asian crisis.[14] Although the most important elements of industrial policy in Korea, for example, had been abandoned in the early 1990s, many observers in the region have argued that the legacy of the developmental state had contributed to the crisis of the late 1990s, primarily through its impact on the domestic financial sector.

The point to stress at this stage is that authors writing from outside the Neoclassical paradigm have usefully kept alive the issue of government intervention as a positive force for industrialisation and have done so primarily by reference to earlier successful industrial development often, but not exclusively, in East Asia. This empirical evidence has encouraged generalisations to other locations based on the concept of a developmental state. Within the narrower context of debates in the Radical literature, this re-assessment of the state's role in industrialisation clears the way for an analysis of the scope for successful capitalist industrialisation in the periphery of the world economy in collaboration with TNCs. The simple generalisation of a subservient Neocolonial regime incapable of supporting the interests of local capital can be rejected as the single explanation for the activities of the state in such economies. Naturally it is not inevitable that all developmental states will succeed in their industrial policies (and the more recent evidence of Crony Capitalism is not encouraging) but, a priori, one cannot rule out the possibility of success at least at certain stages of an economy's development.

Manufacturing as an engine of growth

If the role of the state has partially survived the Neoclassical onslaught, what of the view that economic structure matters for development and that, in particular, manufacturing has a special role to play? In simple terms, even if in the short term you can generate a higher rate of profit making potato chips than computer chips, the long-run implications of producing the latter should be far more favourable. This should not be interpreted as part of a debate on the merits of giving priority to manufacturing over other sectors, particularly agriculture. Some early discussions might have had such an emphasis, but it has long been recognised that simple notions of priority have to give way to an awareness of the interrelationships between sectors. There is no reason why all economic activities should grow at the same rate or require the same amount of resources. What is important is that bottlenecks should not emerge due to the neglect of particular activities. The simple manufacturing-or-agriculture dichotomy has been replaced, in most discussions, by considerations of the contribution of manufacturing to general economic goals, some of which can include the strengthening of other sectors.

Manufacturing can strengthen agriculture, for example, by providing domestically produced inputs like fertilisers or farm equipment, or alternatively by generating the foreign exchange to import these. On the other hand, it is widely recognised that a strong agricultural sector can foster the expansion of manufacturing by providing raw materials for processing and foodstuffs for industrial workers. In addition, growing agricultural incomes can be a source of demand for manufactures and of savings for investment in manufacturing. Industrialisation can be held back by a stagnant agricultural sector, so that overemphasising manufacturing at the expense of agriculture may lead in the longer-term to a rate of manufacturing growth lower than that possible under a more balanced investment strategy. What is required is that investment is allocated in line with expected returns in alternative activities, and the Structuralist case has always been that, in most countries at relatively low-income levels, this will entail an increasing share of additional resources going to manufacturing industry. This is not to imply that other sectors, particularly agriculture, should be neglected in the sense of being denied resources for viable investments. It is rather that, because of the relatively high returns expected in manufacturing, the right balance in sectoral allocations will involve some shift towards industry, and manufacturing in particular.

As noted in Chapter 1, there is a well established statistical relation in an economy between growth of manufacturing and growth of national income. Fast growing economies tend to have a relatively rapid manufacturing growth and, conversely, slow growing economies tend to have a slow growth of manufacturing. This relationship is not found for agriculture where there is normally no relationship between agricultural growth and that of national income. Services, on the other hand, do tend to grow in line with national income, but their role is seen as passive in responding to growth in productive activity.

However, to develop the case that manufacturing has a special role in stimulating the growth of the economy as a whole requires a theoretical justification to explain why causation should run from manufacturing growth to GDP growth, rather than vice versa. Production from a particular sector will be more valuable in economic terms than other forms of production under two broad conditions. First, where the incidence of external benefits, that is higher incomes for producers or consumers not directly associated with the initial production, are greater there than elsewhere and second where there are long-run gains in productivity that result from the cumulative experience in production in the sector concerned, which again are greater than could be obtained in other forms of production. The 'engine of growth' case rests on these two conditions being fulfilled. In setting out this case, we begin by considering the importance of externalities, particularly those related to the spread of ideas and technical knowledge through the growth of manufacturing.

Externalities

Externalities are effects created by individual producers or consumers that are felt elsewhere in the economy. They are significant in a theoretical sense because they demonstrate the inability of a competitive market system to reach an economically optimum situation and have been a central plank in the argument for the importance of industrialisation in developing countries at least since Rosenstein-Rodan (1943) argued for a 'Big Push' – that is a co-ordinated investment programme – that would attempt to maximise the gains from these external effects. Central to the Structuralist position is the view that externalities are more significant in industry than in other sectors, thus providing a major rationale for industrialisation. However, arguments on external effects can be put in very vague terms, and it is necessary to clarify the issues by distinguishing between different types of external effects.[15]

A more precise definition of externalities than that given initially is that they are effects created by individual producers or consumers, which have repercussions on other producers or consumers, that are not reflected in the cost and revenue position of the original creator of the effect. They are examples of a distortion since, for example, if a producer creates an effect on another producer the market price of the output of the original producer will not reflect the cost or benefit to the other producer. This broad concept can be narrowed down by distinguishing between 'technological externalities' and 'pecuniary externalities'. The former have been described in more recent literature as 'real externalities'.

Technological or real externalities are defined as direct external effects that do not arise as a result of market transactions for which prices are charged. Here the output of a producer will depend not only on its own inputs, but also on the physical quantities of the outputs or inputs of other producers. Externalities of this type are termed 'technological' since the inputs or output of a firm enter directly into the production function of another firm. There are several examples of this type of external effect, which are relevant for industry. One is a labour training effect where, for example, the training undertaken by producer A can create a skilled group of workers who, if they leave A's employment, can bring their skills to producer B; second, if several firms use a resource which is free, but in limited supply, the greater the inputs used by producer A, the less there will be available to producer B.[16]

A third, some suggest critically important, area relates to knowledge transfer via externalities. As we discuss further in Chapter 6, much attention is now given to the development of firm-level technological capability, defined broadly as the capacity to apply, adapt, modify and at a later stage develop technology. The significant point to note here is that, whilst some of the important mechanisms for establishing such capability will be internal to firms and result directly from firms' own efforts, others are external operating at sector, regional or even macro levels. Hence, provided it can be shown that technical change in firm A is influenced by the actions of firms B to Z, either through copying, transfer of human skills or other forms of non-market dissemination, then technological externalities will be at work.[17] Hence, where manufacturing production can be shown to generate important externalities that speed up technical change, we have an important strand in the case that it has a special role in development. Finally there is the possibility of significant environmental externalities. The factory that polluted the stream was always the simplest illustration in textbook discussions of technological externalities and was treated as something of a theoretical curiosity. However, now the impact of industry on the physical environment receives considerably more attention in the development context than previously.

Whilst technological externalities reflect direct interdependence between producers, pecuniary externalities, on the other hand, operate through the market mechanism, so that their effects are manifested in price terms.[18] Formally pecuniary externalities arise whenever the profits of a producer are affected by the output and input levels of other producers. They are, therefore, a broader category than technological externalities, which do not operate through the market, and which, therefore, affect only output quantity; where technological externalities also raise profitability, they are subsumed under pecuniary effects.[19]

The central importance of externalities, positive or negative, is that where they exist the net benefits to the economy as a whole, what we term 'economic benefits', can differ significantly from the benefits accruing to private producers. Hence, where firms act individually in response to their own private profit estimates, in the presence of externalities, their investment plans will be non-optimal in broader economic terms.

Linkages

The case for the importance of externalities in manufacturing industry is strengthened by reference to linkages.[20] Linkages can be defined in a broad or a narrow sense. In the former a linkage is simply an inducement to activity on the part of one enterprise created by the actions of another; the narrow sense is technical, referring to a series of production relationships in an inter-industry framework. In the narrower sense there are conventionally two categories of production linkages, backward linkages from a particular industry to its suppliers, and forward linkages from an industry to its users. These linkages reflect production interdependence and are a mechanism through which some pecuniary externalities can be transmitted. The greater linkages created by manufacturing, and therefore its greater potential for generating externalities, has been used as a major argument for the importance of industrialisation.[21] Nonetheless, despite the inducement effect to further investment that linkages create, a strategy of maximising linkages is unlikely to be economically rational. Not all linkages will create economically desirable inducements; for example, setting up an automobile plant creates a demand for steel, and may encourage the setting up of local capacity. However, if the domestic market is small, or local raw materials are expensive, the cost of producing domestic steel may be high by world standards. If local steel is not protected from foreign competition there will be no positive pecuniary externality, since due to its high cost it will not be possible to run a domestic steel plant profitably. With protection, profits sufficiently high to justify domestic production may be generated and in this case the initial linkage has created the possibility of setting up local production by generating a demand for the product. However, if protection is essential, these profits can only be earned through the intervention of the government. If the local steel does not become competitive over a reasonable time period, the economy will have lost potential income through this mechanism. This sequence was relatively common in protected import-substitute economies, where backward linkages induced the establishment of high cost suppliers.

Naturally, in some cases, linkage effects may be economically beneficial, creating a market for goods which can be produced competitively, or which can become competitive over a period of time. The general point is that it cannot be assumed a priori that simply because there is a domestic market for a commodity as a result of linkages, that this commodity immediately should be produced domestically. Where high protection is required to sustain such a linkage, it is likely to be premature and the resulting output high cost. Where uneconomic suppliers are set up, domestic users of the goods will be penalised and their cost competitiveness will be reduced.

Production specialisation and dynamic increasing returns

The second element of the case for manufacturing's special role is based on the gains in productivity that arise through specialisation as an inter-related set of new industries expand together. Here such benefits may be internal to individual firms as well as external in the form of benefits to others. Growth of productivity has been a central feature in many discussions of the role of manufacturing industry. It is empirically well established that productivity per worker is higher in manufacturing than in other sectors, such as services or agriculture. What is of particular significance, however, is the trend in sectoral labour productivity over time, since a rising output per worker means more real income for distribution within an economy.

There is a view with a long tradition in economics that manufacturing is the only economic sector that, in the long run, is subject to increasing returns; that is, rising productivity as output expands. This originates in the distinction conventional in the Classical economists, between increasing returns in manufacturing compared with diminishing returns in agriculture, with commerce treated as an appendage of manufacturing.[22] However, the engine of growth argument cannot be based on a simple notion of economies of scale, where unit costs fall as output expands, since such relations can be found outside manufacturing. What it requires is a dynamic relationship – 'dynamic increasing returns' – between growth of output and growth of productivity. Only in manufacturing, it is argued, are productivity, and thus unit costs, linked with the cumulative growth of output over time. The mechanisms are learning by doing, technological adaptation and modification and the gains from increased specialisation as manufacturing activities are increasingly sub-divided into more specialist forms. Unlike simple or static economies of scale, productivity gains arising in this way are not linked with output at a point in time and are thus non-reversible should output decline temporarily. However, full closure of an activity could, of course, cause the loss of such improvements.[23]

This argument goes beyond the discussions of externalities and linkages considered earlier, to suggest that the key element behind the productivity growth that historically has occurred in manufacturing in many countries is the scope for specialisation within manufacturing as the size of the market expands.[24] This allows increasing specialisation and differentiation between firms, in particular as an increasingly complex network of supplier industries is established. The scale of operation of these specialist producers is dependent upon the size of the market for the products for which they provide inputs, so that as manufacturing in general expands, firms have the opportunity to become more specialised and reap the advantages of specialisation.[25] Individual firms benefit from the external economies provided by the greater specialisation of their suppliers, and similarly at the branch level, growth of one branch may have its immediate impact on the productivity of suppliers located in another branch. The important point is that, in principle, the expansion of the market for a firm or branch can have repercussions in terms of productivity and profits for a whole range of manufacturing activities. This provides a rationale for seeing industrial operations as an inter-related whole, in which new investments are not planned in isolation from each other.

In summary, from this engine of growth perspective shared by many Structuralist and Radical authors, a successful manufacturing sector will generate benefits to firms both within and outside the sector itself as well as to consumers. In part this can arise when productivity gains in one firm lead to lower costs and higher quality manufactured products used as productive inputs by other producers or purchased as final goods by consumers. In addition, manufacturing expansion can lead to productivity improvements in other sectors. This can arise from the supply side if high-quality capital goods, embodying new technologies, are produced domestically rather than being imported at higher cost. The demand effects from manufacturing can also stimulate productivity gains, for example in agriculture where rising labour productivity is likely to result when job opportunities in manufacturing draw workers off the land. Similarly if there is spare capacity in the transport and distribution sectors, productivity there will rise if greater manufacturing production leads to a higher throughput in these sectors.

Clearly, caveats need to be noted. The strength of such effects must vary with the stage an economy has reached and, even if the argument is accepted in full, it cannot imply that manufacturing will retain a key role at all levels of income, since as noted in Chapter 1, there is a well established tendency for the share of manufacturing in total activity to decline as a certain income level is reached. Even if external benefits in the form of learning and technical change remain more important than in other sectors, demand patterns are such that beyond a certain income the proportion of domestic expenditure on manufacturing will decline. Exporting can delay this effect, but up to now it has emerged in all economies. Further there is no presumption of a unique pattern of manufacturing expansion that can maximise these benefits. Typically early growth in low income economies is based on technologically simple labour-intensive manufactures, like textiles and food processing. How rapidly it will be appropriate to deepen the industrial structure to move into the production of parts, components and capital goods will vary with the conditions of a particular economy. All that one can say is that resource endowments, both current and potential, institutional capacity and external market conditions will combine to determine the speed at which it will be economically justified to move into more sophisticated areas of manufacture.

Nonetheless, in general terms the engine of growth argument retains a validity. In the past it has been linked with a justification for protectionist trade policies, as a means of building up an integrated industrial base sheltered from foreign competition.[26] However, this is not necessarily a logical conclusion, since the experience of the East Asian NIEs shows how successful export-based industrialisation can create a very rapid expansion of the manufacturing sector and in some cases a genuine deepening of the industrial structure. In fact, as we have seen in Chapter 3, there is some evidence that benefits in terms of productivity growth are greater when output growth is concentrated in the export rather than the home market, due to the competitive pressure and external links associated with exporting. The question of the relationship between foreign trade and manufacturing expansion brings us to the third theme we wish to consider in this chapter.

The global economy

One of the critical distinctions between Neoclassical authors and their critics in policy terms has been in attitudes towards foreign trade and the world economy in general. The work of both Structuralist and also many Radical authors was seen as a justification for the protectionist import-substitution programmes pursued in the majority of developing countries from the 1950s to the early 1980s.

In the 1950s the majority of economists writing on development problems shared the widely held view of 'export-pessimism' regarding traditional primary exports from developing countries. At various times, some of the major economists working on development issues, for example Nurkse, Prebisch, Lewis and Myrdal, all commented upon the difficulty of expanding rapidly developing countries' exports of these goods.[27] Since traditional primary exports were seen as incapable of stimulating the domestic economy, local production of new industrial goods for the home market was an obvious alternative. New industries would inevitably be high cost in international terms, and would thus need some protection from import competition. This was generally viewed as an acceptable cost, which had to be borne if domestic industry were to become established.[28]

The prospects of significant manufactured exports to developed countries were not considered seriously at this time, given the relatively low level of industrialisation in developing countries, at least outside Latin America. However it is also clear that autarky was not widely advocated, and that the potential gains from trade were not overlooked.[29] It is not that the significance of export demand was ignored, but that from the perspective of the 1950s, exports appeared unpromising as a source of demand for the newly established manufacturing activities of developing countries. Critical to this atmosphere of pessimism is the set of arguments put forward by the Latin American economist, Raul Prebisch, during the 1950s and 1960s when he held senior positions first at the Economic Commission for Latin America (ECLA) and then at UNCTAD.[30]

The declining terms of trade

In pointing to an apparent decline in the prices of poor countries' primary exports relative to the prices of their imports, Prebisch in part provided an ex post rationalisation for an industrialisation policy, which was already being implemented in parts of Latin America. His empirical evidence on the trend in the terms of trade of developing countries was subject to much, often critical, comment, but nonetheless contributed to an atmosphere of scepticism concerning the potential gains from trade for developing countries. His case for industrialisation was predicated upon a basic distinction, also used in the Dependency literature, between the rich countries of the centre specialised in manufactures and the backward countries of the periphery, specialised in primary commodities. Particular structural characteristics of these two groups of countries were seen as determining their trading relationship. First, due to the different functioning of labour and product markets, technology-induced productivity changes were seen as having different price effects for the exports of the two groups. For manufacturing, productivity growth in the centre is taken in higher wages, whilst in the traditional export sector in the periphery it leads to lower employment with a consistent downward pressure on wage rates. Markets for manufactures in the centre are oligopolistic, with prices determined by a mark-up on costs, whilst in the periphery they are competitive. Hence productivity growth in the former leads to higher prices, whilst in the latter lower costs are passed on to consumers in lower prices. In addition, arising from their different production specialisation, there is a clear disparity between the income elasticity of demand in the centre for the traditional exports of the periphery, and the income elasticity of demand in the periphery for the manufactured goods it purchases from the centre. The income elasticity of demand for the peripheries' imports exceeds substantially that for its exports and hence the establishment of new manufacturing industries, that would replace imports, was seen as a key means of reducing demand in the periphery for manufactured imports.

In combination, these features of poor countries provided an explanation for a long-run decline in the prices of the traditional raw material and agricultural exports of developing countries relative to their manufactured imports from the centre. This relative decline in their commodity terms of trade was taken as justifying government intervention in the process of foreign trade.[31]

Prebisch's policy prescription of industrialisation based on import-substitution follows from this analysis of the relations between centre and periphery. If a long-term decline in the terms of trade was an accurate forecast of future trends, as opposed to simply an observation from a particular period, it implies that the route of continued expansion based on traditional exports cannot be relied upon for sustained long-term growth. As Prebisch himself pointed out later, it is rational to shift resources into new industrial activity even if this activity is high cost by international standards, provided that the losses sustained through the excess of domestic production costs over the costs of comparable imports, are less than the income losses, which would result from falling export prices as a result of the expansion of traditional exports.[32]

The Prebisch case relating to trends in poor countries' terms of trade remains highly relevant both theoretically and empirically. Theoretically, once one accepts the assumption of different market structures in different groups of countries, the Prebisch analysis becomes compatible with conventional Neoclassical interpretations of trade. This follows since, if productivity growth systematically shifts the supply curve for primary products to the right more than that for manufactured products, and income growth systematically shifts the demand curve for manufactures to the right more than that for primary commodities, it is a logical conclusion that the relative price of primary commodities in terms of manufactured goods will tend to decline and, to the extent that developing countries export primary products and import manufactures, their commodity terms of trade will tend to fall.[33]

Further, the argument has been extended from primary exports to labour-intensive, technologically simple manufacturers. For example, if world market prices are based on cost of production and new producers can enter markets for labour-intensive commodities with ease, then there will be a tendency for the costs of labour-intensive manufactures (that are still the dominant manufactured exports of the poorest developing countries) to fall relative to skill or capital-intensive manufactures as countries compete through reductions in wage costs. The only way to prevent this process is for individual low-income countries to find market niches that will allow them to generate rents or extra-normal profits. If they do not succeed in finding such niches, there will be a tendency for real wages to be pulled down to the level set by the lowest cost large world market supplier, which it is suggested at the turn of the new century was China.[34]

Empirically more recent analyses of the question have generally found support for Prebisch's position on the terms of trade. Prebisch's original analysis used UK price series for British imports of primary commodities and exports of manufactures as proxies for developing countries' terms of trade. More recent studies have used both different price series and considerably more sophisticated econometric techniques and, in general, have concluded that when the analysis is extended up to the 1980s there remains a secular decline in the export price of primary goods vis-à-vis manufactures, of around 1% annually.[35] Attempts to explain this trend suggest that both the differential growth of wages between manufacturing and primary activity (stressed by Prebisch) and raw material saving technical change that conserves primary inputs (stressed by Singer) are important in explaining this trend.[36] The strongly negative impact of these two effects on the price of primary vis-à-vis manufactured goods is partially offset by the strong growth of world manufactured output, which pulls up primary prices through its induced demand.

However, the key issue to consider here is the policy significance of these results. First, even when Prebisch was writing, the generalisation that all poor countries exported primary goods, whilst rich countries exported manufactures did not hold. With the growth of manufactured exports from some lower income economies starting in the 1960s, the pattern of world trade has shifted even further away from this simple generalisation. What does appear valid, however, is that primary exports remain of great significance to the poorer countries, particularly in Africa and South Asia. Second, whilst most of the debate has focussed on relative export prices (the so-called net barter or com-modity terms of trade) in terms of export earnings, what matters is the income terms of trade. Whilst relative primary export prices appear to have fallen since 1945, export volumes of primary goods have grown significantly over the same period, allowing the aggregate purchasing power of primary exports to grow; for example, at nearly 3% annually up to the early 1980s.[37]

Naturally aggregate comparisons such as this mask problems for particular commodities and countries specialised in these commodities. However, since a declining commodity terms of trade for primary exports means a lower real income growth relative to a situation of unchanged relative export prices, it still provides a strong and persuasive case for diversification out of traditional exports. This was the central insight of Prebisch, Singer and others and as a policy recommendation it remains as valid now as forty or fifty years ago. Finally, however, there is a related question not posed by Prebisch, but of key concern today: is there a tendency for the commodity terms of trade for the manufactures exported by developing countries (which from the poorer coun-tries of the group are predominantly of a labour-intensive type) to decline secularly relative to the prices of manufactures exported by the developed economies? This latter point raises significant questions regarding the pattern of export diversification that should be aimed at. There is, in fact, evidence of declining prices for developing country manufactured exports relative to prices of their manufactured imports, as we have seen primarily it is hypothesised due to heightened competition through low wage levels, associated particularly with the expansion of manufactured exports from China since the mid-1980s.[38]

Infant industries: a justification for protection?

Prebisch used his results on the terms of trade to argue for an accelerated programme of industrialisation to allow developing countries to diversify their exports and save foreign exchange through import-substitution. However, newly established industries will frequently not be in a position to compete with more established producers abroad. The infant industry argument provided a justification for not requiring such industries to face unrestrained import competition, at least not initially. The infant-industry case for protection from imports has a long history in economics, for example providing a rationale for protectionism in the USA and Germany in the nineteenth century against the competition from British goods. It clearly has a relevance to discussions on the import-substitution industrialisation pursued in the majority of developing countries post-1945, and it was influential in the thinking of early Structuralist economists.[39] The infant industry case has evolved over time and one can identify at least four separate strands in the argument to justify special treatment for new industries.

Learning effects

At the centre of the argument is the simple proposition that new activities can only be mastered effectively over a period of time – the 'learning period' – and that new industries therefore cannot be expected to compete on equal terms with established producers in other countries. The policy recommendation is, for a limited period of protection from import competition either in the form of import tariff or quota protection, whilst learning takes place. The expectation is that, over time, costs of production in these infant industries will fall to internationally competitive levels and the economy as a whole will gain from their protection. In principle the argument can be applied to any form of economic activity that produces internationally traded goods, but it has conventionally been associated most closely with manufacturing industry on the grounds, discussed earlier (page 83), that the scope for gaining by experience, or learning-by-doing, as well as specialisation due to an expanded market and technical change, are greater there than elsewhere.

Externalities

In addition, the infant-industry case has been linked with the question of the externalities generated by industrial investments. It is argued not only that the costs of individual producers will fall due to learning, which is an internal economy for them, but that the external benefits they create for others will also grow over time. Positive externalities created by infant industries can arise at different levels. For example, they can be external to an individual producer but internal to the branch in which it operates; that is, the gains accrue to firms in the same branch. The labour training externality, where skilled workers possessing skills specific to a branch leave a producer for work in the same branch, is an example of this. Alternatively the externalities could be external to the producer but internal to the whole manufacturing sector; that is, benefits accrue to firms within manufacturing with no systematic distinction between branches. An example of this would be technical progress in the production of inputs, such as capital equipments, used in a wide range of manufacturing activities. If these equipments are either lower priced or higher quality there should be a gain in profitability in their user activities. Finally, at the broadest level, externalities can be external to an individual producer and internal to the whole economy; that is the extra incomes created by externalities can accrue anywhere in the economy. This would be the case, for example, if external effects are in the form of changes in attitude towards work or decision-taking, so that experience in manufacturing creates new attitudes that can be used productively in a wide range of other activities.

These arguments are normally illustrated using diagrams that relate costs of production in infant producers to either time, or the cumulative output they have produced at any one point in time. Figure 4.1, for example, shows the real

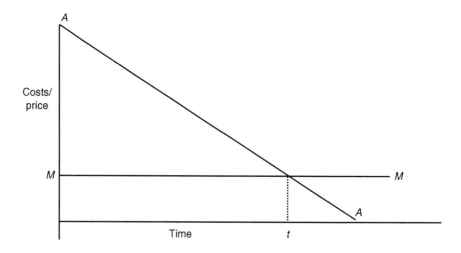

Figure 4.1 Infant industry: learning.

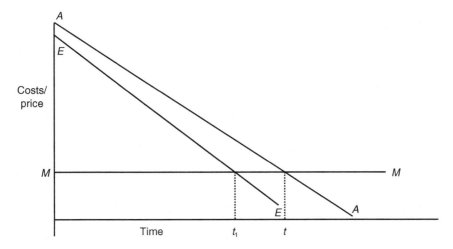

Figure 4.2 Infant industry: learning and externalities.

average cost curve *AA* of an individual producer over time, compared with the cost, insurance, freight (*cif*) price of comparable imports MM. Import prices are here assumed constant in real terms, and domestic costs are shown falling as learning takes place. At the time *t* the infant 'matures' as costs fall to internationally competitive levels; beyond *t* costs are shown as continuing to fall, so that exports should be possible. For the individual producer there will be a short-run cost up to *t*, in the absence of import protection, to be balanced against a longer run gain for the rest of its operation. Where import protection is provided, the short-run cost is borne by the consumers or users of the output, rather than the firm itself, since they must pay prices in excess of world levels. If import competitor prices fall in real terms, MM will slope downwards in Figure 4.1, and the achievement of competitiveness will be delayed.

Externalities are introduced in Figure 4.2. Here it is assumed that not only do the costs of the individual producer fall over time, but that other producers gain from the external benefits the original infant generates. In this situation a second cost curve is required *EE*, which shows the net unit cost to the economy of the production of the infant producer. If other possible distortions or externalities are absent, this net economic cost is the infant's own cost of production minus the external benefits per unit of output that are created for others. The consequences of the inclusion of *EE* in the diagram are that maturation occurs more rapidly at time t^1, that the initial losses are lower and that the gains after t^1 are greater, since net economic costs are significantly below the world price of comparable imports. In other words, what is illustrated is that the case for infant-industry protection is strengthened wherever positive externalities are generated. If externalities are negative, *EE* will be above, not below, *AA* and the opposite results will hold.

Technology and technical change

One can extend the infant industry argument further by introducing aspects of technology and technical change. Since many industries are characterised by indivisible technologies, such that a critical minimum level of output (the minimum efficient level of production) is required to introduce a new technology subject to significant declining unit costs, trade protection or promotion can be critical in ensuring that firms reach this critical minimum output.[40] This argument is illustrated diagrammatically in Figure 4.3.

We take a producer operating initially at a low output level. *DD* represents domestic demand, *Pm* is the cost of imports in the domestic market, inclusive of any import tariff, and *Pe* is the price obtained for exports. Transport and distribution costs account for the remainder of the divergence between *Pm* and *Pe*. At low levels of domestic demand such as *OQ*, unit costs of domestic production are high and the supply line is horizontal at *PdS*. At this level of demand local producers are uncompetitive even with protection. However when demand grows beyond *OQ** a new technology subject to falling unit cost can be applied and is represented by the supply line *SS¹*. If demand grows to *OQ₁*, for example, local production is competitive with imports (although protection may still be required). Once demand reaches beyond *OQ₂*, however, local

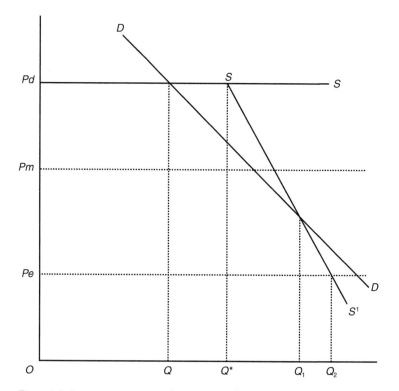

Figure 4.3 Import protection and minimum efficient output.

producers can compete internationally, since their unit costs fall below the export price. Here, initially protected high cost firms have been able to expand to become competitive exporters as a result of the initial support given by protection, since it is assumed that without protection (or promotion) demand would not have reached the level of OQ^* at which a minimum efficient scale of production can be introduced.[41]

Where this story departs from the Neoclassical one is in the ability of protected firms to move down the supply line SS^1. The Neoclassical case asserts that it will be far easier to exploit economies of scale by serving export markets initially, since a protected domestic market gives firms too much scope for inefficiency. This is often referred to as X-inefficiency. However, in their analysis, for exports to occur requires either for firms to take losses on initial sales, at lower output levels, or for some promotional support from governments. The policy issue is whether special protection against imports or promotional support can be used positively as a means to achieve cost reductions.

This latter possibility can occur if we introduce technical change into the analysis. This can be done by relating technical change to the domestic market position of firms, which will clearly be influenced by government trade interventions. Once one allows for market imperfections, one can make a case that technical progress may be stimulated more by protection than by a liberal foreign trade environment. This requires the behavioural response by enterprises that the larger is a firm's market share the greater is its investment in productivity improving technology. Hence if market share rises due to protection, the more rapid will be technical change. The logic is simply that the larger the scale of output, the greater will be the benefits to a firm of a given proportionate decline in costs, so that there is a complementarity between production and technological investment.[42]

Figure 4.4 plots the relation between technological investment or expenditure and sales for individual enterprises. Line TT shows technological investment rising with output in response to the initial behavioural assumption and line QQ shows how output grows as a result of lower costs due to technological effort. Protection by improving domestic market share can shift the latter line to Q_1Q_1, so that for a given level of technological investment output rises. This output rise will, in turn, stimulate more technological investment, so that once again cumulative gains result. As before, if cost reductions are great enough, exports may emerge. Once again this is quite a different story from Neoclassical analysis and links with the late industrialisation discussion above. The key difference is that, whilst Neoclassicals can accept the logic involved, they would argue that technical change under protection will not be economically efficient, since producers would respond to distorted price signals. In the medium term, therefore, even in a technologically dynamic sector, internationally competitive producers will not emerge. The efficiency of technology choice is discussed further in Chapter 6.

Technological
expenditure

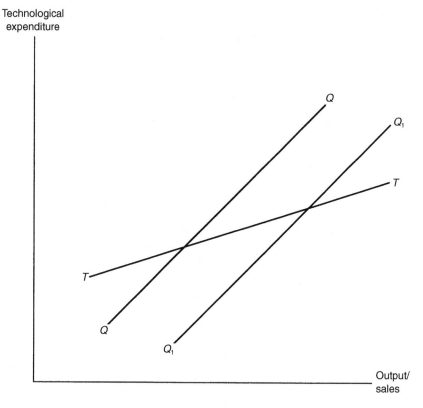

Figure 4.4 Protection and technological effort.

Strategic trade theory: a new version of the infant industry case?

The initial version of the infant industry case, summarised above, was restated from a different perspective in more recent debates on trade theory. During the 1980s, international trade theoreticians posed a series of challenges to Neoclassical theory by dropping the standard assumptions of perfect competition and non-constant returns to scale in models for analysing the welfare impacts of trade flows. The analysis was concerned primarily with developed economies, but several writers suggested it had an applicability to trade policy in the NIEs and perhaps other developing economies.[43] Once one allows for declining unit costs it is possible that comparative advantage in a particular activity can derive from historical accident in that initial production happened to commence for whatever reason (including government protective or promotional measures), but once established, domestic firms could expand to become internationally competitive. This argument links directly with the cumulative causation approach to industrialisation summarised earlier (page 83).

Technically, once one introduces imperfect competition and increasing returns to scale, then a major conclusion follows, which is that, in principle, successful producers can experience profits at above normal levels (since by definition perfect competition ensures that only normal profits can be generated). Such super-normal profits or rents will vary with the market structure of industries, but once they are acknowledged to exist then there is the possibility that strategic interventions in trade by governments can ensure that national producers obtain a higher share of these rents than they would in the absence of such interventions. Since rent is extra domestic income and some industries will generate more rent than others, this provides a rationale for targeting and supporting particular industries. Further, once one allows for government activism each government of trading partners will have an incentive to intervene in trade provided it thinks there is a possibility of other governments intervening. This follows, since even though a country may be better off if no one intervenes (that is, with free trade) it will be worse off if a trading partner intervenes and it does not.[44] In other words, where rents accrue internationally, government policy can influence how they are allocated between trading partners, hence the terminology of 'profit-shifting' applied to this analysis. Much of the policy discussion is conducted in terms of export subsidies, but conventional tariff or quota protection can also be used in this context.

The analysis is of relevance to industries, for example like jet aircraft construction or certain aspects of computer production, where there are only a small number of possible producers from different countries and where the key investors are aware of each others' strengths. The critical role of government intervention in this argument can be illustrated by reference to a simple pay-off matrix in Table 4.1. We consider two producers in countries A and B. The global market is only sufficient to support one firm. If both firms produce they will each make losses ($-\$1$ million), whilst if neither produces their profits are zero. If one produces, but the other does not, the sole producer will earn $5 million and the non-producer will earn zero profits. In Table 4.1 the first figure in the matrix refers to returns to A and the second to returns to B. The absolute values in the matrix are unimportant and the argument holds provided any similar relative figures are used.

The point about this illustration is that the rational response for a producer in one country in regard to whether to produce or not depends on what it thinks the other producer will do. If a producer is convinced that the competitor will produce, the rational response is to avoid entering the market since there will be a choice only between zero profits (from not entering) and $-\$1$ million (from both entering). This is shown in the first column of Table 4.1

Table 4.1 Pay-off matrix – gains for each country under alternative scenarios ($ million)

Country A Country B	Produces	Not produce
Produces	$-1, -1$	0, 5
Not produce	5, 0	0, 0

where country A always produces. If both A and B produce, they each lose $1 million, whilst if B does not produce, but A does, the latter gains $5 million. Column two shows the situation where A never produces. If it does not enter the market, but B does, B gains $5 million. Where neither country enters, both have a zero gain. Government strategic trade interventions in favour of a producer may be critical in establishing the credibility of that producer's threat to enter a particular market, since whilst private firms on their own may not be able to withstand initial losses from the dual entry scenario, with government support they may.[45]

However, as in the conventional infant industry analysis, this policy will only be justified in economic terms in the context of declining costs, either due to economies of scale in production, to learning, or to external benefits elsewhere in the economy. If costs do not fall, so that the economy does not have a potential comparative advantage in the activity concerned, the extra profits accruing to the national producer will reflect simply a transfer from those who bear the cost of the subsidy, who will be either tax payers or consumers. The existence of declining unit costs raises the potentially important result that, under some circumstances, strategic interventions of this sort in support of local import-competing producers may in the longer-term lead to exports from such firms. This possibility can be seen again taking a two-country/two-producer case. If both start from a position of equal sales and unit costs, then in the presence of declining unit costs, if one government supports its national firm via either tariff protection or a production subsidy, this will have the effect of expanding the production of the firm. As output grows, unit costs fall and the firm becomes more competitive relative to the other producer. If both sell to a third market output in the non-subsidised firm will contract as it cannot compete in price, thus allowing a further expansion of the subsidised firm. Finally, if unit costs decline sufficiently, the subsidised firm may start exporting to the national market of its competitor, so that the initial support or protection has created the basis for later exports. Here a strategic intervention has allowed an economy to exploit a potential comparative advantage.

In relation to the strategic trade policy case, it should be clear that the industrial structure discussed here is one of international oligopoly where world markets are dominated by a few large firms. Hence there is the issue of the relevance of this type of analysis for all but a few of the higher income developing countries. The aircraft industry provides one reasonably well documented illustration where the Brazilian government promoted exports of small jet aircraft (such as the Brasilia) by a nationally owned firm.[46] In most other instances in this type of industry one will be considering investments by TNCs and, whether support by host governments will be sufficient to induce a particular TNC to invest in a new product in its economy. How far host governments can actually influence TNC behaviour in practice is a subject for debate, since new product development is rarely undertaken by them in developing country locations. Hence this particular version of the infant industry argument remains something of a theoretical possibility rather than a practical option.

Some qualifications

Theoretically, none of these arguments actually makes a totally convincing case for protection per se. First, to justify the protection of infant industries one must do more than demonstrate that costs fall to internationally competitive levels. Infant-industry protection can be treated as a form of investment by the economy with initial costs offset against later gains, when domestic costs of production fall below world levels, technical change occurs and possibly positive externalities are also generated. Strictly the case for protection requires that over the lifetime of an investment, the discounted value of later benefits outweigh the discounted value of the initial costs. This can only be demonstrated by a detailed cost–benefit appraisal of the infant producers' activities and *ex ante* it can be extremely difficult to anticipate where successes will occur. Second, the Neoclassical position is to question why, if later gains outweigh initial costs, firms themselves would not make the necessary investment in the absence of protection. If the reason is due to market imperfections such as lack of access to credit for new, relatively high risk activities, the Neoclassical policy prescription is to go directly to the cause of the problem and reform the credit market, rather than to adopt import protection as a means of encouraging the new investment, since protection brings with it costs in terms of allocative inefficiency. Similarly, if the explanation for why the investment does not take place is because many benefits are external, such as technical applications that can be copied by others, the recommendation is to subside the activity, like R and D, that generates the externality.[47] In practical terms, however, although protection may be theoretically a second-best means of promoting new activities, it is relatively straightforward to introduce and certainly less difficult than financial sector reform. It is also paid for by consumers rather than governments, whilst subsidies, whether in the form of tax concessions or direct payments, are a drain on government income; hence its attraction to policy-makers.

Empirical work on developing country experience with infant industry protection has been conducted as part of assessments of the efficiency of import-substitution strategies. In general the judgement on infant industries set up as part of import-substitution programmes is strongly negative, in large part because, unless firms know they will at some point be subject to competition from imports, they will have no incentive to improve efficiency and lower costs. Empirical case studies on firms in a number of developing countries have shown that learning is rarely an effortless or costless process. It is now common to distinguish between different forms of learning, with learning-by-doing as a result of production experience only the most elementary. The implication is that successful infants will need to purposefully pursue policies of raising their capacity to understand, adapt and improve the technology they are using. Only such technologically active firms will emerge as successful infants, and the shelter provided by protection provides no incentive to seek out these various improvements.[48] Evidence from Korea suggests that a key factor in explaining the success of infants there was the impetus to export at an early stage provided by government policy. Exporting exposed producers to both competitive pressure and foreign designs and marketing techniques. Export sales at an early point in the lifecycle of firms was made possible by cross-subsidisation, with firms selling above their costs in the protected local market, but often below cost abroad. The incentive to do this was to obtain benefits from the government through, for example, access to low cost credit and the granting of licences for various investment initiatives.[49]

A consensus on infant industry protection is difficult to achieve, given the contrasting views. What can be said, however, is that whilst there is ample empirical evidence that past protectionist policies have been associated with economic inefficiency (see Chapter 3), because of acknowledged market failures including externalities there is no general supposition that protection or promotion of particular activities may not be economically rational. Promotional measures may be less distorting in a theoretical sense, but they are more difficult to apply and may be less transparent than is protection. However, the case has to be made for specific interventions and current discussions of infant industry protection suggest that it should not be applied as it was under old-style import-substitution regimes, but rather that it should be selective, targeting particular activities with competitive potential, and explicitly temporary, so that protection is not seen as a permanent source of income for producers at the expense of consumers.

Conclusion

This chapter has examined what remains valid in the vast literature on industrialisation in developing countries that refuses to accept at face value the certainties of the Neoclassical position. Of the three broad themes discussed here, on the first, the role of the state, there is ample historical evidence most recently from the NIEs that, under some very well defined circumstances, the developmental state has undoubtedly had a positive role. Although developmental states can become over-stretched or outlive their usefulness, as the events of 1997–98 in East Asia have shown. The implication is that a policy mix that uses the market, where appropriate, but is not wholly subservient to it, can still have a role to play in some countries, although simple blueprints for intervention are not available.

On the second theme, that of the special role of manufacturing, again some truth remains in the argument, since whether one produces potatoes or computer chips is bound to affect longer-term growth prospects. Manufacturing still has special economically desirable features. The real policy debate is how best to utilise these and support the sector and how far such interventions should aim to override market principles. The cumulative gains from manufacturing may well be greater, however, in an open competitive trading environment and exports may play a crucial role in such a cumulative process.

The discussion on the third broad theme on participation in the world economy suggests that developing countries in principle have much to gain.

De-linking from world trade and investment is not an option; however, choices remain on how best to encourage new activities and on how to diversify exports. Whilst there is ample empirical evidence that past broad-based protectionist policies have been associated with high levels of economic inefficiency, because of acknowledged market failures, including externalities, there is no general supposition that protection or promotion of particular activities may not be economically rational. Although in theory, as we have highlighted, special support and encouragement for new activities can be justified, particularly on the grounds of technical change, the case has to be made for specific interventions and the form they take needs to be examined carefully. We return to some of these themes in Chapters 7 and 8.

5   Small-scale industry
Is it really beautiful?

Size of industrial units in developing countries has held something of a fascination for economists. From different theoretical perspectives small enterprises have been viewed as alternatively:

- the main appliers of appropriate technology and producers of appropriate products;
- efficient labour-intensive users of limited investment funds;
- a seedbed for entrepreneurship;
- and the mechanism for generating production specialisation and external economies.

We consider these varying claims in this chapter. However, at the outset, it is necessary to clarify what is meant normally by the term 'small-scale enterprises' (SSE) and to give some indication of their continued importance in many developing countries.

Definition of small-scale enterprise

Most definitions of SSE focus on number of workers employed in an enterprise. A common set of distinctions is set out in Table 5.1.

The classification of Table 5.1 differentiates between very small household or cottage enterprises using traditional technology and family labour and very

Table 5.1 Definition of scale

Enterprise category	Number of workers
Household/cottage	0–4
Micro	0–9
Small	10–49
Medium	50–99
Large	above 100

Source: Adapted from Cortes *et al.* (1987) Glossary.

small micro enterprises that use hired labour and a form of factory-based production located in workshops rather than the home. Precise definitions can vary between different academic studies and also between official statistical sources, which sometimes complicates comparative work. The main alternative to the use of employment data is to distinguish between scale on the basis of the value of capital assets. This has an advantage where labour employment is temporary or seasonal, but has the disadvantage, particularly at the larger end of the size scale, that asset data are normally only available at historical book values, which may be a very poor indicator of replacement cost.

An obvious reason why SSE have attracted so much attention in developing countries is that, in many cases, they provide the bulk of employment within the manufacturing sector. Although given their relatively low labour productivity, they are much less important as a contributor to manufacturing value-added. It is now a reasonably well established historical pattern that as economies develop and incomes rise, the share of both cottage and micro enterprises in manufacturing employment declines, as their markets are taken over initially primarily by modern small and medium enterprises and at a later stage by larger firms. The precise mix between these latter three size categories will vary between cases, but the expectation is that beyond a certain income level the role of large enterprises in manufacturing employment will start to increase significantly.

Accurate data on the size distribution of manufacturing employment is rare, but most estimates support the broad trend noted above. In the 1960s and 1970s small manufacturing enterprises (0–49 workers) accounted for over 50% of manufacturing employment in countries for which data were available.[1] More recent comparable statistics are difficult to obtain but there is evidence that the employment share of these firms remains important in many cases and that their employment has grown rapidly in a number of countries, particularly in Africa. Table 5.2 gives some illustrative data from different sources for the 1980s. The usefulness of the data for comparative purposes is weakened by the lack of agreed definitions in the original sources.

Table 5.2 confirms the very large role micro and small firms play in employment creation in low-income economies in Africa and Asia. Even in Latin America where incomes are higher and larger enterprises are more important in terms of employment share, there is still an important small sector (although in many countries these small firms are defined as those with less than 100 workers). However, one feature of developing countries' industrial structure is that, in many countries, large numbers of micro and cottage firms co-exist in some sectors with several large firms. This creates a pattern in the size distribution often termed the 'missing middle', as in employment terms firms employing between ten to ninety-nine workers are substantially underestimated in comparison with the distribution in developed economies.[2]

Not only do small firms continue to play an important role in manufacturing employment in low-income economies, in some cases there is evidence that this role is increasing. In several sub-Saharan African countries during the 1980s,

Table 5.2 Employment share in manufacturing for different sizes of firm (1980s and 1990s (%))

Country	Year	Micro	Small	Medium	Large
Indonesia[a]	1986	53	15	32	
Nepal[b]	1986–87		57	25	18
Zambia[c]	1985	83	1	16	
Mexico[d]	1985		24	9	67
Bolivia[d]	1984		24	15	61
Bolivia[e]	1994		26		
Columbia[d]	1985		22	14	64
Ecuador[d]	1985		35	12	53
Argentina[f]	1993			45	
Ecuador[f]	1996			38	
Paraguay[f]	1997			41	
Uruguay[f]	1995			58	
Venezuela[f]	1995			40	

Notes

a Indonesian data come from Tambunan (1991) Table 1. Micro firms have less than 5 workers; small firms have 5–19 workers; large and medium firms are grouped together as those that have 20 or more workers.

b Data on Nepal come from the Government of Nepal (1989). Asset values are used for the size categories; small firms are in the lowest asset value group; large firms are in the highest asset value group; medium firms are the rest.

c Zambian data are reported in Liedholm (1992). Micro firms are those with 0–9 workers; small firms have 10–49 workers and large and medium firms are grouped together as those with 50 or more workers.

d Mexican data come from Government of Mexico (1989). Data on Bolivia, Columbia and Ecuador are reported in Spath (1993). In all these cases small firms are those with 0–49 workers; medium firms are those with 50–99 workers and large firms have 100 or more workers.

e Data on Bolivia for 1994 come from Peres and Stumpo (2000)

f Data come from Peres and Stumpo (2000). Here medium covers firms in both small and medium categories, that is up to 99 employees.

SSE (defined as enterprises with less than fifty workers in all sectors not just in manufacturing) provided over 40% of the new jobs created. In two cases, Zimbabwe and Swaziland, the share in new employment from SSE over 1981–90 was as high as 86% and 92% respectively.[3] The bulk (nearly 80% averaged across all five countries surveyed) of these new jobs was from new enterprises starting up, rather than the expansion of established firms. How stable this new employment will be is unclear since a significant part of the high job creation in SSE is likely to be in the form of very small micro or household units formed due to the redundancy of the head of household. In response to the loss of a job in a larger firm or in the civil service, a household or owner enterprise may be set up. This type of employment may be low productivity with little scope for future growth, but may still offer an income above what could be earned in any feasible alternative activity. It provides a survival strategy for the households concerned rather than a dynamic growth path. The general pattern of SME births and deaths in poor countries has been described as one of 'churning' with high birth rates (averaging over 20% a year in many countries) and almost as high closure or death rates. Jobs created by new start-ups are seen as less stable than those created from the expansion of existing small firms, on the grounds that the latter are more likely to respond to the pull of demand factors, whilst the former are more likely to reflect the push of supply conditions (that is, the lack of alternative income opportunities).[4]

In Latin America small and medium-sized firms have been a source of dynamism, increasing their production in most countries in the 1990s and in some instances increasing their share in total industrial activity. Labour productivity in these firms rose substantially over this period in most countries, although in a majority of cases, this was accompanied by falling levels of employment. However, the trend is very varied since in Mexico, Chile, Colombia and Peru numbers employed in these firms grew over at least part of the 1990s.[5]

Generalising about the representative SSE is difficult given the diversity amongst enterprises with less than fifty workers. However we can think of stylised facts about representative firms as a means of drawing distinctions between them. At low levels of development and income per capita, such a firm is likely to be a one-person, household-based firm; examples of common activities are tailoring and knitting, woodworking, metalworking, and the production of cheap consumer goods, such as mats and baskets, and simple repairs. Such firms are likely to be financed exclusively from the savings of the household concerned or their family and friends. They will serve local markets with natural protection from larger firms in the form of their low charges and knowledge of local needs. At lower income levels they will tend to be rural rather than urban based and to a disproportionate degree be run by females rather than males. As income per capita rises the representative SSE is likely to be a micro-enterprise based either in the household or in a workshop or small factory. Activities may be similar to that at the earlier stage but with greater scale and sophistication through the use of a modern rather than traditional technology; in addition baking, brewing, and the supply of various building materials may become more important. Here some external savings, either from banks or money lenders, may be used to supplement family resources. Markets will be less local and aimed less obviously at very low income consumers and an increasing proportion of enterprises will be urban-based. Finally, at a more advanced stage the representative SSE may be a small modern manufacturing unit engaged in making clothing, metal products, furniture, baking and other foods, and perhaps also chemicals, paints and various tools. Some external credit will almost certainly be used from either banks or possibly suppliers or customers. Although the local market remains predominant at this stage, the firm may also export a proportion of its output or may compete domestically with higher priced imported goods. This type of firm will be factory-based with hired labour and will probably use modern, but older, technology.[6]

Small firms and appropriate technology

The concept of an appropriate technology has played a major role in a discussion of the merits of SSE in developing countries. It is usually interpreted as a technology with characteristics suited to the conditions of low income economies.[7] Typically the characteristics of such a technology include:

- the use of relatively large numbers of workers per unit of monetary investment;
- the use of local materials and inputs rather than imported alternatives;
- relatively uncomplicated technological processes that can be handled by national technicians and workers;
- the production of low cost, unsophisticated products that are suited to the needs of low income consumers, who are the majority of the population.

In other words, appropriateness is linked with low capital–labour ratios; low shares of imports in total cost; a low use of foreign experts and the production of simple products aimed at the low income segment of markets. Such technology, it is argued, will use less financial resources, generate more employment and suit the needs of local consumers. The significance for the present discussion is the expectation that it will be predominantly small firms that will employ this type of technology. To illustrate we can take the example of textiles, which can be produced in several alternative ways. There is large-scale production in modern mills; an intermediate alternative based on power-looms in small factories and handlooms based in homes or small workshops. The factor-intensity of these three alternatives will be quite different, with the former using far more capital per worker employed. Also the quality of finished goods will differ with the former providing goods to an international standard. By the criteria noted above the latter two can be seen as the appropriate alternatives. Further examples that are analysed in the literature include technologies for sugar, textiles and rice milling.[8]

Small firms and efficient technology

An ambiguity that exists in the definition of appropriate technology relates to its link with economic efficiency in the Neoclassical sense discussed in Chapter 3. Clearly, to be appropriate, a technology must be efficient, otherwise it will involve income losses for an economy. If we define appropriateness in terms of a set of characteristics, such as labour-intensity, there will always be the possibility that, given the resource endowment of a particular economy, a technology identified on the basis of a common characteristic will not be economically efficient. However, it has been argued that small-scale labour intensive technologies are often more efficient in developing country conditions than larger-scale capital intensive alternatives. Examples cited are sugar processing in India and Kenya, pineapple-canning in the Philippines and Taiwan, rice milling in the Philippines, maize milling in Tanzania and spinning in Thailand.[9]

The Neoclassical interpretation of technology choice, whilst highly simplified in that it assumes infinite factor substitutability and the use of only two factors (so one can always produce the same output using more labour to substitute for less capital and vice versa), is nonetheless helpful in bringing out clearly the role of relative factor prices in determining efficiency in technology choice. Figure 5.1 shows the standard two factor analysis with a convex production isocost curve (CC) showing how a given output can be produced by varying combinations of labour and capital; at any point on CC cost and output will be the same, but at each point there will be different combinations of the factors of labour and capital used in production. The desirable combination can only be determined when one knows the relative prices of the two factors, which are shown by the straight line AA. Costs are minimised for a given output at X, which is the point of tangency between the price line AA and CC. Hence with a new price line AA¹ there will be a new point of tangency and a new cost minimising point at X¹. The important issue illustrated here is that, as drawn, the steeper the price line, the higher is the cost of labour relative to capital. AA¹ therefore reflects a situation where labour is cheap relative to capital, whilst AA reflects one where it is relatively more expensive. The two cost minimising points X and X¹ differ significantly in the combinations of capital and labour used in each. X¹,

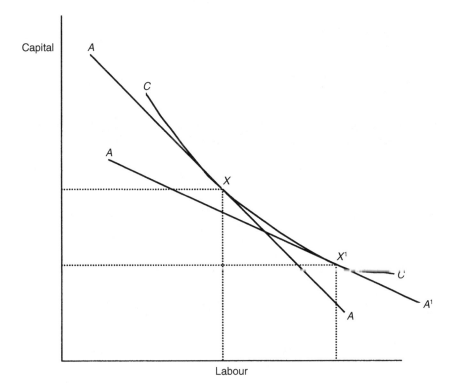

Figure 5.1 Choice of technology.

reflecting the relatively low cost labour scenario, has a much lower capital to labour ratio. Hence the demonstration of the intuitively persuasive point that, in economies where labour is relatively abundant and capital relatively scarce, the appropriate or desirable technology should be labour-intensive in the sense of a lower capital to labour ratio to produce a unit of output. A shift to such technology will increase jobs per unit of investment and thus contribute to employment creation. An important strand in the Neoclassical literature has been a critique of past policies, which shifted prices of capital and labour away from their true scarcity values and thus distorted technology choice. Minimum wage legislation, overvalued exchange rates and interest rate controls, it was argued, all combined to raise the labour–capital price ratio and thus to encourage greater capital intensity and, from that, the use of inappropriate technology.

The analysis in Figure 5.1 is clearly simplified and omits important practical issues. For example, there may be only a limited scope for replacing one factor by another; quality of product may differ when factor combinations change; the choice of technology may influence not just costs but also re-investment possibilities and income distribution; and labour will not be an homogeneous factor, but will reflect workers of varying skills. Nonetheless, whether SSE are both more labour-intensive than larger enterprises and more economically efficient needs to be demonstrated, rather than simply asserted.

The case can be summarised as follows; if SSE are more labour intensive, for a unit of output of standard quality:

$$(K/L)_s < (K/L)_l \tag{5.1}$$

where K and L are units of capital and labour per unit of output and subscripts s and l refer to small and large firms, respectively.

However for efficiency to be higher, a lower K/L is not enough, since efficiency is measured as a return on capital given as:

$$(VA - L*w)/K \tag{5.2}$$

and we require:

$$((VA - L*w)/K)_s > ((VA - L*w)/K)_l > r \tag{5.3}$$

where K, L, s and l are as above,
VA is value-added per unit of output,
w is the economic value of each unit of labour,
and r is the economic discount rate.

Equation (5.2) can be thought of as the rate of economic surplus or returns per unit of capital input. Even if condition (5.1) holds, the lower capital labour ratio may be offset by lower labour productivity in small firms (VA/L), so that condition (5.3) need not be met. The inclusion of the discount rate r in (5.3) is to ensure that not only is the small firm superior to the large, but that it is also economically efficient in the sense of generating a return above the opportunity cost of capital.[10]

An equivalent approach also adopted in some studies is to express (5.2) and (5.3) as benefit–cost ratios. Now, for a small firm, the benefit–cost ratio is:

$$(VA/(r.K + w.L))_s \tag{5.4}$$

and equation (5.3) becomes:

$$(VA/(r.K + w.L))_s > (VA/(r.K + w.L))_l \tag{5.5}$$

Since the discount rate is included in the cost calculation here efficiency in an absolute sense requires that benefits exceed costs, which is benefit–cost ratio of above 1.0.

Size and factor proportions

Within certain sectors there is clearly a range of technology choice implying differing capital intensity. Further, at the aggregate level of all-manufacturing from census and survey data across countries there is a clear tendency for capital to labour (K/L) ratios to rise with firm size.[11] What is less clear, however, is how far this is due to smaller firms being located in labour-intensive sectors and how far within one sector smaller firms are always more labour intensive. More disaggregate data is more ambiguous on the link between size and capital intensity. Table 5.3 illustrates the problem with Mexican industrial census data. Capital intensities are given for all-manufacturing, for the sub-sectors Food, Drink and Tobacco and Machinery and Metal Products and for two branches within these sub-sectors.

Table 5.3 Capital intensity in Mexican manufacturing (1993)

Size of firm (employees)	*Capital–labour ratio (thousands of pesos)*				
	All[a]	Food[b]	Baking[c]	Machinery[d]	Air-conditioning[e]
0–10	24.9	23.7	23.8	32.5	41.7
11–50	35.6	46.0	13.5	32.0	24.9
51–100	56.3	72.2	25.7	44.5	30.8
Above 100	105.5	95.5	94.5	58.9	39.7

Source: Government of Mexico (1995) Table 8.

Notes
a All-Manufacturing.
b Food, Drink and Tobacco, Census category 31.
c Baking, Census category 311503.
d Machinery and Metal products, Census category 38.
e Air-conditioning and Refrigeration equipment, Census category 382206.

It can be seen that at the aggregate level the capital–labour ratio indeed rises with the size of firm.[12] Capital intensity varies significantly between different parts of manufacturing but for the sub-sectors shown the same link between size and capital intensity holds with the minor exception that for Machinery and Metal Products micro firms (ten employees and below) are slightly more capital intensive than small firms (eleven to fifty employees). However, once one looks at the six-digit level of disaggregation, the relation between size and capital intensity is more ambiguous. For the branches selected, micro firms are now by no means the least capital-intensive. For Baking they have a capital–labour ratio nearly twice that of small firms and only a little lower than that of medium firms. For Air-conditioning equipment micro firms are the most capital-intensive with a capital–labour ratio that exceeds even that of large firms (100 workers and above). For both these two branches the lowest capital–labour ratio is found for medium-sized firms.[13]

Size and economic efficiency

The result that small firms may be relatively capital intensive in some lines of activity, because they operate at low levels of both labour and capital productivity, is paradoxical, but far from new.[14] What is of more significance is the evidence on size and economic efficiency, since minimising the K/L ratio on its own is not a rational economic criteria. Even if labour has a zero economic cost (a highly unlikely scenario even with open unemployment due to the higher resource costs associated with higher consumption due to employment), efficiency requires maximising the value-added to capital (VA/K) ratio rather than minimising the K/L ratio (see equation 5.2). What is important to consider, therefore, is the evidence on the comparative performance of different sizes of firm in similar industries.

A priori, despite some rather simplistic notions on the automatic superiority of small firms, there is no reason to expect that there will be an unambiguous relation between size and performance that holds for all forms of manufacturing. Arguments on the benefits of size work in conflicting directions. In some sectors, it may be that technological indivisibility means that economies of scale in production are so significant that small producers are bound to operate at much higher unit costs; steel and cement are examples where such scale effects may be critical. In other activities, for example in parts of electronics, economies of scope, reflecting the ability of large firms to co-ordinate a range of diverse activities, such as marketing, input purchases or innovation, may also create a cost advantage. On the other hand, small firms may have advantages in terms of knowledge of particular local markets, particularly those like simple textiles or engineering repairs aimed at low-income consumers. Furthermore, in specialist niche markets, such as fashion clothing or shoes, small enterprises may exhibit greater specialisation and flexibility in response to changing markets. When this is combined with a geographical concentration of small firms and their suppliers, external economies of location may also create competitive advantages.[15] Given such contradictory potential effects, the expectation must be that there will be clear variations in the size–performance relation between different branches.

A simple means of assessing comparative efficiency is to use Census data for different size categories and to estimate a version of either equations (5.2) or (5.4). This approach has the limitation that, unless very disaggregate Census classifications are reported, firms producing dissimilar products may be picked up in the comparison. Further, the capital stock figures may be particularly suspect. Undervaluation is more likely than overvaluation and if this is more of a problem for small firms, this could exert an upward bias in their estimates relative to those of larger firms. When this approach is used, different size categories are found to have the highest economic return in different countries.[16] The approach is illustrated in Table 5.4 using the same Mexican Census data as in Table 5.3.

The results in Table 5.4 reveal a wide difference between branches of manufacturing. In the aggregate small firms clearly have a higher return to capital that do larger firms. Small firms (11–50 employees) have slightly higher returns than micro firms (0–10 employees). Within sectors and sub-sectors the pattern varies. In Food, for example, micro firms have the highest returns, followed by large firms (above 100 employees); in the Baking branch of Food, small and large firms have the highest returns with almost equal rates of return. In Machinery in the aggregate micro firms have higher returns than large firms, whilst in the Air-conditioning equipment branch the reverse holds. However, in both the aggregate Machinery sector and its Air-conditioning sub-sector, firms in the 11–50 size group have the highest returns. Everywhere it is the medium sized firms (51–100) that have the lowest returns.[17]

A more accurate means of assessing the impact of scale on performance is to compare firms of different size operating under a similar market environment

Table 5.4 Economic returns in Mexican manufacturing (1993)

Size of firm (employees)	*All*[a]	*Food*[b]	*Baking*[c]	*Machinery*[d]	*Air-conditioning*[e]
		Economic return per unit of capital			
0–10	0.65	0.88	0.53	0.50	0.56
11–50	0.67	0.72	0.92	0.63	0.02
51–100	0.37	0.41	0.33	0.36	−0.004
above 100	0.42	0.76	0.92	0.47	0.65

Source: Calculated from Government of Mexico (1995) Table 8.

Notes
a All-Manufacturing.
b Food, Drink and Tobacco, Census category 31.
c Baking, Census category 311503.
d Machinery and Metal products, Census category 38.
e Air-conditioning and Refrigeration equipment, Census category 382206.

and producing identical products. Some examples of this approach are available using versions of either equations (5.2) or (5.4). One of the most detailed studies that is cited frequently in the literature compares economic returns in a range of activities and countries for small (below fifty workers) and large (above fifty workers) firms.[18] The striking conclusion is that, in all cases, small firms were more efficient and, with very few exceptions, large firms were economically inefficient in that they generated a negative economic surplus. Table 5.5 gives their results. One interpretation is that the large firms have benefited from trade protection and hence, in economic terms, their effect on the economy is negative. However, the results appear extreme, since such a high proportion of negative returns in a sample suggests a distinct bias in selection.

A rather different picture emerges from work on Colombia, which looked in detail at relatively large samples of metalworking and food processing firms.[19] Table 5.6 gives the benefit–cost ratio (following equation 5.4) for these firms by size category. The results in Tables 5.5 and 5.6 are not directly comparable since the former uses a version of equation (5.2) and the latter equation (5.4). What is of interest is the comparison within the tables. Whereas the data in Table 5.5 are unequivocal that small scale is always more efficient, the results in Table 5.6 suggest that for both activities in Columbia efficiency generally rises with size of firm. However, the food processing firms are mostly small and there is no com-

Table 5.5 Rate of economic return in large and small firms[a]

	Large	Small
Botswana		
sorghum beer	1.3	1.9
Egypt		
clothing	0.17	0.42
metal products	−0.03	1.03
Honduras		
clothing	−0.21	0.45
furniture	−0.26	0.58
shoes	−0.22	1.02
leather products	−0.21	0.79
metal products	−0.24	0.23
Jamaica		
clothing	−0.11	0.86
furniture	−0.0004	1.73
shoes	−0.06	2.47
metal products	0.17	0.56
Sierra Leone		
clothing	−0.27	0.59
bread	−0.11	0.12
rice milling	−0.30	0.80

Source: Cited in Stewart and Ranis (1990) Table 2.

Note
a Economic return is close to equation (5.2) and is defined as value-added minus a capital charge (at the economic discount rate) and labour costs (at a competitive wage) divided by capital stock.

Table 5.6 Benefit–cost ratio for metalworking and food processing firms in Columbia

Size (number of employees)	Number of firms	Metal working benefit–cost ratio[a]	Food processing benefit–cost ratio[a]
1–10	13	1.47	
11–20	16	1.82	
21–40	15	1.55	
41–60	11	1.96	
61+	8	2.07	
1–7	11		2.11
8–15	11		2.62
16–29	8		2.87
30+	6		3.08

Source: Cortes *et al.* (1987: 104) Table 3.8.

Note
a Benefit–cost ratio is what the authors term the private benefit–cost ratio, since outputs and inputs are not valued at economic prices. It is similar to equation (5.4). Values shown are averages for each size category.

parison between firms above and below fifty workers. In this case all that is shown is that, within the category of small firms, those at the larger end of the size range have higher returns than others. Another detailed study, this time on India, also reports profitability data (which implies a ratio similar to equation (5.2)) for a large sample of Indian firms in six sectors.[20] In three (machine tools, powerlooms, and soap) returns in large firms (above fifty workers) were above those in small firms (below fifty workers) and in three others (printing, shoes and metal casting) the reverse held.

The data from these studies on Colombia and India are in no sense definitive. We put them forward here simply to caution against accepting simple generalisations such as those implied by the results reported in Table 5.5. Furthermore there can also be some variation in performance within the SSE sector. Recent studies for Ghana and Palestine find that within the SSE sector, enterprises above ten workers are, in general, more efficient than micro firms using a profitability measure of efficiency.[21] For Ghana it is clear that the majority of these firms bring in very little income for their owner–managers and that when the latter's time is costed at the minimum wage the return on assets in these firms is generally negative. This is clear support for the view that in many countries (and particularly in sub-Saharan Africa) small enterprise development is predominantly a survival strategy for the owners, rather than a source of long-term dynamism.

Obstacles to small firms

Indirect evidence questioning the inherent efficiency of SSE in developing countries comes from the substantial literature on the problems they face. The vast majority of new firms setting up production in low-income countries are small in terms of employment and capital. There is evidence from a wide range of countries and market environments that the bulk of these new firms either remain small or disappear, either due to closure or to a move into another line of activity. Nonetheless, a minority do grow and some graduate into the category of small to medium or even large firms.

Although there appears to be no shortage of entrepreneurs willing to commit their time and resources to new small-scale activities, the failure or closure rate of such firms is generally high.[22] Closure rates can, of course, be due to personal reasons, such as ill health or new employment opportunities, rather than financial failure. In general, risk of going out of business is highest in the first three years of operations. If this period can be survived, there is a much higher chance of firms growing over time. Direct evidence on the extent to which this graduation takes place is scanty. Not surprisingly, experience varies between countries with a tendency for the move from micro to small–medium categories to be greater in higher income developing countries. For example, to the extent that we have broadly comparable data it appears that graduation, in the sense of micro enterprises growing into firms with more than ten employees, seems more common in Latin America and Asia than in Africa.[23]

Even within a region, patterns still differ. Data from sub-Saharan Africa suggest a higher rate of graduation in Kenya, Botswana and Swaziland than in Malawi and Zimbabwe, for example.[24] However, from the other perspective, in these African economies the vast majority of micro firms, as much as 99%, do not graduate to a higher size category. Where such firms do grow they tend to do so by adding only relatively small numbers of workers to the average firm. In the aggregate, however, these individually small increases in jobs nonetheless may still account for a substantial proportion of total new job creation.[25]

A dynamic SSE sector should be a source of strength to an economy and the inability of the majority of small and micro firms to expand significantly has prompted a focus on particular problems faced by SSE. The literature is extensive and here we consider only some of the more important aspects of the debate. The discussion is organised around the general heading of the functioning of markets, which can be approached from both Neoclassical and alternative perspectives. We commence the discussion with a consideration of what we term Radical arguments, since in general the Radical development literature has had a particular concern with the role of SSEs.

SSE and the functioning of markets – a Radical perspective

In the 1970s, the Radical literature used the concept of petty-commodity production to analyse the position of micro enterprises.[26] The arguments are not really appropriate to firms employing more than ten workers and probably not to the larger micro firms who use wage labour. The analysis can be seen as an extension of the work of those who attempted to adapt classical Marxist analysis to the new conditions of what was termed 'peripheral capitalism'. Within classical Marxism history can be analysed from the perspective of different modes of production, reflecting different structures of social relations. In any actual society different modes may co-exist, although one will dominate. In the history of developed economies the capitalist mode came to supersede all earlier modes and, in doing so, raised material wealth substantially. However, the key argument is that in the conditions analysed as peripheral capitalism this process is stunted and blocked by the impact of external economic forces, so that pre-capitalist and capitalist modes can co-exist over a long period without capitalism playing its expected progressive role in improving material conditions.

The petty commodity mode of production is the pre-capitalist mode, which has been used to analyse small micro enterprises. Petty commodity production can be seen as production for a market that does not involve wage labour, since it is by small independent producers owning their own means of production or capital assets. Labour is provided by owner–employees, family members or non-wage workers, such as apprentices. The relevance of this analysis for the present discussion is that, within this paradigm, it has been argued that petty commodity production is both integrated into capitalism and subordinated to it. Small micro producers are exploited in their relations with larger capitalist firms in the sense that value they generate is transferred to the large-scale sector. Hence, the network of links between large and small firms is seen as the primary reason why so few micro firms graduate to the ranks of larger capitalist enterprises.

Theoretically what is involved is a further application of the unequal exchange model noted in Chapter 4, but applied here to internal not international market transactions. Various forms of market power exercised by large firms will combine to lower the prices small firms receive for their output and raise the prices for the inputs they purchase from large firms, for example under sub-contracting arrangements.[27] Such manipulations of market relations generate very low incomes in the micro sector and, in this argument, this has the important consequence of lowering wage costs for the capitalist sector. Wages are kept low both because the income that can be earned in petty production, which can be seen as the alternative foregone, is low and because micro enterprises will supply low quality consumer items or wage goods at low prices.[28] Hence the petty producers play a central role in maintaining the profitability of the capitalist sector, whilst, given its peripheral and externally dependent nature, domestic capitalism is incapable of creating the conditions under which petty production will become increasingly unimportant, due to growing wage employment. The logic of this case implies that whilst individual small enterprises may prosper, the small-scale sector in general will remain permanently impoverished, since this condition is essential for the growth of the large-scale capitalist sector.

As with much of the Radical–Dependency literature this argument is now taken rather less seriously than it was thirty years ago.[29] First, it is certainly not universally the case that the petty production sector is sufficiently large or specialised in wage goods for it to have the central role in lowering wage costs to the capitalist sector that is implied in the above analysis. This may still hold in many of the lower income economies, particularly in Africa, but is less likely to

be true in Latin America or East Asia; there, wage goods are produced predominantly by capitalist enterprises, since incomes are sufficiently high for the low
quality products of petty producers to be only a small proportion of labour's consumption. In addition, in much of this literature, there is an explicit tendency
to equate market transactions between large and small units as inherently
exploitative. Sub-contracting by large firms who supply petty producers with
materials is the obvious example. Theoretically, within the logic of the unequal
exchange model as applied to domestic transactions, the existence of lower
remuneration in the petty commodity sector in itself does not prove that the
latter is exploited. Low remuneration may be simply a reflection of low productivity and low alternative income earning opportunities. Historically there are
well-documented examples of sub-contracting proving beneficial to both the
large and small enterprises involved. Hence the assertion that it is inherently
exploitative and a block on the development of the small sub-contractors
requires a clear theoretical substantiation. Finally, the crux of the theoretical
case rests on the peripheral model of capitalism that asserts that normal capitalist development in low-income economies is impossible due to external dependence. Growth that is subject to the dynamic of external forces means that
petty commodity production must persist if the overall system is to function.
However, as we discuss in Chapters 4 and 7, this dependency interpretation of
recent economic history is dubious and hence if we reject the peripheral capitalism model there seems little reason to take seriously an analysis of the small-
scale sector that rests upon it.

SSE and market distortions

From a totally different starting point, Neoclassical theory can also be used to
construct a case for policy biases against SSE.[30] The argument is that, due primarily to government interventions in markets, prices of factors or key resources
are distorted in a way that is biased against small firms. In some instances, small
firms also face different prices to those paid by larger firms although here it must
be recognised that these differential prices do not always work against SSE.
Taking the differential pricing argument first, small firms will typically have
lower wage costs per worker than large firms due to their exemption from any
national insurance or related contributions. Further, those at the micro end of
the scale will not normally be fully incorporated into the tax system and will
thus have a zero or very low marginal tax rate. On the other hand, these advantages may be offset by the higher interest charges on loans taken out by small
firms due to their perceived higher credit risk. The position of different types of
small firm may also be distinguished with the smaller micro enterprises escaping
the tax and social security net and receiving no credit from formal credit institutions, whilst the small to medium firms may both receive high cost loans and
be subject to tax and related regulations. It is thus the latter type of small firms
that may be the most disadvantaged.

The Neoclassical case goes much further than this, however, in arguing that the functioning of certain markets has an inherent anti-SSE bias. Two markets in particular have been the central focus of attention, those for foreign exchange and credit.[31] Until recently, the foreign exchange market in many countries was subject to significant government control, with the price of foreign exchange pegged by the Central Bank and access to the foreign exchange market limited to those who could obtain import licences. This, it was argued, had the dual effect of subsidising users of foreign exchange, since the pegged exchange rate frequently valued foreign exchange at well below its true economic value, and in addition, since licences for imports were rarely issued to small firms, ensuring that this subsidy went to the large-scale sector. A consequence, it was suggested, was that large firms were encouraged to adopt excessively import-intensive, generally capital-intensive, technology. In addition, since only a minority of SSE produce internationally tradable products, it was primarily larger firms that competed with imports and thus benefited from the trade barriers that sustained the import-substitution strategy. In so far as SSE purchased protected inputs or infrastructure and other facilities whose costs were raised indirectly by protection, they would have been disadvantaged by import protection rather than benefiting from it. The Neoclassical response to these problems is to liberalise the foreign exchange market and abolish the licensing system, so that the price of foreign exchange can rise in response to excess demand and decisions taken in the marketplace, not the judgement or whims of bureaucrats, can determine who could get access to foreign exchange. In addition, tariff reform is intended to lower protection from imports and thus reduce the indirect effect on non-traded costs. Since many small firms in low-income economies use few imported inputs and those that do have difficulty in obtaining credit to finance the purchase of imported inputs, small firms would not necessarily benefit very directly from such a reform, but nonetheless larger firms would lose the direct subsidy inherent in the control system.

Much attention has also been given to the functioning of financial markets and the inability of small firms to obtain adequate credit. Most surveys of SSE find a shortage of credit for either working or fixed capital cited by owners as one of the most important constraints they face.[32] The Neoclassical case is that this is, at least in part, due to the imperfection of credit markets. However, different causes of this malfunctioning need to be distinguished. One possibility is to blame government intervention in the form of interest rate ceilings and directives to institutions to lend a proportion of their total credit to priority borrowers, that may include SSE. The argument is that, with fixed lending rates, financial institutions cannot add an appropriate margin for risk to cover the possibility of loan defaults. Hence, in such circumstances, banks and other institutions require high levels of collateral as security and, since most SSE do not possess sufficient assets for this purpose, they are by-passed. Further, with small loans, the administrative costs of lending are a much higher proportion of the loan and, since these cannot be recovered by charging higher interest rates, institutions will have a preference for lending to larger borrowers. Direction of credit to priority borrowers, it is argued, may worsen the situation of many SSE even if they are nominally included as priorities. This is because, within the priority category, institutions may prefer known or well-connected borrowers, who are likely to be at the upper end of the size scale of SSE. In addition, if such directed credit leads to loans to financially weak investments, this will undermine the viability of the lending institutions concerned, who will then not be in a position to play an active role in channelling funds to efficient borrowers, including SSE.

A more sophisticated version of the Neoclassical case recognises that the credit market may be inherently imperfect even without such government controls. The argument here is that, as information on the likelihood of project success is not fully available to lenders, and as the returns they receive are a fixed interest charge not a proportion of future profits, even in an uncontrolled credit market it will be rational for lending institutions not to raise interest rates to a market-clearing level, but to ration credit on the basis of the credit-worthiness of applicants.[33] The implication is that some high risk, but high return, activities, including some profitable SSE investments, will be excluded even from a non-distorted credit market.

Given these arguments, what are the Neoclassical policy recommendations in the credit area? First, there is a confidence in the ability of markets to mobilise and allocate savings in an efficient manner. Removal of interest rate controls and directed credit are seen as essential, coupled in many cases with the reform of public sector banking institutions. The aim is to develop a competitive banking sector, in which competition drives down the spread between lending and deposit rates, thus lowering the cost of credit to borrowers, and forces institutions to seek profitable opportunities for long-term lending. However, second, it is recognised that even these reforms may still exclude many SSE from access to credit. Thus there has been considerable interest in the development of informal credit sources, ranging from the savings of friends and relatives, money lenders and local savings associations to unconventional banking institutions, based on group lending schemes. These sources may be a more efficient means of supplying small amounts of short term funds to SSE since they may involve lower administrative and monitoring costs per dollar lent and, through the links between borrower and lender, may ensure less defaults on repayments. In other words, banks and other formal institutions may have a comparative advantage in reaching larger credit-worthy firms, whilst informal lenders may be more suited to serve SSE. Informal financing sources appear to have been particularly important in East Asia, where important links developed between the formal and informal financial sectors through on-lending. Large firms or traders would obtain credit from formal sources and then lend it on as trade credit to SSE, who were their sub-contractors or suppliers.[34]

Precisely how far market imperfections and controls hamper SSE remains unclear. Controls on foreign markets are now much less prevalent and hence of less concern, although shortage and cost of credit for SSE remains a key issue. One view is that it may not be so serious if micro and small firms have initially to rely on the savings of owners or family and friends, since a lack of formal credit may act as a screening device to ensure that only the more efficient become large enough to need to seek external sources of finance.[35] However, this rests on the assumption that those firms that do not grow are inherently inefficient, with no potential to become efficient if they could only survive through their initial learning period. This assumption is controversial and many others continue to be concerned with the credit problem for SSE. Nonetheless, another strand of the literature points to the success of SSE in certain countries and sectors and implies that despite the difficulties and biases discussed above they can be a dynamic force. We discuss this approach below.

SSE and flexible specialisation

As discussed in Chapter 7, an important distinction in the literature on industrial organisation is between mass production systems based on large firms, lengthy production runs, standardised products and narrowly trained workers (often described as Fordism, after the assembly-line system introduced by the Ford Motor Company) and flexible specialisation involving multi-purpose equipment, non-standardised products and an adaptable workforce. The latter form of production is seen by many as increasingly relevant in a global marketplace in which responsiveness to changes in market conditions is critical for enterprise success. Flexible specialisation can be applied in both large and small firms, but it is its application by the latter which is of relevance here, since it is seen as an important means of organising successful small-scale production. It is difficult to categorise the flexible specialisation approach. With its emphasis on externalities it shares some of the features of earlier Structuralism and, by locating a system of production within global capitalism, it draws on elements of the Radical literature. It has little in common with Neoclassicism, however, and technical indicators of performance associated with the latter are rarely applied in flexible specialisation case studies.

In relation to developing countries, flexible specialisation amongst small firms is often discussed in the context of the 'industrial district model', which attempts to capture the essential features of developed economy experience amongst groupings of small firms pursuing flexible production. An ideal type of industrial district involves a geographical cluster of small to medium firms, specialised in a particular sector and linked to each other as suppliers and customers, whose owners and workers share common skills and cultural backgrounds.[36] The success of small firms based in such districts, it is argued, arises from collective rather than individual efficiency; that is, cost reductions and quality improvements associated with the functioning of the district. The two key mechanisms are:

- external economies arising from the local interaction of firms within the district; these include the transfer of skilled labour between firms, technological adaptation as ideas are copied or shared, and the communal use of infrastructure facilities;

- joint action as firms deliberately co-operate; for example in sharing information on markets or technology, in specialising in different production lines, and in training or recruitment.

The difference between these two dimensions of collective efficiency is that, by definition, external economies are unplanned by-products of production, whilst joint actions are explicit attempts at co-operation.[37] The expectation is that in a successful cluster of small firms both dimensions will be present.

The initial impetus for this approach to SSE stems from the experience of industrial districts in Europe, particularly Italy, on which the stylised facts of the industrial district model are based. However, a number of studies have been conducted in developing countries in recent years to establish the relevance of this approach in a low income economic environment.[38] Although many of the results are tentative, a number of general points can be made.

First, researchers have located a significant number of clusters or districts in a range of sectors and countries, although not surprisingly examples of successful clusters are located in Latin America and Asia rather than Africa. The sectors involved include footwear (in Brazil and Mexico), metalworking, engineering and electronics (in India), textiles (in India and Korea) and sports and surgical goods (in Pakistan). In Africa, few examples of successful clusters exist.

Second, empirical work reveals a wide variety of experience within these clusters, which often departs from the simple stylised facts of the industrial district model. In other words, developing country experience has often differed significantly from that found in Italy. Collaboration between firms varies greatly from casual exchanges of tools and information to direct collaboration in sharing orders and training. In some instances clear specialisation emerges with firms buying parts and components from local suppliers in the cluster, whilst in others there is a clear tendency as firms grow for them to move into making their own parts and components.[39] In some cases clusters have ceased to be collections of small and medium firms, with large firms emerging to establish a dominant sub-contracting relationship with smaller firms. Cultural cohesion has also ceased to be an important unifying factor in some cases where more impersonal market relationships have come to dominate links between firms. In some cases external actors, particularly export agents or traders, have played an important role in stimulating cluster activity. As a general proposition, it has been suggested that clusters are particularly important for small and medium sized firms at low income levels as a means of reducing their risk of failure by allowing expansion in small increments; for example, this may involve sharing equipment, skills and ideas.[40]

Third, most studies offer few quantitative indicators of the performance of small and medium firms within districts or clusters. However, at least qualitatively, they suggest that some groupings of small firms operating flexible production methods have operated successfully and, in some instances, have broken into export markets. Whilst it is clear that this form of production grouping offers the potential for efficiency gains and growth, this may not be realised equally by all such groupings or by all firms within a district or cluster. Further the policy implications of the successful cases are not clear. Experience suggests that successful clusters of small firms have arisen almost exclusively through the initiative of firms themselves. State support may have played a secondary role, but chiefly in strengthening already existing private sector groupings. Most discussion of public policy initiatives in this area stresses the need to strengthen the market for SSE products, rather than rely on more conventional supply-side initiatives, such as provision of funds for training or credit.[41]

Fourth, it is now becoming clear that clusters can be relevant for different types of firms. They can be important for very low-income producers for whom collective activity provides a modest survival strategy. At a higher level of income and technological development they can also create a dynamic environment from which successful medium and even large size firms can emerge. Finally, clusters can also be relevant for relatively sophisticated firms, many of whom would not be classed as small. In Latin America, for example, it has been pointed out that subsidiaries of international firms and their suppliers can also benefit from location in clusters.

This is quite a different view of SSE to that offered in the rest of the literature and it needs to be seen in perspective. The problems of SSE, whether lack of credit, excessive state regulation, scarcity of materials or poor demand prospects, are not removed simply by location in industrial districts and collaboration with similar firms. However, they may be partially offset by the gains discussed under the heading of collective efficiency.[42] The link between collective efficiency and the broader economic and policy environment needs much closer investigation. This is particularly the case where the outputs of firms are internationally tradable and changes in trade policy may have important impacts on clusters of firms. Further, there is evidence that performance within groups or clusters can vary significantly with size of firm. It may be that clusters will do little for micro enterprises operating a survival strategy to provide only a basic living for owners and their families. Such firms may be too small and economically weak to respond to the external effects and potential for collaboration offered by a cluster.[43] Nonetheless the approach has introduced new thinking on the problem of SSE and provides a rationale for encouraging a new form of small-scale private sector development.

Conclusions

SSE are an important part of the manufacturing sector in most economies. In developing countries they assume a greater significance in part because of the appropriateness of their activity, as defined above, and in part because of their role in household survival strategies. Rapid employment growth in SSE in some countries over the last ten to fifteen years or so has been more a response to economic crisis with job retrenchment in the public sector and in large, previously protected firms, than a sign of economic dynamism in the small-scale sector.

Few small firms graduate to the ranks of the medium scale, but the small minority that do are obviously a sign of efficiency and dynamism.

It is difficult to argue plausibly that, in an absolute sense, SSE are inherently superior to large firms, since much depends on the circumstance of a sector and an economy. One can say with confidence, however, that industrial expansion in developing countries will require a vibrant SSE sector that can be both a supplier of inputs for larger branches of manufacturing and of consumer goods for workers. In addition, growing incomes in SSE will help revive domestic markets for larger manufacturers. The policy implications of this role are that almost certainly some special focus on SSE revival remains important, particularly in terms of access to credit.

6 Technology

Can we open the black box?

Technology can be defined simply as a collection of processes for transforming inputs into outputs and the knowledge and skills necessary for their application. From whatever perspective one approaches development issues, there is rare unanimity that technology and, more specifically, technical change (that is, improvements in processes of transformation) have a central role in any explanation of economic growth and industrialisation. Technology remains something of a 'black box', however, much discussed but often not fully understood. In this chapter we first survey some technology concepts before turning to Neoclassical and competing perspectives.[1] We discuss some of the evidence on technical change in newly industrialised and low income economies and conclude with a policy assessment.

Technological capability

Before surveying alternative approaches it is necessary to clarify different stages and modes of technical change. A five-stage division is often used.

1   A search for new products and processes which, for poor countries, normally means the identification and importation of products and processes developed abroad. This is the mechanism of technology transfer and its possibility is seen as a critical advantage for follower or latecomer economies.
2   The adaptation of new, often foreign, products and processes to local conditions.
3   Improvement in products and processes in the light of experience in local production, which will normally require a conscious investment rather than simple learning by doing.
4   Development of new products and processes superior to those available elsewhere.
5   Conduct of basic research into the theory underlying particular processes.

Stages 1 to 3 broadly correspond to mastery of what has been termed 'know-how' (largely knowledge of production) and stages 4 to 5 to 'know-why' (largely knowledge of basic processes). Mastery of these different stages will require different capacities or what are termed 'technological capabilities'. In the words of one of the key authors in this area:

> Technological capabilities (TCs) in industry are the information and skills – technical, managerial and institutional – that allow productive enterprises to utilise equipment and technology efficiently. Such capabilities are firm specific; a form of institutional knowledge that is made [up] of the combined skills of its members accumulated over time. Technological development may be defined as the process of building up such capabilities.[2]

A categorisation of TCs distinguishes between:

- production capability covering aspects of product design, production management and engineering, repair and maintenance, input sourcing and output marketing;
- investment capability covering activities relating to project selection, design and engineering, extension services and training;
- invention capability concerning local capacity to adapt, improve and develop technology.[3]

Clearly, for low-income economies, TCs will be expected to be low in most areas. However actually quantifying TC at the firm level is extremely difficult. A relatively simple approach is to use the range of products supplied or the number of staff in research related positions as a proxy for TC.[4]

As we have noted already, globally the requirements placed on firms operating in industrial activities have altered with shifts in production systems. In the early part of the twentieth century, much of industry was organised on a mass production basis in the manner pioneered by the Ford Motor Company. This form of production was characterised by long production runs, single products and continuous flow of production based on the synchronisation of all activity. The key technological capability required to operate the system was the ability to synchronise production of a single product. This system spread well beyond the automobile sector and was the dominant form of large-scale industrial activity until well into the 1970s.

The challenge to the Fordist mass production system came initially from developments in another automobile firm, Toyota, who pioneered the 'just-in-time' system. This was based on a multi rather than a single product system and was organised in production cells rather than on a single assembly line. The aim was to both minimise stocks (hence the reference to 'just-in-time'), whilst at the same time introducing flexibility by focussing on the production of small batches of finished goods. The system, copied initially by other car producers, has been highly influential in other sectors as well, and has led some observers to write about a revolution in production organisation with a shift to flexible as opposed to mass production systems.[5] A new range of technological capabilities is required for this form of production, since flexibility requires the ability to adjust the number of workers in a cell, rapid changeover in the use of machines and multi-skilled workers. High levels of managerial and production skills are needed to operate the system properly. More recently the application of micro-processor technology has led to production based on a continuous process of product redefinition and improvement. The successful companies in high-technology sectors have developed the capability to manage this continuous innovation by combining the results of applied research directly into the pro-duction process.[6] This type of technological capability is clearly well beyond the vast majority of firms from the lower income developing economies, although not beyond many firms from the NIEs. However it is a matter of controversy whether such new, more flexible forms of production organisation have actually made optimal sizes of production smaller or not.[7] Hence one must be cautious about accepting general arguments about the scope for small-scale flexible pro-duction in poorer developing countries based on a new technological system.

Research and development expenditure

Assessing the quantitative extent of technological activity is difficult, but by any accepted standard the share undertaken by most developing countries, outside the NIEs, is very small. The most commonly used indicator is expendi-tures on R and D which, itself, has been categorised in different ways. A common subdivision is between:

- basic R and D, defined as experimental or theoretical work to acquire new knowledge without any specific direct application;
- applied R and D, defined as original work with a specific practical purpose directed towards commercial production;
- experimental R and D, defined as work drawing on existing knowledge directed towards the creation of new products.

Accurate comparative statistics on these subdivisions are not available, but the bulk of R and D in developing countries can be expected to be of the applied, production-oriented type.

However, it should be remembered that high R and D expenditure in an environment of economic inefficiency and distortions may not be a good guide to technological dynamism. The experience of the ex-Soviet bloc economies, which spent large sums on an indigenous technological base that became increasingly out-dated, is an obvious illustration of this point. Further, it is also recognised that major changes in design and production can arise from a number of sources, of which formal R and D activity will be only one, and not all activity aimed at adapting and modifying technology will be captured under the R and D heading.

Nevertheless, comparative R and D statistics bear out what one would expect. Approximate estimates for the early 1990s suggest that developing countries account for no more than 5% of world R and D expenditure and less than 3% of registered patents.[8] Most R and D expenditure is concentrated in the developed economies and it is only in a small number of NIEs – principally Singapore, Korea and Taiwan – that R and D expenditures per head are significant. In lower-income economies such expenditures are trivial (see Table 6.1). An alternative to considering total R and D expenditure is to focus only on that conducted by productive enterprises, since this category is more likely to be focussed on applied operationally relevant expenditure. Again a similar pattern emerges. Enterprise-financed R and D averaged only 0.04% of GDP in all developing countries in the mid-1990s, as compared with 1.04% in developed economies. In some of the NIEs the share of this expenditure in GDP is high by international standards, with figures of around 2% in Korea and 1% in Taiwan. Apart from Japan, no other economy is close to the figure for Korea (although this may have changed after the financial crisis of the late 1990s). The high Korean, and to some extent Taiwanese, figures reflect the effort that has gone into developing an autonomous technology strategy in these economies that has relied heavily on the adaptation and modification of foreign technologies.

Table 6.1 Total R and D expenditures: selected economies

Country	Year	R and D/GDP (%)	R and D per capita (US$)
Hong Kong	1995	0.1	19.8
Singapore	1992	1.0	153.6
Korea	1995	2.7	271.1
Taiwan	1993	1.7	179.6
Malaysia	1992	0.4	11.2
Thailand	1991	0.2	3.1
Indonesia	1993	0.2	1.5
China	1992	0.5	2.4
India	1992	1.0	3.1
Pakistan	1987	0.9	2.6
Ghana	1991/92	0.2	1.0
Kenya	1990/91	1.3	4.6
Tanzania	1991/92	2.4	2.6
Uganda	1991/92	2.2	2.9
Japan	1995	3.0	1225.6
France	1994	2.4	544.8
Germany	1991	2.3	674.8
UK	1994	2.2	383.6
USA	1995	2.4	655.2
Argentina	1995	0.4	n.a.
Brazil	1995	0.6	n.a.
Mexico	1995	0.3	n.a.

Source: For all countries except those in Africa and Latin America, Lall (1998); for African countries Enos (1995), where the definition is 'expenditure on advancing science and technology'; for Latin America, Amsden (2001).

Singapore has a share of 0.69% of GDP, well above the developing country average, and also above that of several other NIEs. This is significant, since Singapore's reliance on TNC involvement in its industrial strategy is well known. However it appears that the government has been successful in encouraging such firms to undertake a significant amount of R and D within Singapore and not in their home markets. This is quite different from the situation in Latin America where TNCs do very little R and D in host economies, which is part of the explanation for the low R and D to GDP ratios shown for Argentina, Brazil and Mexico in Table 6.1. The position in the poorer developing countries also differs very substantially from that in the NIEs. A number of countries, including Thailand, Sri Lanka and the Philippines, devoted only 0.02% of GDP to enterprise financed R and D and, in the larger Latin American economies, the proportion is only marginally higher.[9] Hence, at present, there can be only limited expectations concerning indigenous technical change within these economies.

Technology exports

Levels of technology exports are another means of gauging a country's technological development. Technology exports are again difficult to quantify since they can include all or some of the following:

- exports of plant and equipment with some element of design or commissioning work, sometimes termed 'project exports';
- sales of technical and managerial services, usually termed 'consultancy exports';
- sales of patents, brand names and technical assistance covered under 'licensing'.

Most technology exports from developing countries are of adaptations and modifications to known technologies based on production experience of use in the local market of the exporter. As such they may be suited to the factor conditions and markets of lower income economies. Not surprisingly it is firms from the NIEs that dominate technology exports from developing countries; for example, firms from India, Brazil, Argentina and Singapore have been successful in certain sectors in exports of idiosyncratic, locally developed technologies.[10] Furthermore, as we have seen, firms from the East Asian NIEs have been highly successful in exports of relatively technologically sophisticated products, particularly in electronics. These firms often started in a form of sub-contracting for developed country firms, thus gaining access to foreign technologies and designs, which they later adapted to their own designs and incorporated in exports.

The significance of technological activity in the process of industrialisation and economic growth, in general, is widely recognised. Globally it is the higher technology branches of manufacturing that are expanding most rapidly, both in terms of production and trade. Chapter 1 has drawn attention to the divergence in industrial structure between the NIEs, where roughly 20% of manufacturing was in high technology (defined as R and D intensive) activity in the late 1990s, compared with only 5% in the poorer developing countries. This divergence is both a reflection of past performance and an indication that poorer countries risk being left further behind in the process of globalisation. R and D activity of an applied nature appears to have a relatively high economic return, even though at low income levels the focus will be on adaptation rather than on any more original. The high returns are evidenced by cross-country studies that relate economic growth to an economy's technology gap (defined broadly as a measure of its TC relative to TC in technological leader economies). TC can be proxied by R and D expenditure, and a change in TC can be measured by the change in an economy's R and D to GDP ratio relative to the leader economy (usually taken to be the USA). Such studies normally find a fall in the technology gap to be positively associated with economic growth.[11]

Competing perspectives on technology

As noted in Chapter 3, Neoclassical growth theory has been extended to incorporate the role of technical change. Internal to growth models is a simple explanation for technical change based, for example, on investment in education or research and development. Whilst this analysis is clearly superior to leaving technical change as the unexplained residual element in growth, it provides little guidance on technology policy. A fuller understanding of the Neoclassical policy position can be gleaned from a consideration of the basic model set out in general terms in Chapter 3.

Technology can be treated as a commodity like any other, although it will have both embodied (for example, plant and equipment) and disembodied (for example, the knowledge of skilled staff) elements. Two features of the technology market are significant. One is that, by general agreement, technological development creates external benefits, as ideas and skills are diffused within an economy. Linkage relations between firms and their suppliers are an obvious mechanism for the spread of these external benefits, so that, through local networks, knowledge of new products and processes and the skills to create or apply them can be transferred. There is ample historical evidence of the functioning of these mechanisms for this to have become one of the accepted stylised facts of development. Its significance for Neoclassical theory is that, once a positive externality is acknowledged, a market-solution will be sub-optimal, since an individual profit-maximising firm will only invest up to the point at which its additional revenue (not that of society at large adding in other producers' or consumers' change in income) equals its additional cost. This can be illustrated simply in Figure 6.1. The demand line DD is a private one and its intersection with private costs gives output OQ. Inclusion of positive external benefits gives the social demand line DD* and a social optimum of OQ*. If left to itself the market will under-provide. The conclusion is that a subsidy in this case given by the difference between DD* and DD at OQ* is warranted. This provides a justification for tax allowances for R and D or training expenditure, for example.

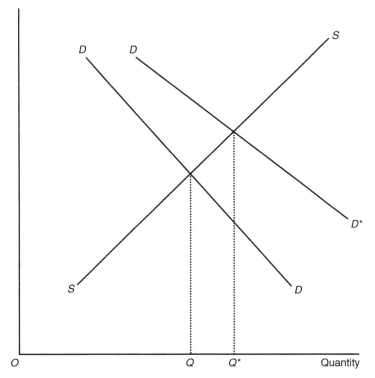

Figure 6.1 Technology market and external benefits.

The second feature of the technology market that is recognised in standard Neoclassical discussion is that there is inevitably a lack of information. Producers themselves may lack the information needed to assess the potential gains from investment in TC, or if they do not lack information they may still feel there is a high risk element in such activity. In terms of Figure 6.1, both *DD* and *DD** may be known only very approximately. Lack of information makes an unwillingness to take risks wholly rational and provides a reason why a subsidy solution may be inadequate. Where this holds, there is a case for direct state investment to either set up research and other facilities or, in some instances, to encourage production of commodities embodying new technology.

This simple market framework can be extended to incorporate firms' own decision-taking and objectives to understand what influences the demand line in Figure 6.1. Figure 6.2 introduces the link between a firm's sales on the horizontal axis and its own technological expenditure on the vertical. The line *TF* reflects the fact that, as sales and output rise, firms will be willing to spend more on R and D and related technological activity, as they can spread the overhead costs over a larger volume of output. However, the relation between technological activity and sales runs both ways, since one would expect that

Technological
expenditure

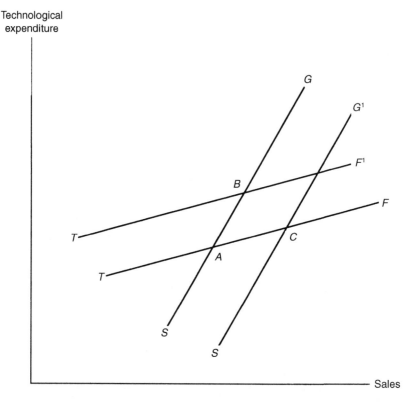

Figure 6.2 Imports of technology and firms' technology intensity.

technological expenditure increases sales by either lowering costs, and hence price, or by improving quality. This second relation is reflected in line SG, which can be expected to have a larger slope than TF.[12]

The firm's profit maximising point will be at A, where the two lines intersect, and this determines the firm's optimum technological expenditure to sales ratio. Firms in developing economies, as latecomers to most industries, have the option of importing technology. This can affect the analysis in two possible ways. If technology imports complement domestic efforts at R and D, they will induce more technological expenditure than would otherwise have taken place, implying that TF shifts upwards to TF[1]. Now with SG unchanged there is a new optimum point at B and a higher ratio of domestic technological expenditure to sales due to the effect of technology imports. Alternatively, imports of technology may serve to diversify products and hence increase sales relative to domestic technology expenditure. This is shown by an outward shift in SG to SG[1] and a new optimum point at C. Now at C there is a lower ratio of technology expenditure to sales than in the original case at A, although the absolute amount of technological expenditure has increased at C as opposed to A. Some of this higher expenditure will be needed to adapt imported technology to local conditions.[13] The policy aspect of this is whether firms themselves will have adequate information and incentives to reach these optimum points. Further, where externalities are important, from the economy's point of view there will be a new social optimum determined by the relation between a firm's techno-logical expenditure and total sales, not just sales by the firm itself. Further, in principle, imports of technology by one firm may be complementary to the technological expenditure of other firms again causing a new optimum. As we have seen, in the presence of such externalities, subsidies will be required to move from a private optimum for an individual firm to a social optimum for the economy.

In theory, therefore, the Neoclassical framework is sufficiently flexible to both recognise market failures and to allow some interventionist solutions. However, in practice, many working from within this paradigm are content to recommend limiting the scope of government intervention in pursuit of technology goals to modest tax allowances, on the grounds that whilst markets will fail in the presence of externalities, governments will fail in a range of situations, whether due to administrative incompetence, corruption or, more chari-tably, simple lack of information on which technologies to promote. In a liberalised market environment, it is argued, firms can take their own decisions on building technological capacity with only modest government support, chiefly in terms of tax allowances for particular types of expenditure that promote TC.

Although the Structuralist authors of the 1950s and 1960s have little in particular to say on technology policy, their general scepticism of market solu-tions has been carried into this area by a range of authors, who may be broadly labelled neo-Structuralist for present purposes.[14] In general we can identify two broad strands in this literature. The first, and most radical in terms of its policy implications, sees technical breakthroughs as central to economic development. Distinctions are drawn between incremental innovations (stage 2 of our schema, page 121), radical innovations (broadly corresponding to stage 4), new technological systems of innovation and changes in techno-economic para-digm. The latter two categories extend beyond the activities of individual firms and have major macro economic consequences. A technological system is a combination of innovations, which have major implications for different branches of activity, as well as giving rise to new branches (an example would be genetically engineered and other new bio-technology products). A techno-economic paradigm change refers to a combination of innovations that are so profound as to alter the conditions of production across whole economies; the introduction of steam power, the electric motor and more recently micro-electronics and its computer applications and bio-technology are examples of such paradigm shifts.[15]

The significance of these distinctions, it is argued, is that, over long periods of economic history, a small number of new techno-economic paradigms will emerge fuelled by an accumulation of incremental and radical innovations. At the early stage in the emergence of a new paradigm (such as the 1980s with new computer-based production systems), there will be a window of opportunity, it is suggested, for latecomer economies to 'leapfrog' over technologically more established producers. This arises because, at the early stage in a new system, much basic research knowledge is relatively freely available as researchers publish within the specialist research community. This is prior to its commercial exploitation and the establishment of proprietary rights over this knowledge. Established economies with a commitment to the old, now dated, paradigm may be less flexible in adapting to the new situation. How far this window of opportunity for latecomer economies can be taken advantage of will depend on the domestic resources available; that is what has come to be termed the 'national system of innovation' reflecting a society's combined TC.[16]

If valid, these arguments imply that at least some latecomer economies should attempt to establish themselves in frontier technology at the heart of a new paradigm. To some extent this leapfrog analysis, like the Dependency based de-linking discussion of the 1960s on foreign trade, was a product of a particular decade (in this case the 1980s), when the impact of new computer-based systems were beginning to be felt. However, it provides a rationale for the ambitious plans of a few countries to establish a national presence in frontier technology sectors. On page 132 we discuss evidence on the Brazilian attempt to establish a national computer capacity.[17]

The second strand of the neo-Structuralist case more modestly and realistically attempts no ambitious claims for leap-frogging. Rather it focuses on the simple proposition that in terms of industrial and technological development, low income and newly industrialised economies are latecomers, who through technology transfer by imports of technology and equipment can draw from the technological shelf developed in the industrialised economies.[18] Transfer can arise by many routes: licensing of technology blueprints, imports of equipment that embody a technology, direct foreign investment, and management contracts for operating a project, as well as more informal channels such as imitation of foreign goods and contacts between producers and buyers abroad.

From this perspective technological development involves moving through the sequence of stages set out at the onset of this chapter. Progress is primarily based on an accumulation of incremental innovations, with only limited radical breakthroughs. In this literature, evidence for the importance of technology transfer is drawn more from recent experience than from formal theory. The East Asian model pioneered by Japan and followed successfully by Korea and Taiwan relied heavily on adaptations to foreign technology, and this provides the major plank of the argument. More recent developments in East Asia suggest that some firms are following a technology diversification strategy, in the sense of diversifying product mix as a means of spreading the overhead costs of technology development over a larger range of products. For latecomer economies, this is seen as preferable to aiming at a technology leadership role in specific market niches, although there is a recognition that the autonomous path to technological development, as followed by these economies, is more difficult to pursue in the current international climate than it was forty or fifty years ago.[19] As we discuss in Chapter 8, this is partly because import protection, which provided much of the boost to profits that allowed and encouraged firms to take the risk to develop their own technologies, is now much more difficult to apply under the international trading rules of the World Trade Organisation (WTO) that most developing countries have now joined. Further patent protection, which limits the copying of new technology, has been strengthened considerably by the introduction in the WTO of rules on Intellectual Property Rights. This means that countries breaching developed country patent laws can face trade sanctions under the WTO agreement.[20]

On the other hand, WTO rules allow government support through subsidies and non-financial measures for the development of science and technology in general, including R and D, provided it does not infringe copyrights or patents. Singaporean experience is usually cited as a key illustration of what can be achieved. There, import protection played little or no role, partly because it was largely foreign not national firms that were supported. Rather, government support involved a combination of tax incentives and direct grants for local R and D, and the provision of a high standard technology infrastructure based on public sector research institutes and universities. Government institutes established successful joint research projects with TNCs and, in the 1990s, financial incentives were such that for every dollar invested in R and D by a TNC, government provided another 30 cents. Surveys of TNC executives revealed consistently that they decided to invest in R and D in their Singapore operations, rather than follow the normal pattern of siting R and D in their head office location, principally because of this level of government support.[21] However, outside East Asia, the technological upgrading and R and D activity has been much less.

We survey below some of the evidence on the domestic technology position of firms, starting with experiences during the import-substitution era.

Import-substitution and technical change

General surveys of firms functioning in economies operating protectionist trade policies have found little evidence of any positive infant industry effects in terms of technical change and falling costs.[22] There are, of course, exceptions to this failure. Many firms in Korea and Taiwan clearly became competitive after only relatively brief periods of protection. However most observers now agree that this is likely to have been due to the strong export-orientation in both economies, which meant that there was pressure on firms to export at an early stage in their working lives. We have noted already that in the Korean case this pressure took the form of export targets. In the case of Taiwan, market pressure from the incentive structure, which avoided serious anti-export bias through various financial incentives to export, is likely to have been more important.

In Latin America, various firm-level case studies of production operations in the 1970s and early 1980s pointed to various forms of technical adaptation and modification. Often these adaptations referred to adjustments to foreign technology to make it appropriate to local market conditions. Examples included adaptations to allow the use of local rather than imported raw materials, scaling down of plant size to match the size of the domestic market, use of simpler machinery because of poor ancillary services and diversification of the product mix to meet the needs of the local market.[23] To some extent such adjustments will be inevitable if firms are to become internationally competitive, but where they are adaptations to the constraints imposed by a protectionist trade regime, for example the requirement to adapt to local raw materials, they will not be compatible with production that can export competitively; for example, if local materials are poorer quality than imports, requiring their use will penalise exporters. Some firms, however, were shown to have adapted technology in a relatively efficient manner. A public sector steel company in Brazil was cited in particular, as an example of indigenous technical effort which transformed a situation of initial dependence on foreign technology into one where all engineering work for expansion could be done internally. Similarly in Mexico there was also evidence of local technological effort by both domestic and foreign firms. Technologies that were not just adaptations of foreign technology were developed for processes that produced sponge iron from natural gas, a process for non-woven textiles and a process to manufacture newsprint from the sugar by-product bagasse. These were processes that were claimed to be equal or close to the international best-practice.[24] However, the Latin American pattern has relied very heavily for R and D on the activities of TNCs, most of whose activity in this area has been in their home economies rather than in the region. Table 6.1 has shown the low R and D to GDP ratios in the main Latin American economies in comparison with developed economies. Another indicator is the cumulative number of patents registered in the US. By 1995 the figures were as low as thirty-two for Argentina and sixty for Brazil compared with over 1200 for Korea and over 2000 for Taiwan.[25] Using labour productivity growth as a simple proxy for technical change, more recent macro work on Latin America in the post import-substitution era suggests that only three Latin American economies – Argentina, Colombia and Mexico – managed to achieve an overall growth of labour productivity in manufacturing higher than that in the USA over 1970–96. Hence only in three countries was the labour productivity gap with the US reduced, although in all branches in these economies, US productivity levels remain higher, suggesting only very modest technological catch-up.[26]

The Brazilian computer industry

A more dramatic example of technical change under import-substitution is the case of the attempts in Brazil to foster a domestic computer sector. During the 1970s, computer production in Brazil was dominated by foreign, predominantly US firms. However, from the end of that decade to the early 1990s, a deliberate effort was made to foster domestic capability for computer production through a policy of reserving segments of the domestic market (principally mini and personal computers and their peripherals) for national firms.[27] Foreign owned firms were restricted essentially to mainframe production through an investment licensing system, and import competition was removed by quantitative import restrictions. Import controls over computers were introduced in 1975 and the market reserve system began in 1977. As a consequence, the growth in number of nationally owned firms was dramatic with such firms employing more than 50,000 workers and taking roughly two-thirds of the domestic computer market by the end of the 1980s.

The market reserve policy was always controversial, although it found favour amongst economic nationalists and advocates of interventionist industrial policies. It was strongly opposed by both foreign computer firms and national computer users, who protested that they were having to rely on uncompetitive local products. The policy was always time-bound since the original Informatics Law envisaged that the market-reserve policy would be revised in 1992, but it was in fact abandoned slightly earlier as part of a more general trade liberalisation process. The whole episode is a good test for alternative views on industrial policy, as it reflects an attempt at technological leapfrogging by infant protection in a technologically sophisticated frontier activity.

As is frequently the case in this debate, the evidence is subject to varying interpretations. In both cost and quality terms there is no doubt that local Brazilian computer firms could not produce internationally competitive products in the period that the market reserve policy was in operation. By the end of the 1980s there is considerable evidence that prices for both personal computers and peripherals in Brazil were at least double the prices in the US. Further, there was also a gap in terms of technological standards between Brazilian and frontier technology, which was estimated at between two and four years in the mid-1980s and perhaps two years by the end of the decade. Not all of this uncompetitiveness was due to inefficiency or slow learning in the firms themselves, since one estimate suggests that, of the price differential with the US noted above, roughly half was due to high cost in the locally supplied inputs used in domestic computer production. These local inputs were often supplied at high cost by transnational, not national, firms operating in monopolistic markets.[28]

Taken at face value this evidence provides scant support for a new variant of the infant industry case. There is some evidence in mitigation, however. First, the Brazilian–US price comparisons, whilst revealing, may also be misleading. As a highly oligopolistic industry, computer prices vary substantially between national markets, with US prices normally being considerably lower than elsewhere. The correct comparison to establish the costs imposed on computer users by the market reserve policy is to compare Brazilian prices with either import prices or with prices from local supplies produced by multinational subsidiaries if they had been permitted to operate in the local market. As it seems highly unlikely that multinational corporations would have exported to Brazil at US prices, or would have allowed their subsidiaries to sell in Brazil at US prices, the 2 to 1 ratio must overstate the costs involved. Second, there is little doubt that the market reserve policy did stimulate the growth of many local firms which, in general, tended to invest relatively heavily in R and D.[29] This activity was redesign or minor innovation rather than frontier developments, but the argument is that it allowed some firms to build up specialist skills for niche markets, and that the very process of such local R and D initiatives created a cadre of human expertise in electronics that would not have been available without the reserve policy. Whether these qualifications would be enough to justify the policy is unlikely, but the episode illustrates that the incentive to invest in local TC must be created and that protection of this sort is one way forward, even if it is not the most efficient.

Ghanaian manufacturing

Technical change in manufacturing in Africa is generally at a qualitatively lower level than elsewhere. A survey of firms in Ghana in the early 1990s gave a detailed insight into the situation there.[30] It depicts a sector where local TC is very low in the key areas of investment, production and product development. Further, although the sector has been exposed to foreign competition through trade liberalisation, there is no systematic policy to build-up local TC. Ghana has managed to develop a limited production capability only in a few mature technologies. In terms of investment capability, virtually all equipment used is imported and of old vintage. In textiles and garments, simple sewing machines as opposed to more sophisticated programmable ones were normally used with initial installation and training by foreign technicians provided by the equipment suppliers. In food processing several subsidiaries of transnational firms were in operation, although they relied exclusively on their parents for launching their investments with no local participation in the technical aspects of investment. Several locally owned firms relied on turn-key contracts to establish their plants, some of which seemed to function satisfactorily. In general, investment capability was rated as weak, with the exception of the TNC affiliates, although the latter had not invested in developing local skills amongst their workforce. Local firms largely used simple technologies that some had installed adequately. In wood and metalworking, in particular, there were small local firms that were judged not to know how to go about investing efficiently.

In terms of production capability, the story is similar and even the better firms were weak by international standards. For example, the most capable garment firm in the sample was estimated to have costs 15–20% above those of imports from Hong Kong. Other garment firms were likely to be much further behind imports in costs and quality. Similarly in food processing one affiliate of a global TNC in 1992 had the lowest productivity of around 100 affiliates of the company world-wide. Finally, product design capability was again poorly developed. Many firms in garments simply copied imports. In food processing there has been some modest innovation with adaptation to local conditions; for example, one firm adapted its yoghurt to use local pineapples. These results are particularly disappointing as Ghana had already undergone a significant trade reform in the 1980s, with little evidence that, by the time of the study, it had had any impact on the technological base of the sector.

Japanese manufacturing techniques in Zimbabwe

An important form of disembodied technical change is the adoption of new forms of management and production techniques. In recent years the shift towards more flexible patterns of operation has been led by the use of techniques pioneered in Japan. As discussed earlier, these aim to raise quality and reduce costs, primarily by reductions in inventories and work-in-progress. Production tends to be organised in cells, so that the shop floor comprises a series of mini-factories, with a flexible and multi-skilled workforce, whose initiatives are encouraged as a means of raising efficiency. The pace of factory operations is driven by orders not the capacity of equipment, and inventories are held on a 'just-in-time', not a 'just-in-case' basis.

In the case of Zimbabwe, introduction of these techniques in the 1990s was due to the initiative of an international consulting firm Price Waterhouse, who leased the operational procedures used by the Japanese engineering firm Kawasaki and wrote its own documentation for non-Japanese users. A Zimbabwean affiliate of Price Waterhouse took the initiative to market the programme in Zimbabwe and, by the early 1990s, had sold these services to over fifty firms. Initial success with the application of these techniques was mixed but at least some firms experienced significant growth in labour productivity and reductions in cost. This was achieved at a relatively modest cost in terms of consultancy fees. For example, a metalworking subsidiary of a UK transnational had been experiencing difficulties in meeting customer orders in an adequate response time, with high levels of work-in-progress. However, with changes in factory layout, a reduction in lot size (that is, the units of work-in-progress passed between different points on the shop-floor) and a new 'production-pulling' system, major cost savings were achieved.[31] The key factor in explaining this performance was said to be high-level managerial commitment to the re-organisation, although whether improvements were maintained after the study period is not known. Three other firms were examined in detail and, of these, two producing agricultural equipment and automotive components, were said to be weakly successful, whilst the other making cartons and cardboard boxes, was judged to be a failure in its use of the new system. Key factors explaining this varied performance were said to be a combination of managerial commitment to change and the degree of worker participation, with the successful firms persuading their workers of the need to do things differently. The study is almost certainly biased in that it focussed on foreign owned larger firms, who were likely to be more receptive to new ways of doing things. Further it was carried out before the impact of the limited trade reform in Zimbabwe had made major inroads into the market position of domestic firms. It shows two basic points, however; one, that Japanese techniques can be applied successfully in a relatively unlikely operating environment and, two, that the degree of up-take of such techniques and their success in reducing costs was quite mixed, even between the managerially more sophisticated firms in Zimbabwe.

Is there a blueprint for a technology policy?

As we have noted the Neoclassical position on technology policy tends to focus on the role of subsidies to finance formal R and D expenditure. This view is disputed by most working on this topic from a Structural perspective on the grounds that such limited interventions are simply not effective enough to overcome obstacles to technical change.[32] This approach sees a Neoclassical tax-subsidy intervention as only a partial solution, as the development of TC and hence the achievement of technological progress is too important to be left to the market. It suggests that direct provision of support facilities, plus grants and tax concessions as practised in Singapore, are essential. Some go further and argue that to promote technological development, selective tariff protection to grant time to up-grade TC will also be required.

There is no simple agenda for a Structuralist technology policy. However, some of its dimensions can be sketched out by reference to the list of infrastructure requirements for the development of technology-intensive industries given by Justman and Teubal (1991: 1173). The authors stress the role of governments in ensuring the availability of this infrastructure and of building up a minimum critical mass of technological capabilities. Seven areas of infrastructure are identified as important to support technological change. The first is physical infrastructure, which can range from power, roads and communications from the basic to the more sophisticated, such as integrated digital services. Naturally governments need not provide all or any of these themselves but they have a responsibility to ensure that there is an adequate system of physical infrastructure in place.

Second is human capital infrastructure in the form of sufficient technically and scientifically qualified personnel to cope with the demand of the new technologies. This is the area of education and training. Whilst in many countries private institutions of this type are active, it is rare to find that the state is not a significant provider, and at the very least governments have to ensure adequate standards even when delivery is in the private sector.

The third area relates to the acquisition of TC as defined earlier. This covers capability in relation to investment, production and ultimately innovation, and generally is closely related to the acquisition of experience. Central to the Structuralist case in this area is the argument for selectivity in support to particular industries or firms to allow them to build up such expertise. For example, this may take the form of temporary tariff protection or selective credit allocations and interest subsidies, which affect a firm's operating profitability. Alternatively, it could imply grants, loans, tax credits or direct government provision of R and D activity. This selection of 'strategic' technological activities is justified on the grounds that, if different activities have different barriers to technical change and different capacity to build up TC, they should be treated differently.[33] It is not meant to imply a return to blanket import-substitution, but it should be remembered that, whilst there may be a strong case in principle, selectivity may imply considerable resource costs, if it goes to support enterprises that fail. Whatever support is offered should be flexible to take account of the situation of the technology users.[34]

A significant qualification to this argument is where a distinction is drawn between government support at the infant or initial stage of technological development and at the more advanced or mature stage. It has been suggested that, at the infant stage, government support for R and D should be neutral, that is, available to all new firms and relatively large. A figure of 50% of R and D costs covered by state grants is mentioned. The argument is that at the infant stage a critical mass of TC needs to be built up, so that general non-selective support is required. In this view, genuinely selective support is only justified at a more mature stage of TC development, when more risky but potentially higher return activities should be supported.[35]

Fourth, we have development of science and technology. Although, naturally, R and D can be done in the private sector, either with direct government finance or tax credits, there is also a strong case for publicly funded and freely disseminated R and D to develop product quality and competitiveness rather than to erect a barrier to competing firms, as has proved to be the case in some sectors in developed economies. The key proviso is that the R and D is operationally helpful to firms, which in turn requires that a close working relationship is established between government and industry. Models of such a relationship that are often cited are the industry associations in Japan with their close links to government and the successful small firm sector in Italy, for example in textiles, clothing and footwear, where state-funded support centres are seen as instrumental in the success of the so-called Third Italy region.[36]

The fifth and sixth area of policy relate to marketing infrastructure and financial infrastructure. These are important aspects of support to firms' operations but are less directly aimed at technological development than the other support activities noted above. Finally, the last area of policy is a general reference to institutional development. This refers to an important range of institutions to be either provided or supported by the state including public laboratories and research institutes, standards institutes, science and technology parks and consulting services. All may contribute to an environment of innovation and application of new technologies.

This collection of measures has been referred to as a national system of innovation; that is, the institutional base supporting the technical change in an economy.[37] Many argue that national capacity in this area is a critical factor in explaining international competitiveness and the success of firms from the East Asian NIEs has been ascribed to the effectiveness of the national system of innovation in these economies. A common comparison has been between these economies and Latin America, where technological capability and depth of institutional support for technology have been much weaker. In so far as any

Table 6.2 Quantitative measures of national systems of innovation (1980s)

Indicators of TC	Brazil	Korea
Age group in third level higher education (%)	11	32
Engineering students as a share of total population (%)	0.13	0.54
R and D/GNP (%)	0.7	2.1
Industry R and D to total (%)	30	65
Robots per million workers	52	1060
Per capita sales of telecommunications equipment (US$)	10	77
US patents	36	159
Telephone lines per 100 of population	6	25

Source: Freeman (1995) Table 4.

economy conformed with the Neostructuralist model of technology policy, it is Korea.

Table 6.2 gives some quantitative indicators of the extent of this system for Korea and Brazil in the 1980s. Korean policy involved not just government investment in various levels of education and the establishment of a high standard research infrastructure in public sector laboratories. In addition, efforts were made to ensure private R and D initiatives. Access to government investment funds required that firms established their own R and D laboratories. Further, there was direct collaboration between public sector research centres and national firms in a series of 'National R and D' projects in strategic industries. Initially the public sector financed the majority of Korean R and D but, by the 1990s, its share had fallen to below 20% as private firms built up their own R and D networks. However, over the period from 1960 to the mid-1990s, it has been estimated that roughly two-thirds of private R and D was financed by state-subsidised credit. In Brazil, on the other hand, private sector initiatives in R and D were considerably more modest so that, by the 1990s, remarkably only 366 Brazilian firms were judged to be research-active.[38] Even in the more liberal environment of the new century, the Korean government has continued to take major technology based initiatives, principally the Highly Advanced National Projects, designed to develop world frontier technology in strategic industries in collaboration with the private sector.[39]

Conclusions

There is a clear consensus that technical change is a critical element in the process of industrialisation. In the context of most developing economies, in all industries TC is modest by global standards and often the technology in use is well behind international best-practice. Latecomer status for these countries raises both opportunities and obstacles. The only feasible path to development lies in applying and adapting imported technologies, a process which on balance has probably been helped rather than hindered by the recent trends towards globalisation and the expansion of transnational activity. The way forward is largely one of gradual progress building on the cumulative production experience of local firms combined with know-how from abroad. Within this process development of domestic TC will be critical. However state intervention of some form, whether in the 'light' Neoclassical variant of tax credits or the 'heavier' Neostructuralist policy package involving greater public expenditure and selectivity, will be required. There can be general agreement that, for well-understood reasons, markets will under-provide the supply of technology.

7 Globalisation and industrialisation

Like many concepts that have slipped into popular discussion, the term 'globalisation' is subject to different interpretations. In the development context it is normally taken to refer to the rapid expansion of flows of commodities, services, capital and technology between nation states in the world economy. A helpful broad definition is given by the UK government's White Paper on Globalisation and Poverty:

> In fact, globalisation means the growing interdependence and interconnectedness of the modern world. This trend has been accelerated since the end of the Cold War. The increased ease of movement of goods, services, capital, people and information across national borders is rapidly creating a single global economy. The process is driven by technological advance and reductions in the cost of international transactions, which spread technology and ideas, raise the share of trade in world production, and increase the mobility of capital. It is also reflected in the diffusion of global norms and values, the spread of democracy and the proliferation of global agreements and treaties, including international environmental and human rights agreements.[1]

These trends have both economic and social consequences that have been the subject of much discussion in relation to their implications for the poorer economies in the world economy. It is worth entering a simple qualification, however, that the novelty of this process can be exaggerated. Economic historians point out that, in the nineteenth century and up to 1914, the world economy also experienced a rapid increase in trade, capital and at that time labour flows. There was a clear tendency of prices of similar goods to converge in different countries and interest rate differentials between the capital markets of the major economies also came to be relatively modest; both features that are normally taken as key characteristics of open, closely inter-related economies.[2] This era was ended by the First World War and the Depression of the 1930s, and it was not until around 1960 that the rapid growth of trade and financial flows resumed. This process of closer economic integration on a world scale accelerated in the post-1980 period with dramatically declining transport costs, improving communications and the development of sophisticated international financial markets. It is this recent acceleration of the process that observers have in mind when they discuss globalisation, but its historical antecedents should not be overlooked, since arguably it was the protectionist and recessionary era from 1914 to the 1950s that was the unusual period.

Nonetheless, what is clear is that the current trade and financial flows are now proportionately more significant than they were in the pre-1914 era and that the spread and speed of communications has meant that, unlike in the previous period of global opening, few economies remain untouched by the process.[3] International production in the sense of production controlled by transnational firms and subject to the logic of these firms' global production systems has become increasingly important and is now one of the critical features of the global economy. Value-added attributed to foreign subsidiaries and affiliates of TNCs was about 10% of world GDP in 1999, roughly double the percentage of the early 1980s. Within manufacturing, global production is proportionately more significant than in other sectors, with roughly 22% of capital formation in the world economy in 1999 contributed by FDI inflows. In developing countries the proportion was as much as 36%.[4] In terms of trade in commodities, now roughly two-thirds of world trade is conducted by TNCs and international production, defined as global sales controlled by TNCs and their affiliates, is substantially higher than total world exports.

The chapter proceeds as follows. The first section discusses some theorising on the links between globalisation and industrialisation and on the concept of competitiveness in a global economy. The second section discusses questions of FDI as a source of capital and technology flows and the third focuses on globalisation and trade prospects in relation to manufactures.

Some theoretical perspectives

From a Neoclassical viewpoint, globalisation presents few conceptual difficulties. In a world in which barriers to trade and capital flows are lowered due to a combination of lower transport costs, better communications and policy changes to liberalise trade and capital flows, theory predicts that exports in which countries have a comparative advantage will rise, as will imports of goods where the country concerned has no comparative advantage.[5] If capital is mobile internationally it will shift in line with perceived profit opportunities, so that, other things being equal, one would expect the export of capital from high wage to low wage economies, where capital scarcity implies it will have a higher marginal productivity and thus a higher rate of return. Theoretically through trade and capital flows there exists the prospect of income convergence, so that, in the process of globalisation, poor countries grow more rapidly than rich countries and incomes per capita move closer together. This possibility arises in Neoclassical growth theory, discussed in Chapter 3; provided savings rates and technology are identical between countries, growth will be higher in capital-scarce (that is, poorer) countries where returns to capital are higher. More recent extensions to growth theory qualify this analysis, however, so that convergence becomes 'conditional'. This means that other things being equal, that is assuming a whole range of similar conditions like levels of human and physical capital and access to technology, countries with a lower income per capita will grow more rapidly than richer countries. However, since global inequality means that other things are clearly not equal, this is clearly not a strong prediction of convergence. Recent evidence suggests that, on the contrary, divergence has been the predominant global trend. Over the last twenty-five years or so, whilst incomes in East and South Asia have grown strongly relative to the developed economies and have clearly converged, in Africa and Latin America this has not been the case, as growth of incomes there has fallen well behind the developed country average.[6] These qualifications are well known, but it is argued that the beneficial effects of globalisation are still valid despite the existence of real world conditions, such as activities of oligopolistic TNCs or the protectionism still prevalent in some developed economy home markets, which depart strikingly from the assumptions on which most Neoclassical growth models are based.

For many years it was a central tenet of the Structuralist and Radical literature that such conventional Neoclassical discussions seriously misrepresented the way in which the world economy functioned. Chapter 4 has already examined the more significant of these arguments, relating particularly to infant industries and declining terms of trade. In general, the broad dependency position that poor countries of the periphery are held back by the activities of the rich countries of the centre has given way in the Radical literature to a much more agnostic position.

The Dependency perspective of the 1960s and 1970s implied that the unequal relations between poor countries (the periphery) and rich countries (the centre) imposed almost insurmountable barriers to industrialisation for the former. Dependent poor economies were the marginalised component of the world economy, whose surplus income was drained away by unequal trading relations and by the operations of foreign firms, whose transnational activities made them a key mechanism for the exploitative activities of the centre. Dependency theory seems of interest today primarily as an expression of thinking at a particular point in time, essentially one of pessimism regarding the prospects for developing countries.[7] It failed almost completely to explain the successful industrialisation in East and South East Asia and has not provided tools for a sensible assessment of the globalisation process that now drives the world economy.

Of much greater contemporary relevance are the more recent offshoots of earlier Radical work under what was termed an 'internationalisation of capital' perspective. This focussed on capitalism as a global system and examined the implications of its functioning for developing economies. The simple point is that all economies, whether high or low income, are part of a global system and, as such, are subject to its laws of motion. From this perspective international economic relations have an outcome which depends on circumstances, with scope for mutually beneficial collaboration between capitalists in rich and poor countries. The notion of a dependent development thus becomes meaningless once global interdependence is accepted and it becomes far from inevitable that interdependence works against the interests of individual low-income countries. Growth may be uneven, as far as what used to be termed the periphery is concerned, but for individual countries it should not be seen as inevitably stunted or blocked by the laws of motion of the global system.

It is interesting to note that much of the early literature, written from a Dependency perspective, focussed on the ills imposed on poor economies by powerful international firms or TNCs. This included arguments about de-nationalisation (the taking over of local firms), introduction of inappropriate products (luxury consumer goods in poor countries), inappropriate technology (capital-intensive techniques in labour-surplus economies) and the use of various restrictive practices, such as transfer pricing. Some of these arguments were always more important than others and collectively they never created a plausible case that transnational firms per se stunted or restricted growth of individual economies.

As capital has become international in its search for profits and markets, international production by TNCs is a response to wage rates and market opportunities in different countries. In this view, the impact of TNCs on host developing economies can be contradictory, with the potential for both positive and negative effects. However, one important implication is that dependence, in the sense used in Chapter 2 of a heavy transnational involvement in the economy, can be associated with growth. Furthermore this analysis sees a strong tendency for large and successful nationally-owned firms to become increasingly similar to TNCs; for example in the technology, marketing strategies and product designs that they employ. In fact, with the spread of non-ownership, links between local and foreign firms, for example technology agreements and management contracts, it is argued that the distinction between national and transnational firms becomes blurred. This blurring is further reflected in the emergence of some transnational firms whose head offices are based in countries of the periphery, as discussed in Chapter 2. Hence, in a global market, ownership of firms may cease to be the critical element it was once thought to be. Thus, from quite different standpoints, both Neoclassical and Radical authors can agree on the potential benefits for developing countries from globalisation. Quite how 'independent' this development is, is another question. If the 'internationalisation of capital' perspective is adopted, the question itself is meaningless, since a national capitalism will be linked with other capitalisms through the various mechanisms of the world market, including the activities of transnationals. This is not to imply that the interests of individual governments and transnationals needs always coincide, nor that the activities of transnationals are always economically beneficial to the host economies. It is simply that a capitalist industrialisation in developing countries, closely linked with the world market, is feasible and in a few countries has proved highly effective as a means of economic transformation.

Chains in world industry

In discussions of international competitiveness in global markets, two concepts of chain analysis have been used. Although superficially similar, they originated from different perspectives and shed light on different issues. We first discuss the concept of 'value chains' before turning to that of 'commodity chains'.

Value chain

The idea of a chain analysis is that a product passes through a series of links or chains in its move from conception to sale to the final consumer. The final sale value of a product can be decomposed into value created at the different points in the chain.[8] Competitiveness means that, through the functioning of this chain of activities, a particular firm produces a superior quality product at the same cost as competitors or an equivalent product at a lower cost. Activities in the chain can be sub-divided into primary and support activities. Primary activities refer to organisation of input supplies (inbound logistics), actual manufacturing operations, delivery and distribution of the product (outbound logistics), marketing and sales and after-sales service. Each of these primary stages will be supported by a range of support activities covering a firm's planning capacity, its human resource management, its technology development through its own R and D work and its procurement activity. Figure 7.1 illustrates the value chain.

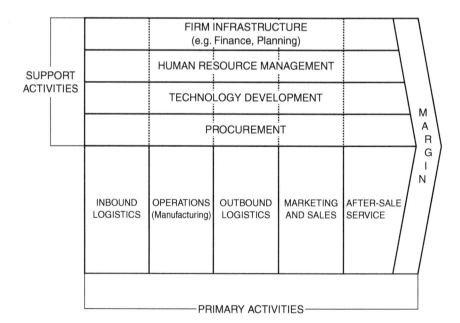

Figure 7.1 The value chain in global industries.

Cost and quality advantage requires firms to manage effectively all stages in the chain, rather than, for example, focusing narrowly on just getting production operations working to international standards. Sustained competitive advantage requires firms to build on their current strengths and to develop others. The successful integrated firms have distinct advantages all through the chain; for example, using new technology, extensive dealer networks and high standard after-sales service. The sources of a firm's competitive advantage can be drawn from a number of sources and their relative importance will vary between industries. Simplifying slightly, the key ones will be:

- cost advantages, for example, in terms of low wage rates or access to low cost local raw materials;
- product advantages in terms of brand names based on cumulative marketing effort or distinctive product design;
- technological advantages in terms of technology specific to a firm or the capacity to continuously modify and improve upon existing widely available technology.

The first of these is the one that firms in developing countries will rely on most, particularly in relation to wage rates. Although it is also the most ephemeral, in that successful economies will expect to see rising wages over time and thus the erosion of this particular advantage. On the other hand, advantages based on brand names and technological capability are much longer lasting. However, to achieve them requires sustained investment and often specialised and highly trained staff.

The value chain approach helps to focus attention on a few basic but important points. Success in world markets requires firms from developing countries to master not just production but also a range of other activities. With the ability to import and adapt imported technology it may be, for example, that the production side of a firm is one of the least problematic, with greater difficulties lying in the provision of support facilities or in developing marketing channels. Further, competitiveness has to be seen as a dynamic process, so that only firms that continue to upgrade can be successful. Advantages based on costs of production are essentially short term and can be eroded quickly. This has the important implication that competitiveness is only given to firms through national resource endowments in the case of certain labour and resource intensive activities. Elsewhere, and even in these activities in the longer run, competitiveness has to be created. Firms may be the prime movers but clearly in some contexts governments also have a role to play. Competitiveness in firms in a range of activities can be cumulative so that, where an individual firm establishes a dominant position, domestic rivals may shift to other market segments, new suppliers develop to supply cheaper inputs and improve process technology and more sophisticated buyers may suggest how to open up new product lines. A process of cumulative causation may thus spur increased competitiveness within a particular industry. Competitiveness studies for developed countries suggest a pattern of sector grouping, so that in a particular economy competitive firms tend to be grouped in closely related sectors (for example consumer electronics in Japan and fashion-based clothing and footwear in Italy). Sustained competitiveness at a national level requires upgrading by individual firms. Hence, export diversification is not just a process of shifting from a few traditional exports to a wider set of goods. It also requires that, within particular export categories there is a continual upgrading in either a minor (for example, modest redesign) or a major (for example, dramatically lower costs or higher quality) form.

Globalisation and 'splicing up the value chain'

Whilst successful firms need to be competitive at all points in the chain they do not need to do everything themselves. Subcontracting particular activities to others has always been an option and international subcontracting or sourcing has been used for many years. However, the closer integration of economies with falling communication, transport and transactions costs in the current wave of globalisation has greatly extended the scope for dividing or 'splicing up' the value chain between operating units located in different economies. The fully integrated firm that controlled and operated all aspects of the value chain within its own organisation provides a vertically-integrated model. However, its relevance in a globalised environment is coming increasingly under question with a considerable literature focussing on ways of 'de-verticalisation' as a means of building competitiveness.

Three possible routes for de-verticalisation or 'splicing-up' the value chain have received particular attention. One is based on a lead firm–supplier relationship. Here, at the manufacturing stage of the value chain, a close relationship is formed between a supplier and its lead firm. The lead firm and the supplier may be part of the same industrial group (in the Japanese and Korean models) or may have only a close commercial relationship. The lead firm may provide the supplier with technical assistance, product design and possibly financial support. This is an integral part of the 'lean production system' where, through its close links with its suppliers, the lead firm minimises inventories and maintains flexibility in the face of market volatility, as suppliers can be redeployed at short notice. A second route involves a less formal set of links between lead firms and suppliers, based on geographical proximity and close relationships. This is the network of regional clusters noted in Chapter 5 in the discussion of industrial districts and flexible specialisation, although the concept can be extended to cover less geographically based relations, such as those based on family relations between overseas Chinese in East Asia. In general, what is involved here is a production of a highly specialised nature involving small batches and fast delivery. Finally, there is a third route developed particularly by US corporations in recent years in response to their loss of share in global markets, which involves a more commercial or 'merchant' relation between the lead firm and its suppliers. Here, splicing up the value chain can involve more than production but also the subcontracting of a range of services including process engineering, assembly, packaging, distribution and, in some cases, after-sales service. The suppliers involved will be far less likely to be tied to one lead firm and will often provide either goods or services that can be sold to a range of users. Hence, long-term contracting relations between supplier and lead firm are not needed and flexibility on both sides is retained. This route allows firms to access the advantages of global specialisation with the minimum input of FDI, whilst controlling R and D and innovative capacity within their own organisation.[9]

There is no suggestion that one particular route is ideal but each provides a means of explaining much of the subdivision of the value chain that has occurred globally in recent years.

A key issue is how far it will be possible for nationally owned firms from developing countries to go in building successful value chains and how far they will have to restrict their activities to certain links in the chain, such as subsidiary production operations supplying lead firms in developed economies. As yet, only a limited number of firms from the NIEs have achieved success at all stages of the chain and the expectation is that latecomer firms will have to rely substantially on subcontracting links with TNCs. A helpful means of clarifying how such links can operate is provided by the related concept of global commodity chains.

Global commodity chains

Relatively recent offshoots of the Radical literature have used the concept of a commodity chain to explain how firms from developing countries can be integrated into specific industries in a global market.[10] This is linked with the value chain discussion in the sense that different chains can be dominated and co-ordinated by different parties (principally either producers or buyers). This involves a distinction between the twin forms of international capital, one based on production and operating a 'producer-driven' chain and the other on trade in a 'buyer-driven' chain. These chains are seen as the main means through which developing countries are linked with the global economy as exporters of manufactures. Within both there is scope for either flexible or mass production systems.[11]

Producer-driven commodity chains are organised around either TNCs or less commonly large national firms, who control a whole production system based around a set of backward and forward linkages; in other words the producer controls both its inputs and the uses for its output. The dominant firm will establish formal relations with its suppliers either through direct ownership or subcontracting. In addition it will have similar formal relations in the distribution and retail parts of the value chain. Hence, both nationally and globally, certain key, normally transnational manufacturers can control the functioning of whole sectors. Producer-driven chains are based on the market power of producers in capital and technology-intensive sectors, such as automobiles, aircraft, computers and heavy machinery. Market power here is based on the barriers to entry created by a combination of high capital investment and proprietary knowledge of key aspects of the industry's technology, and principally it is the control over technology that allows the large firms to dominate the chain. Firms from developing countries wishing to participate in such sectors will initially have to commence in the production of the more labour-intensive components and inputs sourced through sub-contracting.

The alternative to a producer-driven chain is where the organisational dynamic stems from the buyer in a buyer-driven commodity chain. Here large retailers, branded marketers and trading companies set up a series of production networks, typically in low wage locations. Hence buyers in the chain can be either retailers that design their own commodities (for example Marks & Spencer or the Gap), companies that market their own brands but do not have their own retail outlets (such as Nike, Reebok or Umbro) or transnational trading companies that have an intermediary role between producers and retailers. This pattern is found in consumer goods sectors with labour-intensive production, such as garments, footwear, toys, consumer electronics and a range of hand-crafted items. Production is normally carried out by locally owned firms in low wage countries that make finished goods to the design and specification provided by transnational buyers. The market power of the buyer is determined by its brand name, and central to the success of this form of commodity chain is the effectiveness of the buyer firm in managing the series of production and trade networks involved. Profits are determined less by volume or technological breakthroughs, as in the producer-driven chain, but more by design, sales, marketing and financial services that allow the identification of product niches in global markets. Developing country firms are already major participants in this form of global chain through the supply of labour-intensive finished goods to transnational buyers.[12] Figures 7.2a and 7.2b illustrate the two alternatives.

International production with such chains is growing increasingly competitive as alternative lower wage locations can always be found for a particular product; for example if, some years ago, Thailand could offer cheaper labour than Taiwan, currently China, Cambodia or Vietnam can under-cut Thailand in relation to wage costs. This competitive process puts continual downward pressure on wages and may be putting pressure on the terms of trade of those

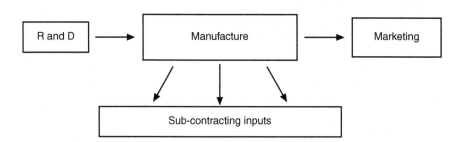

Figure 7.2a Producer-driven chain.

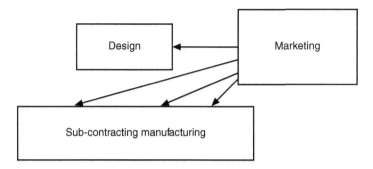

Figure 7.2b Buyer-driven chain.

developing country exporters, who have succeeded in building up manufactured exports. One response is so-called 'triangle manufacture', where as part of either a producer or buyer-driven chain the TNC sub-contracts a local supplier, who in turn sub-contracts a firm from a lower wage economy. In this sequence the original low cost producer, who has established an expertise in the sector, ceases to be a producer, but assumes the role of intermediary in the chain as the production role moves to the lower cost site. This process means that success in particular export activities based on low wage labour will inevitably be transitory and sustained export expansion will require a continual up-grading of export composition. Success for individual countries in the export of higher value goods will require the ability to move into 'own equipment manufactures' (the production of the finished goods in the chain combined with the establishment of alliances to cover distribution and retailing) or 'own brand-name manufactures' (the production of a firm's own branded goods combined with either some form of marketing alliance or more ambitiously a firm's own distribution network). As yet the success stories of firms from developing countries in these areas are relatively few and limited to the higher income NIEs. However, the fact that they can be identified illustrates the potential for success in the global economy. Examples of the development of own brand goods include Hyundai cars and Samsung household electricals from Korea, Acer computers from Taiwan, beers from Mexico (principally the Corona and Sol brand names) and the Brasilia aircraft from Brazil. The implication is that there are opportunities in the world market to be exploited by firms from poor countries, although, as yet, relatively few have been able to take full advantage of them.

Globalisation and TNCs

If developing country governments and their firms have the opportunity to position themselves in relation to global commodities chains, how should they relate to the transnational firms that are the key engines of globalisation as suppliers of technology, brands and marketing networks? A simple distinction between strategies followed by different countries in relation to TNCs is between autonomous and dependent strategies.[13] In the autonomous case, the entry of FDI, whilst not banned, is restricted and local firms are championed against TNCs through various forms of financial and other support. Local firms are encouraged to import foreign technology through licensing rather than through partnerships with foreign investors and the entry of the latter into strategic sectors is limited. A wide range of countries including most in South Asia and Latin America followed a version of this strategy during their import-substitution periods, generally unsuccessfully. It is only in the cases of Korea and Taiwan where this relative autonomy path is agreed to have produced positive results in terms of economic performance.[14]

The dependent strategy can itself be subdivided into passive and strategic variants. In the passive form, which has been the more common, TNCs provide the skills, technology and capital to exploit local resources either in terms of natural resources or low cost labour. Policy involves a welcoming incentive regime for FDI, measures to reduce the transactions costs of doing business in an economy, the provision of a reasonably educated, trainable labour force and the development of infrastructure often in Export Processing Zones.[15] Such zones allow firms located there the right to access to all imported inputs needed for production at free trade prices as well as tax holidays and sometimes subsidised factory sites and other inputs. Examples where economic zones for export are important include both large and small countries, such as Sri Lanka, Mauritius, Jamaica, Dominican Republic, Mexico and China. Exports that arise from this passive strategy will almost certainly be based on existing or static cost advantages, since these will be what attracts the initial FDI.

In contrast, an alternative version of strategic dependence, where countries adopt a more directive approach to FDI can also be identified. Here TNCs are strongly welcomed, but their investments are encouraged in particular activities that involve higher value-added and technological complexity, so that FDI plays an important role in upgrading a country's export structure. Singapore is the clearest example of this approach, although elements of the strategy are also said to be found in Malaysia and Thailand. However, for this more directive approach to work effectively, governments must provide the infrastructure and related support, as well as the local investment in education and training, to make it attractive for TNCs to invest in activities that are based on a dynamic rather than a static version of comparative advantage.

Arguably in today's world of globalisation an autonomous strategy in relation to TNCs is both undesirable and impractical. It is undesirable because of the pace of technical change, which will leave behind countries that close the door to foreign technology or attempt to 'leapfrog' into new areas through their own technical efforts. It is impractical because of the widespread competition to attract foreign capital, so that countries which impose what are seen as excessive restrictions simply will not receive FDI, and because of the introduction of international regulations under the World Trade Organisation (WTO), which reduce the scope for the type of policy interventions associated with the autonomous strategy, particularly the ability to require TNCs to source a proportion of their inputs from local supplies. What is now abundantly clear is that TNCs have led the export drive into relatively sophisticated manufactured goods in East Asia and may also have a significant future role in the development of labour-intensive manufactures and the processing of primary products for export in other regions. The key issue is how best to marshal the resources provided by these firms in the industrialisation process, since they do not provide a simple panacea for industrialisation.

Advantages and disadvantages of reliance on FDI

TNCs are seen traditionally as providers of a package of resources, capital, technology, marketing and management skills. As global firms they choose to exploit their firm-specific advantages through international production. The ultimate national objective must be to ensure that such firms create the maximum income within the economy on a sustainable, long-term basis. As TNCs bring in internationally mobile assets, governments have the responsibility of ensuring that the immobile assets of an economy, essentially its human and natural resources, are used as effectively as possible.

TNCs can cover their equity involvement in projects through transfers of funds, either from the TNC itself or raised on international capital markets, investment in kind, for example through equipment or technology, and through local borrowing. The latter does not contribute foreign exchange for the economy and may crowd out domestic borrowers. At one time, particularly at the height of import-substitution regimes, considerable attention was given to establishing the net balance of payments impact of FDI as a means of judging its attractiveness. Where it was negative, so that the original foreign exchange inflows were exceeded by outflows in the form of repatriated profits or expenditure on imported inputs, considerable concern was expressed concerning the developmental impact of the FDI concerned, which was seen as a drain of economic surplus from poor countries. This perspective is, however, excessively narrow.

Theoretically, if one is concerned with the balance of payments, it is the full impact, direct plus indirect, that matters. Hence, one must allow for the full range of indirect foreign exchange effects, which can include import replacement for final goods supplied by an FDI project, and the foreign exchange effects of using local inputs, some of which may be exportable and all of which will have some foreign exchange content.[16] Some import substitute projects with apparent negative direct foreign exchange effects can create a positive foreign exchange balance, once import replacement is allowed for. However, in general, from a foreign exchange perspective, export-oriented FDI normally significantly outperforms import-substitute activity, particularly where the latter requires high tariff protection.

Further, in an era of globalisation and improved access to international commercial borrowing, it is arguable that the key advantage of FDI is not financial, since finance can be obtained from other sources, either commercial borrowing or portfolio investment (that is equity investment without any management input), but rather the full package involving finance, plus technology, marketing and management skills. Also, the events of the late 1990s in East Asia have shown that FDI is a relatively more stable source of foreign finance than short-term loans or portfolio investment, which are much more likely to be withdrawn from an economy at short notice at a time of financial crisis or contagion.

In terms of technology, in the most dynamic sectors where technical change is most rapid, it will be difficult for firms to purchase technology through licensing or under technical assistance agreements with capital goods suppliers, since technology owners will not be willing to dilute their market power. In terms of the earlier analysis, they will wish to retain control of their producer-driven commodity chains. Further, as a source of technology FDI has the great advantage that it ensures that the skills needed to operate the technology will be provided from within the TNC. However, normally TNCs tend to centralise R and D activity in their home countries and undertake little innovative work in host economies. Singapore is the notable exception. This relegates most host countries to follower positions accepting technical change designed elsewhere. This is unlikely to be a major factor for many developing countries, however, since, for all but a few higher income NIEs, attempting to undertake genuinely innovative technical progress is impractical and is often economically irrational.

How far locally-owned firms benefit from the new technologies brought in by FDI has always been a subject of considerable concern. It is likely to vary with factors like:

- the degree of domestic competition, so that local firms operating in the same market segment as a TNC are forced to strengthen their own technological base to survive, perhaps through involvement with other foreign technology suppliers;[17]
- the links between a TNC subsidiary and local supplier firms, who receive technical guidance from the TNC to ensure inputs of adequate quality; this mechanism links directly with the commodity chain analysis noted above;
- the mobility of labour from the TNC subsidiary to local firms, where workers trained by the former take their specialist knowledge with them;
- the scope for clustering of firms both foreign and national where close proximity facilitates technological collaboration.

All of these can be interpreted as forms of externality from the presence of TNCs in an economy.

In terms of exports, nowadays in all but large economies, such as China, India and Brazil, the bulk of manufacturing FDI will be exported-oriented aiming at selling in world rather than domestic markets. TNCs have been involved in a wide range of product lines from simple garment production to assembly of computers and other electronic products. As we have seen they can provide vital links in the value chain; not just the technology relevant for production operations but also the brand names and distribution networks essential for export success in competitive international markets. At one time subordination to a global company strategy was seen as an obstacle to exporting, so that a particular subsidiary would be banned from exporting to a market, which would be better served by another member of the TNC group. Whilst in principle such barriers may still exist, they are now probably much less stringent than the barriers posed by lack of access to TNC brand names, technology and marketing channels.

The benefits noted above are no more than potential. How such firms actually behave in particular economies will depend in part on the nature of the economic environment they find. Some, but not all, of the potentially harmful practices associated with TNCs can be traced to causes within the domestic economy. For example, if there are capital controls on profit outflows, there is a strong likelihood that firms will use transactions between affiliates or subsidiaries in the same group to manipulate declared profits, so-called 'transfer pricing'. If a subsidiary buys components from another enterprise in the same international group the price charged will be an accounting, not a market value, and as such can be manipulated in the interests of the global operation. If profits taxes are high and capital controls on profit repatriation are in place in the economy in which a subsidiary is based, the interests of the group as a whole will be to inflate the cost of the components to reduce the subsidiary's declared profit in this host economy. This practice received a great deal of attention in the 1960s and 1970s, as a means of siphoning funds out of host developing economies that had formal balance of payments restrictions on capital outflows. However, currently in the new environment of lower profits tax rates, freedom of capital movement in most developing countries and double-taxation agreements (so that tax savings in a host country are simply picked up as tax obligations in another) this is much less of an issue. Currently the problem is of more concern in developed economies like Japan and the US, where tax rates are higher and anti-trust regulations are tighter than in developing economies, and where as a consequence TNCs may be more reluctant to declare their profits.

Similarly, the weak foreign exchange effect of TNCs was sometimes due to the strong incentive they obtained from the import tariff system to sell in the protected domestic market at prices well above comparable world levels. Although high rates of effective protection might have also been caused by a TNC's own lobbying activity, removal of such protection will be a strong stimulus for such firms either to reduce costs or to export, both of which should improve the net foreign exchange position. Also, the fact that some TNCs may produce luxury consumer items, inessential in a broader developmental sense, can be linked with the existence of a sheltered domestic market for such goods, which is a function of both trade protection and an inegalitarian income distribution. Again, changes in either factor will lower the incentive for TNCs to produce such items.

A perhaps more significant charge relates to the tendency for TNCs to invest

in economies to use low cost labour for export production and not to shift sub-
sequently to more technologically sophisticated goods. The issue here is partly
whether the economic environment is conducive to this shift. TNCs on their
own will have little incentive to look to diversify and upgrade exports, where
the technological and skill base in an economy is weak. However, if these
aspects can be built up and financial incentives, such as tax credits for diversification, are offered then governments can stimulate this shift. This is the strategic approach to TNCs noted above, which it is suggested has been highly
successful in Singapore and to a lesser extent in Malaysia and Thailand.[18]

Obviously, not all aspects of undesirable TNC behaviour can be explained in
this way. The issue of local linkages to domestic supplier industries is always a
source of contention since, given a free choice, TNCs would normally prefer to
source from within their own global operation, which would imply imports
rather than local supplies. Local content rules can force TNCs to establish linkages, but these will be difficult to impose under the new WTO rules.[19] Creation
of an efficient local supply network that can compete in price and quality would
clearly help, but this may take a long time to emerge and, in the short run,
TNCs may continue to establish linkages abroad rather than at home. This may
create lower national gains than if local linkages were created, but premature or
inefficient local linkages will only penalise industries that export by reducing
their competitiveness and are therefore unsustainable. Identifying what is a premature or an inefficient linkage is difficult, but the general point is that where
cost and quality factors can be overcome TNCs may themselves establish efficient local linkages in the longer term.

Also, as noted above, whilst there is the possibility of positive externalities
via technological and related spin-offs from TNC activity, the scope for negative externalities cannot be ruled out. The key mechanism here is where TNCs
enter the domestic market and force the closure of national firms, either by
direct take-over or through exit of the latter from particular areas of manufacturing activity. This process of denationalisation generated considerable
concern in the 1970s and 1980s, particularly in Latin America, and can be a
serious problem under certain conditions. These are principally where the
national resources affected, both labour and financial, are not absorbed in
equally productive uses and, critically, where the national level of technological
capability is reduced, leading to lower future productivity growth. This latter
situation may arise if the dominant TNC undertakes less R and D activity than
the national firm would have done. How serious an issue this actually is will
vary with circumstances of economies and particular firms.

These qualifications should be sufficient to show that TNCs do not provide a
simple panacea for developing countries wishing to industrialise. Further, even
if the balance of these arguments is overwhelmingly favourable, there is a limit
to the extent to which individual developing countries can expect to benefit
from FDI. First, there is evidence that TNCs are likely to require a minimum
threshold in terms of local skills and infrastructure before they consider investing heavily in an economy for anything other than the extraction of natural

resources. This rules out the poorest economies automatically. Second, and fundamentally, there is an important fallacy of composition argument. Countries are now competing strongly with each other to attract new FDI. This involves generous tax holidays and various indirect forms of subsidy, such as low cost factory sites. All developing countries cannot realistically expect to replicate the level of TNC involvement achieved by some of the NIEs. For example, if one takes Malaysia as a point of comparison, if all developing countries reached an equivalent level of FDI inflow per capita as in Malaysia in the early 1990s, FDI outflows from developed to developing countries would reach over half their total investment spending, which is clearly an implausibly high figure.[20]

Attracting more FDI per capita is a realistic option for many countries; however, it will not solve the more intractable development problems, as for example in much of Africa, where per capita FDI is very low in US$ terms. This is because of the well-known pattern of FDI flowing to growing markets and competitive low risk environments. Most African economies still do not fit this description and domestic efforts backed by further concessional funding will have to be the main engines of economic progress in the region. This implies that the trend noted in Chapter 1, of the poorer developing countries falling further behind the higher income ones and the NIEs, is likely to be exacerbated in the future.

Globalisation and trade in manufactures

The acceleration in the growth of world trade in manufactures raises the prospect for developing countries of export-led growth based on closer integration with the world market. Although the process of globalisation still has many critics, over the last twenty years or so there is evidence that, within developing countries as a group, those countries which participated most fully in the world economy did best.[21] Countries with a rising share of trade to GDP had a faster rate of economic growth. The more general point is that, for developing countries, closer integration with the world economy in the second half of the last century was associated with higher economic growth, disproving predictions of the emergence of stagnationary global forces holding back their material progress.

Evidence on this is provided in Table 7.1, where twenty-four globalising economies are identified, whose foreign trade to GDP ratio rose significantly post-1980. Of these, two-thirds experienced accelerated growth in per capita income. An aggregate comparison between these, and developed and non-globalising developing countries (weighted by population) is given in Table 7.1. It is clear that the twenty-four economies have done much better post-1980 than in earlier decades and much better than the group of non-globalisers.[22]

There can be general agreement that rapid growth of manufactured exports is an essential requirement for successful industrialisation. The key policy issue is how best to stimulate export growth. Does one do it through heavy involvement

Table 7.1 Globalisers and growth

| | Per capita GDP growth rates by decade and country group[a] | | | |
	1960s	*1970s*	*1980s*	*1990s*
Developed countries	4.5	3.4	2.5	1.9
Post-1980 globalisers	1.0	1.8	2.5	5.1
Other developing and transitional economies	2.2	2.6	−0.1	−1.1

Source: Dollar and Kraay (2001).

Note
a Growth rates are population weighted.

with TNCs, for example through institutional arrangements like export process-ing zones and tax incentives? Does one rely on macro economic reform and trade liberalisation to create a more competitive and open economy and the set of incentives that all firms, both foreign and local, can respond to? Alternatively does one attempt to create the immobile national assets, in terms of physical infrastructure and human skills, that will provide the base for internationally competitive production and also attract foreign investors? Most observers would suggest that export success requires a combination of all of these measures, although the emphasis has varied between successful countries at different times, particularly in relation to ownership and degrees of intervention.

Here we note that, whilst many observers conclude that TNC involvement may well be critical for sustained export success, there are clear limits to the passive-FDI dependent strategy, based on export processing zones or tax induce-ments to inward investment. One relates to the footloose nature of such invest-ment. If TNCs can shift their export platforms from the Caribbean to Sri Lanka or China in pursuit of lower wage costs or further tax holidays, when the ori-ginal concession periods run out, then clearly there will be limits to the extent that they can create sustained export success in any one economy. Also, the relatively low technology nature of such activities implies that, in the longer term, demand prospects for such goods will weaken, particularly as new market entrants arrive, and that countries will be locked into exports with sluggish demand prospects. Both factors suggest that countries need to look to ways to harness FDI to move up the stages of comparative advantage.

Export achievements

Chapter 2 has summarised some of the basic data on trade in manufactures and its uneven spread between developing countries. As we have seen, developing country exports of manufactures have grown rapidly since the mid-1980s and over the same period their share in world exports of these goods has risen to nearly a quarter. Remarkably, developing country shares in electronic exports have grown from 14% in 1985 to 34% in 1998 reflecting the expansion of what

Table 7.2 Wage competitiveness in selected countries and sectors (1995)

	Footwear	Textiles	Clothing	Metals	Wood	Rubber	Plastics	Electricals
Korea	1.03	0.81	0.91	0.79	0.83	0.74	0.58	0.59
Taiwan	2.21	1.45	1.29	1.71	1.81	1.86	1.85	1.80
Chile	0.69	0.83	0.79	0.75	0.61	0.69	0.75	0.93
India	0.99	1.01	0.49	0.97	0.91	0.88	0.88	0.85
Indonesia	0.85	0.47	0.95	0.55	0.53	0.72	0.64	0.76
Kenya	1.13	1.61	1.17	0.91	1.20	0.61	0.63	0.56
Malaysia	1.08	0.73	1.42	0.83	0.85	0.76	0.92	0.97
Mexico	1.62	0.96	1.20	0.76	0.76	0.96	0.83	0.83
Philippines	1.36	0.69	1.12	0.79	0.90	0.71	0.69	0.84
Thailand	1.23	0.87	1.70	0.71	0.57	0.56	0.83	0.65
Turkey	0.69	0.42	0.38	0.46	0.96	0.57	0.34	0.51
Zimbabwe	0.95	0.56	1.26	0.99	0.73	0.74	1.36	1.05

Source: UNCTAD (1999) Table 6.2.

have been classified as high technology exports.[23] Despite this export expansion, predominantly from the NIEs, for a majority of developing countries manufactured exports are still principally of the labour-intensive, low technology type based on the availability of low wage labour and natural resources.

In such activities, where products and their technology are relatively standardised, developing countries can compete successfully on the basis of low wage costs. However, it is not inevitable that simply because wages are low, producers will be cost competitive. Table 7.2 summarises the position in terms of wage competitiveness for a range of sectors and economies in the mid-1990s. The measure of competitiveness used is unit wage costs in US$ relative to the level of unit wage costs in the same activity in the US.[24] Three factors determine this measure of competitiveness: wage rates, labour productivity and the exchange rate. Hence the boost to competitiveness from low money wages can be offset by low productivity and appreciating exchange rates.

A wage competitiveness figure of below 1.0 means that, in unit wage costs, a country is competitive with the US and the lower the figure relative to other countries the more competitive will be producers in the country concerned. This particular indicator is crude since, for example, it assumes product homogeneity within each sector and that prevailing exchange rates represent underlying equilibrium values. Nonetheless, it highlights some basic points. By the mid-1990s, some of the NIEs had become uncompetitive in wage costs in a number of sectors; for example, Taiwan for all sectors covered and Korea for Footwear. On the other hand follower economies in East Asia such as Indonesia and Thailand appeared highly competitive in most sectors. More strikingly some manifestly low wage economies, such as India, Kenya and Zimbabwe, were not always wage competitive with the US, let alone with other low-income competitors.[25]

Hence low productivity and exchange rate overvaluation clearly can mean that even in relatively technologically simple, labour-intensive activities, low

Table 7.3 African economies: manufactures in total exports (early 1990s)

	(%)[a]
Angola	2.5
Congo	7.7
Côte Ivoire	13.7
Ethiopia	4.8
Ghana	10.9
Kenya	19.4
Madagascar	13.9
Malawi	6.2
Mauritius	59.6
Mozambique	27.5
Nigeria	1.6
Senegal	20.6
Sierra Leone	21.0
Somalia	2.0
South Africa	31.5
Tanzania	12.1
Zambia	6.6
Zimbabwe	30.8

Source: Calculated from UNCTAD (1998) Table 49.

Note
a Figures are averages from five or six alternative sources.

wages per se are unlikely to be a guarantee of international competitiveness. The most obvious manifestation of this is the low share of manufactures in the exports of most African economies despite declining real wages in many of these economies since the 1980s. Table 7.3 brings together alternative estimates of the share of manufactures in total exports for some of the main African economies. Because of data uncertainties a number of alternative estimates are available for the manufacturing export share in these economies and here this problem is overcome by averaging the figures from the various sources.

Clearly one would expect such export shares to vary between countries on the basis of natural resource endowments (the share of manufactures in total exports will be low in countries like Nigeria and Angola, for example, due to the availability of oil resources) and with the availability of human skills relative to other resources. The very high export share in Mauritius, for example, based on FDI in export processing zones, can be explained in part by the greater availability of skilled labour. However, even allowing for the fact that most African economies are poorly endowed with human, physical and financial capital relative to land, in the majority of cases the export share for manufactures is lower than would be expected allowing for these characteristics. Policy errors in the 1970s and 1980s, particularly in relation to the exchange rate, are one explanation for this larger than expected divergence, but this is probably not the full story.[26]

One of the few detailed studies of the manufacturing export sector in Africa concluded that most export firms were set up initially to serve the domestic market, with many moving first into the less demanding regional market, before attempting to sell internationally. However technological and marketing capabilities were often weak, technology used was often well behind the international frontier and domestic networks of suppliers and support services often functioned poorly.[27] In terms of our earlier discussion, there were weaknesses at various points in the value chain and as a result there is a long way to go before export-oriented manufacturing development can make a major impact in raising income levels in most of Africa.

Nonetheless, elsewhere simple labour-intensive exports have expanded very rapidly, particularly since the late 1980s and have been a major source of employment growth. Very high rates of growth of garment exports were recorded by Bangladesh, Sri Lanka and Vietnam, for example, on the basis primarily of low cost labour working-up imported patterns and product specifications and often imported fabrics usually as part of the buyer-driven commodity chains discussed above.[28] In the first two of these economies, textiles and garments in combination have come to provide the bulk of manufactured exports (around 70% in Sri Lanka and over 90% in Bangladesh in the mid-1990s), although arguably this is an unhealthy degree of dependence.

At the other extreme, in Chapter 2 we pointed to the dramatic shift in export composition towards technologically more sophisticated, capital-intensive goods that has occurred in the NIEs of East Asia. Table 7.4 shows the composition of exports for the top thirteen developing country exporters (of these all but the Philippines are included as NIEs in Table 1.10). Table 7.5 gives the

Table 7.4 Composition of manufactured exports top thirteen developing country exporters (1998) (%)

Country	Total manufacture exports US$ million	Resource-based (%)	Low technology (%)	Medium technology (%)	High technology (%)
China	167,881	10	50	20	20
Korea	120,700	11	21	38	30
Taiwan	105,553	6	30	27	37
Mexico	103,681	7	19	44	30
Singapore	103,488	14	7	19	60
Malaysia	65,940	17	11	20	52
Thailand	44,759	19	25	21	35
Brazil	38,881	40	15	37	8
Philippines	28,118	7	15	11	67
Indonesia	26,894	39	33	18	10
India	25,855	30	49	15	7
Hong Kong	23,167	5	56	13	26
Turkey	22,885	15	58	21	6

Source: Lall (2000a) Table A.3.

Table 7.5 Composition of manufactured exports by region (%)

Region, 1985	Resource-based	Low technology	Medium technology	High technology
East Asia	23.1	38.3	23.0	15.6
South Asia	32.3	55.8	9.2	2.8
Middle East and North Africa	70.1	17.1	11.3	1.6
Latin America[a]	61.1	16.2	18.9	3.8
Sub-Saharan Africa[b]	70.7	10.1	13.8	5.5
Region, 1998				
East Asia	12.1	28.3	23.6	36.0
South Asia	21.7	61.6	12.1	4.6
Middle East and North Africa	44.3	33.7	18.8	3.3
Latin America[a]	47.2	16.8	29.1	6.9
Sub-Saharan Africa[b]	51.3	35.0	11.5	2.2

Source: Lall (2000a) Table 5.

Notes
a Excludes Mexico.
b Excludes South Africa.

same information aggregated by region. Resource-based manufactures remain a major component of exports in the large economies of Brazil, India and Indonesia, whilst China, India, Hong Kong and Turkey have the majority of their exports in the simple low-technology category. However, the same is not true for most of the East Asian economies. Of the East Asian economies in Table 7.4, in all but Hong Kong and Indonesia, medium and high technology goods are a majority of manufactured exports.

The Malaysian example is particularly relevant here as a successful follower economy. Malaysia had become the developing world's sixth largest exporter of manufactures by the early 1990s. After an early reliance on resource-based manufactures, particularly rubber-based, from the 1970s onwards the major manufactured exports were in the relatively high-skill and technologically complex areas of electrical and electronic products, which by the early 1990s came to take over 60% of Malaysian exports. As a result Malaysia emerged as one of the world's leading exporters of semi-conductors, disk drivers, telecommunications equipment, air-conditioners and various household electricals. Further, within these categories, Malaysia upgraded its export structure by shifting beyond simple manual assembly of such goods.[29]

In Malaysia, the Philippines and Singapore, the bulk of these exports are from TNCs, who provided the institutional mechanism for export diversification and it is in these economies that producer-driven commodity chains have had the greatest effect. On the other hand, in Taiwan and Korea, local firms have been the driving force behind most of the export growth as these economies pursued their own largely autonomous technological and export path.

In Latin America, despite a shift in export composition and the emergence of manufactured exports from some previously protected industrial sectors, in form of 'import-substitute restructuring', with the exception of Mexico, the performance of manufactured exports in the 1980s and 1990s has generally been disappointing. In Mexico a combination of effective incentives, access to the US market via the North America Free Trade Area and the decisions of TNCs appear to have ensured that large manufacturers, at least, have successfully made the shift to exporting.[30] Automotive products, cars and parts, as well as consumer electronics and electronic machinery have been particularly significant. A major part of Mexican manufactured exports come from maquila firms established initially to process or assemble imported inputs chiefly from the US for sale again primarily to the US. Such firms operated under a special import regime, which guaranteed exemption from import duties, but also imposed restrictions chiefly on the sale of output to the domestic market. With the introduction of a free trade area between Mexico, the US and Canada such special arrangements are increasingly redundant and the intention is to put all US–Mexico trade on this footing by 2010.[31]

Elsewhere in Latin America there has been much less success in export diversification. In Chile, most non-traditional exports are still based on processing of agricultural goods and natural resources, with only 17% of exports classed strictly as manufactures in 1998. Colombia has a tradition of manufactured exports stemming from its attempts at export promotion in conjunction with import-substitution. This appears to have been an element in generating later success. However, nonetheless, manufactures were still only 30% of exports in the late 1990s. In Brazil, whilst manufactures were normally around 50% of exports in the 1990s their growth has been disappointing partly, as Table 7.4 shows, because a majority are in the lower technology areas. The precise reasons for disappointing manufactured export performance in Latin America will vary between countries, but key factors usually cited are the level and instability of the real exchange rate, the condition of infrastructure – roads, ports, railways and so forth – and, in some cases, continued anti-export biases in the incentive structure.[32]

Conclusions

What can one conclude regarding globalisation and the industrialisation process in developing countries? The most basic point is that, despite potential difficulties with market access and some adverse price movements for traditional primary exports, increased integration with world markets for both commodities and capital offers poor countries considerable potential for future growth via industrialisation. That this potential has not always been realised is clearly true. The causes for this under-achievement will vary between countries and will include policy errors, political instability and adverse external economic and non-economic shocks. Links with TNCs through either buyer or producer driven chains offer a way forward. Whilst it is clearly desirable for national firms to attempt to build their own expertise all along the value chain, they may struggle to achieve competitiveness if they rely on their own technological capability or marketing capacity. There is no simple set of measures that guarantees that countries will benefit from the process of globalisation, but what is becoming increasingly evident is that those countries that fail to seize the opportunities opened by the expanding world trade system and the major increase in international capital flows will almost certainly fall behind others that take their opportunities. What this implies in terms of policy mix for industry is discussed further in the following chapter.

8　Creating competitive advantage

If there is a consensus around the proposition that for sustained economic success industries and firms must move up the ladder of competitive advantage, shifting away from a reliance on goods with a simple lower-order advantage based on low wages or natural resources, the critical policy question becomes how this can best be achieved. Once posed in this way, the problem can be linked with the role of government and the future of industrial policy. Here we use the latter term to refer to an explicit attempt by governments to alter the pattern of resource allocation away from that which would result from a market-based system. Since all governments intervene in some way (even if only to collect small amounts of taxes to pay salaries of civil servants), we can say that by this broad definition there will always be a version of industrial policy in operation, even if only a very weak one. In the literature perhaps three broad strands of argument can be found; one which suggests that industrial policy will inevitably produce inferior outcomes to those generated by markets – the extreme 'government failure' case; that which argues that industrial policy will be essential to overcome the obstacles faced by poor countries wishing to industrialise – the extreme 'market failure' case; and third, that which acknowledges the success of industrial policy at certain times and in certain contexts, but which recognises that there can be no universal validity in claims for its importance. It is this pragmatic approach that we wish to stress. We take the view that there is no basis in either theory or practice to expect competitiveness to be created on the basis of firms' initiatives alone. Hence the question becomes what can governments try to do, apart from keeping the basic macro economic fundamentals like inflation, and the exchange rate at sensible levels? The answer will inevitably depend on the circumstances of the case.

Alternative versions of industrial policy

For the purposes of discussion we can highlight four idealised types of industrial policy:

- a minimalist version where the government has essentially a 'nightwatchman' role, protecting property rights of investors, whilst providing basic infrastructure and social services;

- a 'market-friendly' policy, where the state intervenes to counter the effects of market failures, for example in the dissemination of information, and in support of activities with external benefits (for example, education, training and research and development investment) and possibly with non-discriminatory support for new industrial investment;[1]
- an interventionist policy in which the state both picks and attempts to create winners by channelling resources (for example, in the form of domestic credit, foreign exchange or technology licences) to particular sectors or firms within sectors;
- a full command system where the state sets detailed production targets for industrial enterprises (which will have to be state owned) and controls the aggregate level of industrial investment.

These four versions of industrial policy run from the extremes of virtual *laissez-faire* (that is, a position of leaving decisions on industrial competitiveness to firms themselves) to the other of a central planning system, where firms have no independent role. In between are the more plausible alternatives – the market friendly and interventionist versions. The nightwatchman model may have an appeal in a context of a very weak, incompetent or corrupt regime, but it finds little support from any theoretical position. Contrary to some popular discussions on the topic, Neoclassical economic theory does not support this approach, but implies that where markets fail to function effectively, as, for example, in the presence of externalities or lack of information, government intervention will be required to help imperfect markets. As discussed in Chapter 3, however, this theory argues strongly for tax-subsidy solutions rather than direct controls in these situations. At the other extreme, the central planning model has been shown to be highly effective in raising rates of industrial growth over the short term, as evidenced by experience in the Soviet Union and elsewhere. However, it has been extremely ineffective over the longer run in generating internationally competitive, technologically dynamic products. Further, application of central planning requires a political system in which social ownership of the industrial sector is the norm. As we have discussed in Chapter 2, with the changes in previously nominally socialist countries over the last twenty years, these political preconditions are clearly absent.

On the other hand, the interventionist model of industrial policy finds conceptual support from the revised Structuralist arguments discussed in Chapter 4 and empirical support from the post-1960 experiences of the NIEs, principally Korea and Taiwan, and of Japan. Whilst no simple East Asian model of industrial intervention can be identified, since there were significant institutional and historical differences amongst the countries that practised this form of policy, the success of different forms of intervention in the particular circumstances of these countries and in specific time periods has been seen by some as crucial evidence on the importance of such a policy, at least under certain conditions.[2]

Table 8.1 Characteristics of alternative versions of industrial policy

	Market-friendly	*Interventionist*
Relationship with private sector	Non-discriminatory, arm's length	Highly discriminatory, close
Position on FDI	Welcoming	Restrictive
Objectives	Offset externalities, improve information	Create economic rents, stimulate dynamic efficiency
Mechanism	Price system	Controls
Measures	Taxes, subsidies	Licensing, directed credit, quotas, targets plus some taxes and subsidies
Examples	Subsidy for training and R and D.	Directed, subsidised lending, differential import tariffs.

Here in our discussion of policy alternatives we focus only on the two more plausible alternatives. Table 8.1 summarises the key features of stylised versions of both.

A market-friendly industrial policy

The market-friendly approach follows directly from Neoclassical theory. It stems from the insight that markets will never work perfectly in the formal theoretical sense and may work sufficiently poorly to require state intervention. However, where the state does intervene, from this perspective it should only do so in a way that supports the functioning of markets. Intervention should not override or distort markets and should be as transparent as possible. The theory underlying this is the analysis of market competition, which will be imperfect whenever all participants in a market have less than complete information and whenever individual, that is private, costs and benefits from actions in the market diverge from social ones. Chapter 4 has already noted the large literature on external effects in the context of industrialisation and Chapter 6 discusses some of these issues in the context of technology. What do these theoretical points imply for discussion of industrial policy?

As information imperfections can be significant, governments can play a facilitating role in spreading data on, for example, export markets, employment opportunities and technological norms and standards. Further, lack of information can heighten risk of failure causing firms to abandon investment plans. However, the market-friendly approach implies that this information problem is more acute for public sector planners than for entrepreneurs. The latter, it is argued, are closer to their sectors and hence are better placed to observe market trends. Picking winners or identifying potentially successful firms, or even sectors, to support is generally beyond the capacity of most public bureaucracies. This can account for government failures in this area in supporting economically non-viable projects.

Beyond this limited role, in terms of information dissemination, there is the issue of externalities. If firms themselves under-invest relative to what is socially desirable, for example because trained workers leave to go elsewhere or because newly developed technology can be modified or copied by others, then governments can offer compensation to encourage additional training or R and D activity. In these illustrations, instead of raising profits by import tariff protection or credit subsidies, which it is argued can have negative effects on efficiency, market-friendly interventions would be targeted as directly as possible, for example by offering subsidies for labour training or R and D. Such subsidies need not involve cash transfers, but could be in the form of tax allowances for private expenditure under these headings. In addition, there will be areas where private provision is not envisaged either due to their public good characteristics and or to the fact that investment is risky or benefits are external and cannot be captured fully by individual investors.[3] Public financing of industrial research institutes where the knowledge generated is pure rather than applied is an illustration of the first case and public provision of road infrastructure is an example of the second. In theory even export subsidies could be justified as a means of offsetting the cost of breaking into new markets, thus providing an externality to other producers who draw on this experience, although they now contravene WTO regulations and their use would invite retaliation against the user by its trading partners.

In the market-friendly approach, transparency in method of support and neutrality as between enterprises is critical to avoiding the misuse of resources in rent-seeking, that is lobbying for special favours. The whole purpose of interventions is to create extra incomes or rents for the beneficiaries of industrial policy. Hence favouring one enterprise over another in an industry is both inequitable and creates a strong incentive for competition between enterprises to obtain the special support. This process can create the conditions for significant corruption, as well as diverting resources from productive uses. These costs of rent-seeking have been of concern to many observers of past policies.

Also central to a market-friendly regime is a well-developed system of financial institutions that can transfer funds from savers to investors and monitor the effectiveness of investment. Governments have a role, less in providing the direct finance through publicly owned institutions, but more through regulation of the financial sector to ensure that banks have adequate capital reserves and follow sound banking practice. In this way, saver confidence in the system can be maintained and banks can act on the basis of commercial criteria to allocate credit between borrowers. In a market-based system, it is essential that financial resources can flow to the investors who can use them most productively, so that financial sector reform is seen as a prerequisite for economies wishing to establish an effective industrial policy.

Specifically in relation to the industrial upgrading necessary for export diversification, the argument is that this can be achieved primarily through the information provided by markets and by the discipline imposed by market competition. In other words, the market provides the 'command' system for enterprises. Left to take commercial decisions in a competitive market environment and faced by price signals that reflect relative economic scarcities, firms will themselves seek out export opportunities and the alliances and organisational change necessary to establish the relevant links along the value chain. Government policy should support not direct this process, for example by providing an exchange rate that allows exporters to be competitive, a trade regime that allows them to import foreign inputs (so that any import tariffs on inputs used for export production are either waived in an exemption scheme or refunded in a drawback scheme), and an investment regime that encourages inward foreign investment in manufacturing. In addition, where necessary, governments should fill the gaps, in terms of information and under-investment, left by market-driven decisions. In relation to TNCs, the market-friendly approach implies a welcoming attitude with minimal restrictions on firms' ability to take their own decisions. However, where governments can detect a divergence between short-term returns to the foreign firms themselves and longer-term returns to the economy, which can be rationalised as a form of externality, then logically under a market-friendly policy, intervention would be called for to bridge the gap between private and economic returns. The clearest example of this is the Singapore government's encouragement to TNCs to shift into more technology-intensive lines of production than the firms themselves would initially have chosen.

Overall, the aim is for a level playing field as between firms and, extending the metaphor, the role of policy is to ensure that the pitch has a smooth playing surface on which the skills of the players can thrive. This, of course, is a description of an ideal type, not a reflection of a real world scenario and, in practice, it is difficult to state categorically which countries have gone down this path in a purist sense. Singapore with an open, but nonetheless directive, industrial strategy probably comes closest to this ideal type. More controversially, World Bank (1993: 84) in its assessment of the rapid growth of the East Asian NIEs suggests that most of the government intervention in that region should be seen as market-friendly rather than interventionist. This is on the grounds that policies were applied pragmatically, if they worked they were retained, whilst if they did not they were rapidly abandoned. Further, levels of price distortion as a quantitative measure of intervention in markets (for example, the effective rates of protection discussed in Chapter 3) were lower there than in other countries. This is a widely disputed judgement, however, with critics arguing that most of the NIEs are paragons of an interventionist policy.[4]

An interventionist industrial policy

The rationale for an interventionist policy can be based on a judgement about the ineffectiveness of tax-subsidy measures to overcome particular market imperfections. For example, simply offering firms a tax concession if they choose to invest in developing new technologies may be insufficient to overcome the risk of failure. Put in these terms, rejection of a market-based solution may be on empirical rather than conceptual grounds. A broader rationale can be derived by reference to economic history and the concept of latecomer industrialisers. Countries that industrialise late will have the advantage of existing international technology to draw on, but the disadvantage that they will have to apply it in competition with well established competitors in other economies. Resolution of this dilemma requires state support for the industries in these economies, which in turn will necessitate state involvement in guiding the evolution of the industrial sector.[5]

An active industrial policy is often associated with Japan and the NIEs of Korea and Taiwan, and more recent discussions have also linked it with follower economies in East Asia of Malaysia, Thailand and Indonesia.[6] India and countries elsewhere in South Asia had an active state-led industrial policy, where public enterprises were the leading force for a time. An explicit industrial policy has also been used at various times in Latin America, for example in Mexico, Brazil and Chile, although less so in Argentina.[7] It is important to stress this range of applications, since there is no simple blueprint or design for such a policy and even within East Asia there were significant institutional differences in the way the policy was practised. Also there is now agreement that where it worked best this approach was applied flexibly and pragmatically, so that if one method of influencing the private sector failed, either objectives were altered or another method was tried.

As in the case of our discussion of the market-friendly approach, we set out an ideal type by focusing on essential features rather than precise details of such a policy. These essential features are summarised below.

- The provision of information on markets and related opportunities to the private sector as part of a close working association between the state bureaucracy and the private sector, so that each are aware of the other's concerns in particular areas through a system of industry associations and 'deliberation councils'. In Japan the concept of the bureaucracy informing the private sector of its wishes and often imposing these was termed one of 'administrative guidance'.[8]
- Public investment in, and often public financial support for, private investment in activities with important external benefits (such as physical infrastructure, training, education and R and D).
- A willingness to alter price signals (for example import duties or interest rates) as well as quantitative controls (such as investment licensing) to influence firms' decisions. This has both positive aspects, encouragement to invest in certain activities, and negative aspects, in the sense of a restriction of additional investment in certain areas.
- A focus on particular firms or groups of firms that receive special favours, because they are seen as strategic or priority; these are the 'national champion' firms.
- A system of 'contests' whereby firms receiving state support compete against each other to meet performance targets set by governments (the

best known example of this is the export target system whereby export sales at particular levels are required to gain access to subsidised credit).[9]

- A deliberate attempt to deepen the industrial structure by shifting investment into activities with higher technological complexity.
- A willingness to negotiate with TNCs over the details of their technology transfer to national firms and over the form and direction of their investments in the national economy. However, in some versions (particularly in East Asia), industrial policy involved a distinct preference for national ownership in key industries, which implies the need to restrict FDI in certain areas, either through outright prohibitions or the restriction of TNCs to minority share-holdings.

Whilst some of these features are shared with the market-friendly approach, others are not. The key points of difference are selectivity as between firms and sectors, with planners anticipating and in some instances trying to create market trends, and use of a variety of non-market mechanisms to shift resources into particular areas. We can illustrate the variety of forms of intervention used in different countries.

Central to all versions of industrial policy has been the use of subsidised and directed credit targeted at particular branches and often at firms within those branches. Conceptually, this can be seen as a form of compensation for the fact that, in developing countries at early stages in their development, capital markets for finance will not be available so that firms cannot attract external finance by share issues. Finance for investment will thus have to come from retained earnings and loans. If privately-owned banks are unwilling to lend long term for industrial investment, because of the perceived risks or because they themselves lack the funds, an alternative mechanism will be required. The institutional mechanism used to channel public funds to new industry in many countries was the state-owned development bank. Such banks typically lent long term at concessional rates of interest with the explicit objective of building up the industrial base of an economy.[10]

Not all credit interventions involved state banks and, in parts of East Asia, a private sector version of this mechanism evolved as part of the conglomerate group structure. Where a bank was also part of the same group as a manufacturing enterprise, it would lend to that enterprise often at concessional interest rates. In so far as industrial policy allowed governments to influence the decisions of these large groups it could affect credit flows to individual enterprises through this intra-group lending.[11]

Whilst the supply of finance was probably the main weapon of an interventionist industrial policy as it operated in the past, a whole range of more specific controls can also be applied.

Licensing – licences for the import of goods or technology or for investment approvals can be used to determine which firms or sectors get access to foreign exchange or technology. Negotiations over the issue of licences provide a forum for establishing performance criteria that recipients will be expected to meet.

Import quotas – quotas can be used to restrict access to the domestic market for imports that compete with local producers. In practice, quotas were often imposed primarily at times of balance of payments difficulty, as a means of conserving foreign exchange, but they can be, and at times were, used to guarantee local producers a share of the domestic market.

Import tariffs – differential rates of import tariff can be used to generate economic rents, for particular import-competing producers. This is the infant industry mechanism, discussed in Chapter 4.

Direct guidance – directives can be given to firms in a particular sector to merge, if it is felt that the market can only support a smaller number of producers or to rationalise production by market sharing to avoid excessive competition. How these directives can be imposed on firms will vary. In most versions of interventionist policy, they will either apply to public enterprises, where there should be no control problem, or be applied to private firms as part of the working relationship between government and industry. Hence, to impose these directives, governments will need to 'sweeten the pill' by offering other concessions, for example in relation to credit or import protection, in return for the desired mergers or rationalisation.

Targeting – encouragement of activities can be granted in return for achievement of targets specified by the government, as part of the contest system referred to above. Targets used in the past have varied but have included particular levels of export, use of local inputs and raw materials, employment generation and development of new products and technologies. In Latin America, limits on enterprise debt–equity ratios were used by development banks as a means of restricting the size of individual firms.[12]

R and D investment – public investment can be focussed on operationally relevant technologies, which can be disseminated to the private sector by the work of public research institutes. The development of science parks, with the aim of encouraging locational external benefits, through various forms of encouragement to private firms to locate there, is an extension of policy in this area.

Where this policy has worked best, the relationship between the state and private sector has been based on a well-recognised notion of reciprocity. Governments support firms, who both compete for these favours and recognise that they have an obligation to fulfil various performance targets. Where this reciprocity is absent, interventionist industrial policy can rapidly degenerate into rent-seeking or crony capitalism, so that the establishment of a form of control mechanism is vital. In terms of export upgrading, industrial policy should seek to encourage producers to think of exports at a relatively early stage and to enter new higher value-added areas.

Japan, Korea, and Taiwan are the countries most often cited as examples of an interventionist industrial policy.[13] However even between these economies, where there were superficial similarities, the form of policy differed. For example, in Korea and Japan, the Ministries of Finance and Industry were the dominant actors in the bureaucracy, whilst Taiwan relied more heavily on task forces outside the normal system of ministries. Similarly, Taiwan relied much more heavily on state investment in key industries as opposed to encouragement to private initiatives in these areas. On the other hand, large private groups have been much more significant in Korea (the *chaebol*) and Japan (the *keiretsu*) than in Taiwan. In terms of the impact of targeting, as we have noted, the Korean export targeting system has been widely praised for forcing Korean firms to export at an early stage (through cross subsidisation of exports by the profits from sales in the protected home market) and thus gaining efficiency benefits in the form of access to foreign markets and technology. In each of the three cases, reliance on FDI was modest and at a relatively early stage in their industrial development, governments were reluctant to allow heavy foreign investment because of its apparent threat to the national champion firms they were attempting to encourage. Hence, whilst there was a clear readiness to accept foreign technology through licensing agreements, the strong preference was for this to allow national firms to build up national competence.[14]

However, in each of these countries the state–private relationship has evolved over time with the state gradually playing a smaller role. As economic development has taken place and the power of private groups has grown, so has their ability to resist state initiatives. The financial scandals in recent years highlighting corruption in the government–business links in Korea can be interpreted as weakening in the contest system there and a successful attempt by the private sector to capture key elements of the state bureaucracy. Recent Korean experience also suggests that the administrative guidance model may have limits, particularly because of its reliance on a controlled financial sector where banks are subject to government guidance on where to lend. We return to this point later (page 174).

Elsewhere in East Asia the activism of industrial policy has been somewhat less apparent. As we have noted, Singapore, with its heavy reliance on foreign investors and its less intrusive state–private relations, is probably closer to the market-friendly model, although state initiatives have been instrumental in encouraging foreign firms to move into higher value-added technologically sophisticated areas. Malaysia, on the other hand, is more ambiguous since, from the mid-1980s onwards, there was an attempt to deepen the industrial structure by developing linkages between exporters and domestic input suppliers and by technological upgrading by TNCs. The instruments used for this purpose are familiar from the discussion above and include selective tariff protection, skills provision and selective investment incentives to encourage more technologically intensive activities.[15] In Indonesia, whilst interventions proliferated, at least one eminent observer concludes that selectivity, whether in differential rates of tariff protection or directed credit allocations, was likely to be haphazard and ad hoc, guided more by issues of patronage and special pleading than by notions of strategic intervention in support of dynamic activities.[16] In Thailand, new industrial activities were offered a range of incentives provided they met many of the performance criteria noted above.[17]

Outside East Asia the success of an interventionist version of industrial policy is at best mixed. Indian experience, before the weakening of controls in the 1990s, has been heavily criticised for either dampening down private initi-ative or encouraging it in the wrong areas, as firms could make high profits in activities highly protected from foreign competition.[18] In Latin America, Brazil and Mexico at various times have attempted versions of industrial policy. Chapter 6 has already discussed the largely unsuccessful attempt in Brazil to build a national computer industry behind protective barriers and import restraints that were designed to reserve segments of the local market for national firms. Even after liberalisation in the early 1990s, local investment was still encouraged by government procurement policy favouring locally supplied computers over imports provided the former were price competitive. In Mexico, in the 1980s, at a time of general trade liberalisation, industrial programmes were applied to grant special support to the sectors of automobiles, computers and pharmaceuticals. Firms in these sectors were granted special treatment in access to imported inputs and eligibility for tax credits. As a condition for this support, firms were required to match their expenditure on imports with export sales and to maintain a minimum level of differential between domestic and import prices for their goods. These special programmes were only removed in the early 1990s, several years after the general import liberalisation and have been praised by some observers for facilitating restructuring in these sectors.[19]

Does an interventionist industrial policy work?

Establishing that countries used the tools of an interventionist industrial policy is not the same thing as demonstrating that such a policy was effective in raising the growth rate and altering the structure of economies in an economically pro-gressive manner. Conventional economic efficiency criteria were often ignored in such programmes, leading to the type of inefficiency results reported in Chapter 3. The long periods of protection granted to firms and the ineffective-ness of control mechanisms in forcing improvement in efficiency have been documented for many countries. East Asia is the only region where sympathetic observers have been able to point to significant success in terms of structural change arising from industrial interventions. The early focus on exports, which turned conventional infant industry ideas on their head, is generally seen as critical to industrial success. Even the policies of directed credit at concessional interest rates, which were widely criticised elsewhere, were found to work effect-ively in at least some of the East Asian NIEs. A significant part of the growth in these economies appears to have been due to high rates of savings and reinvest-ment, but their productivity performance in their high growth years was also good by comparative standards.[20] Several policy initiatives to move into heavy and chemical industry, for example in Korea in the 1970s and Malaysia in the 1980s, have been criticised as premature and misguided but, these apart, the robust performance of these economies has been linked with the application of industrial policy.

Assessing the impact of a very diverse set of policies is difficult, particularly because a policy that works in one place at one point in time need not be universally successful. What emerges clearly in considering recent experience is that industrial policies cannot be judged in isolation from an economy's stage of development and the international economic environment it faces. A plausible case can be made that industrial interventions, which may have contravened short-term efficiency considerations, appeared to work effectively in the East Asian NIEs at relatively early stages of their industrialisation. In the 1960s and 1970s risks associated with industrial investment were relatively high and financial markets were poorly developed. Industrial policy provided a transfer mechanism for shifting resources to industrial investment, often, it should be noted, at the expense of domestic consumers. High private savings and high investment aided by government strategic interventions provided a very strong boost to industrialisation, most obviously in Korea and Taiwan. However, arguably once an industrial base has been established through this mechanism, short-term efficiency considerations assume greater significance and longer-term success will require a more flexible, market-friendly approach. Hence the Japanese pattern of an interventionist policy followed by a shift to a more market-based approach was followed in both Korea and Taiwan, which both had virtually abandoned the main elements of their interventionist policies by the early 1990s. If this interpretation is valid, it raises a number of questions. First, did industrial policy during its activist heyday in these economies actually make that much of a difference? Second, how easy is it to turn on and turn off industrial interventions in this way? Third, what are the lessons for today's follower economies, who are having to industrialise under a different global trading and investment environment to that faced by Korea and Taiwan in the 1960s and 1970s?

Did industrial policy make a difference?

Recent empirical work, whilst recognising individual successes in particular firms, has questioned whether the aggregate impact of industrial policy was really that significant in the East Asian NIEs and Japan. World Bank (1993) started this by arguing, first, that industrial structure in the East Asian NIEs did not differ significantly from what would be expected from economies of their income level and factor endowments and, second, that in these economies there is no tendency for total factor productivity growth to be higher in promoted sectors, favoured by policy, than in those not favoured.[21] To other observers this revisionist interpretation is not convincing.[22] In qualifying this view it is possible to argue that the main impact of industrial policy may show up in the overall growth rate rather than in the pattern of growth within manufacturing. If an interventionist industrial policy allows high levels of savings and investment by its pro-investment stance and by overcoming a foreign exchange constraint on importing capital goods, then it will be its macro not its micro effects that matter.[23] Second, since the sectors concerned are all tradable, a better test of the impact of industrial policy than a comparison of productivity growth between sectors is an examination of their comparative efficiency in relation to import competition. By this criteria industrial policy can be judged a success if it changes comparative advantage, so that, in a protected activity, domestic costs fall below costs in a competing economy. This approach has been followed for Korea with the finding that, within the manufacturing sector, growth was unrelated to initial comparative advantage, which strongly supports the view that industrial policy did influence resource allocation. However some, but not all, of the favoured industries achieved competitiveness over the period 1970–90 and the important activities of general machinery and transportation equipment did not. Hence although unlike other economies some protected infant industries did mature and reach competitiveness, success was not universal.[24] Nonetheless, the case that industrial policies did not influence resource allocation in these economies is counter-intuitive and implies either that rents created by interventions were not great or that, where they were significant, they had little impact on enterprise decisions. Neither of these propositions seems very plausible.

What is the legacy of industrial policy?

Perhaps a more important question is what legacy interventionist industrial policy bequeathed to the economies in which it was pursued. If industrial policy creates a climate of rent-seeking and corruption, even its abandonment may not resolve the problems it creates, since economic actors will have the costs and uncertainty of adjusting to a new way of operating. The significance of this question was heightened by the Asian financial crisis, which badly affected a number of countries, principally Korea, Thailand, Indonesia and Malaysia, where it has been argued that an interventionist policy had an important role. The issue has been debated most intensely in Korea, since it is not only seen as the paragon of such a policy, but the crisis exposed what many saw as serious structural weaknesses in the Korean industrial sector and, by implication, in the old interventionist model.

Two key features of the Korean-style mixed economy came in for particularly heavy criticism. One was the *chaebol* or conglomerate group system, in which companies operated as part of larger groups often with poor accounting practices, heavy reliance on external borrowing and what some have seen as outmoded, family-based, rather than professional, management. The other was the banking system, itself part of the group network, which failed to exercise adequate control over borrowers. Subject to government control in the days of the interventionist policy, the *chaebol* system appeared to work extremely effectively. However, once controls were dismantled, an alternative control mechanism proved difficult to find. In a fully market-based system, financial discipline will be imposed by banks operating at arm's length from companies and by the capital market through which poorly performing companies can be subject to hostile take-overs. Neither a commercial banking system nor an effective capital market can be put in place quickly and hence, in their absence in Korea, with the relaxation of the old interventionist model, there was no adequate control mechanism to replace it.

The old financial system was simply not ready to cope with the demands placed on it by the removal of capital controls and the ability of firms to borrow internationally. Thus, with the liberalisation of foreign borrowing in the early 1990s, the large Korean firms entered into what were in effect high risk, short-term loans denominated in US dollars, often for speculative purposes. In the late 1990s, with the build-up of short-term foreign debt by corporations, neither the government nor the financial sector knew the full extent of outstanding loans. These corporate borrowers were highly vulnerable to the wave of panic selling that affected currencies in Thailand and Indonesia and then spread to Korea, despite the fact that the country itself did not have a current account problem on the balance of payments.[25]

How far industrial policy per se, as opposed to reckless borrowing by private sector corporations who failed to appreciate the risks involved with foreign borrowing in global financial markets, can be blamed for the crisis in Korea in the late 1990s is the subject of considerable dispute. A plausible interpretation is that, whilst the detailed aspects of industrial policy, such as targets and government credit allocations, had been abandoned by the early 1990s, several years before the crisis, more than thirty years of such a policy had left a legacy of an undeveloped financial sector. In this view, a shift away from government intervention occurred before the essential financial institutions necessary to make a success of a more market-friendly strategy were in place.

The post-crisis policies in Korea have focussed on a full opening of the financial sector to foreign competition and capital inflows and on restructuring the *chaebol*. In a revival of interventionism, the government pushed the *chaebol* into industrial restructuring programmes involving mergers and business swaps in several important sectors, including semi-conductors, automobiles, aircraft and petrochemicals. Further, a new management and governance style was imposed on the *chaebol* with the prohibition of loan guarantees by one enterprise in a group on behalf of another, and the enforcement of lower debt–equity ratios for enterprise operations to ensure a lower reliance on external borrowing. Also in an effort to reduce the influence of family owners, the rights of minority shareholders were strengthened. All of these measures can be seen as deliberate attempts to change the nature of the Korean economy as part of a transition away from the old industrial policy model. However, it is significant that the forced mergers and restructuring referred to above in part represented a move back to the old style of interventionism, with the implication that the transition from an interventionist industrial policy model, even where the latter appears outmoded, itself creates a number of transition costs.

The Korean difficulties of 1997–98 appear in part to have been overcome, with the relatively rapid revival of economic growth. However, the whole episode and the weaknesses in the Korean industrial sector that it appeared to reveal undermined some of the credibility associated with an active interventionist form of industrial policy.

Lessons for follower economies?

Nonetheless, if the relevance of industrial policy varies with the stage of development of an economy, what lessons (if any) can one draw for lower income developing countries wishing to strengthen their industrial sectors? Experience of policy in South Asia and Latin America has rarely been offered to other developing countries as a model, but much has been written on replicability of the East Asian story. Even establishing that a particular set of interventions worked well in East Asia at a period in time is clearly not conclusive proof of their universal desirability.[26] Observers have stressed some of the unique features of the Korean and Taiwanese cases, in particular. There the state apparatus was staffed by a highly capable and respected bureaucracy committed to a national project of independent industrialisation. Economic growth through industrialisation became linked with nationalist goals as a means of establishing the identity and security of these countries.[27] Unique in the relationship between the state and the private sector was the strength of the idea of reciprocity, which, because of the nationalist dimension, was far more powerful than elsewhere. This detached relationship can be seen in political economy terms as the ability of the state to retain significant autonomy in its relations with the private sector. This is evidenced in Korea, for example, by the rise and fall of many of the Korean large groups, as they lost state support.

However, others have suggested that it is easy to overstate arguments about the uniqueness of this experience. First, the effective bureaucracy of both these economies had to be created and was not simply an inheritance from earlier times.[28] Second, relations with private firms were not always either frictionless or transparent. In Korea, in particular, corruption issues, whilst more publicised in recent years, were always of significance. Also, as noted above, the balance of power in the relationship changed over time as would be expected with the growth in wealth of the national private sector. Hence, the idea of a super-competent, incorruptible bureaucracy in these economies, always able to constrain and manipulate private investors, is an exaggeration. Third, the range of institutional mechanisms and policy measures actually applied in East Asia makes it feasible to think of other countries experimenting with their own versions of industrial policy. The implication is that, with the investment of resources and the political commitment, other countries can also construct a capable state apparatus and devise their own version of an active industrial policy.

What then does this experience imply for other countries? Clearly a successful industrial policy requires a meritocratic, well-respected and capable state bureaucracy, with continuity of personnel and political insulation from the pressures of lobby groups. In political terms, for this bureaucracy to function effectively requires governments to build both a good relationship with the private sector and probably also to sustain a climate of economic nationalism so that firms and public servants can be perceived to be working in combination for the good of the nation. This may well be a very demanding requirement for countries, such as many in sub-Saharan Africa, where state bureaucracies have crumbled in recent years in response to macro economic decline and corruption. Having said this, of course, one can also argue that the requirements of a market-friendly industrial policy, whilst less daunting in terms of contact with the private sector than an active interventionist model, are still substantial. Governments that wish to devise effective tax-subsidy interventions will require sophisticated data on market failures, which will not be forthcoming unless significant efforts are made to create it. Hence, the implication is that either version of industrial policy can pose demanding requirements for economies in which the civil service has shrunk, public pay scales are low and traditions of probity in public life are absent.

In terms of the need to raise competitiveness and upgrade the export structure of an economy, it should be clear that well targeted and designed policy interventions can have a role to play, for example, in encouraging exports through tax incentives, R and D subsidies and training programmes. Sensibly designed directed credit financing may also help in high-risk activities. However the limits of such a policy should also be clear. State support must be for specific and transparent periods of time and conditional upon performance requirements being met. Lobbyist and vested interests cannot be allowed to dominate policy. Price interventions must not be so high as to shift private investment into non-viable areas and all policies must be operated flexibly and pragmatically.[29] With these important provisions we can say that sensible interventions could make a difference.

International economic environment

An important new dimension is the new international trading environment and the World Trade Organisation rules that countries are increasingly acceding to.[29] As members of the WTO, the very poorest or least developed countries can still use export subsidies provided they do not reach a certain world market share for the goods concerned. Other developing countries are expected to eliminate export subsidies by 2003. Import tariffs amongst members are negotiated to 'bound' levels, which are maximum tariff ceilings, although in many developing countries actual tariffs are often significantly below these maximum permissible levels (see Table 2.2). Hence modest tariff protection is still possible under these rules. However, 'import-substitution subsidies', which discourage imports and give financial inducements to domestic producers other than through import tariffs (for example, through subsidised credit), must be abandoned. Again the timetable is longer for the least-developed countries, but such measures are expected to be removed by 2003. However, quantitative barriers to import to sustain local production through import quota restrictions are now very difficult to apply. The type of industrial programmes, for example, used in the automobile and computer sectors in Latin America in the 1980s or applied in Korea and Taiwan in various sectors before the early 1990s, that enforced local content agreements on foreign firms or required them to match import expenditures with export earnings are now prohibited under the Trade Related

Investment Measures (TRIMs) agreement. Under this agreement, local content requirements and measures to control the level of imports and exports in foreign-owned firms, are judged to be restrictions of trade. These were to be removed in developing countries by 1999 and in the least-developed countries by the end of 2001.[30]

The only scope that remains for specific non-tariff encouragement for local producers against imports is in the form of emergency protection against an 'import surge'. This is defined as a situation in which a rise in imports threatens serious injury to domestic industry. Under such circumstances affected enterprises can request that their governments impose safeguard measures under this clause. A public hearing, where evidence is taken from interested parties, must be held and the situation assessed against defined criteria for 'serious injury'. If the latter is demonstrated safeguard measures can include quota restrictions, although these cannot be so restrictive as to reduce imports below the annual average for the last three normal years, unless exceptional circumstances can be shown. Safeguard measures must be temporary and would normally be approved for four years, although a further four-year extension is possible, where necessary. Nonetheless, after the first year of their imposition there must be evidence of a gradual liberalisation. This is a very modest form of support for local producers in comparison with what was available in earlier decades, although it does allow some limited support for the restructuring of firms in the face of import competition.

Further, as noted in Chapter 6, industrial patents are now protected for a standard twenty-year period under the Trade Related Intellectual Property (TRIPs) agreement protecting intellectual property rights, so that the scope for copying and modifying foreign technology as part of national industrial programmes is greatly reduced. The agreement states that patent protection must be available for inventions for at least twenty years, whilst industrial designs can be protected for ten years. The only allowable exceptions are where the holder of the patent or protected design abuses their rights by refusing to supply a product in the domestic market. This enables governments to issue 'compulsory licences' allowing competitors to produce the product. Here, however, subsidies in support of R and D activity do not invoke WTO retaliation and thus, along with emergency import safeguards, provide the only real means of providing direct support within the WTO framework.

The implication is that only modest and subtle interventionist policies will be feasible in the new environment, so that even where governments have the capacity to intervene the scope for this will be circumscribed significantly. The acquisition, assimilation and development of technology is widely accepted as critical to progression along the comparative advantage ladder. However, if an interventionist industrial policy that encouraged and nurtured successful domestic firms is largely a thing of the past, this places probably insuperable limitations on an autonomous industrial strategy that attempts to develop a complex technological base around local firms and indigenous technology. Hence, the alternative must be to recognise the possibilities created by the current wave of globalisation and the activities of TNCs and to rely heavily on such firms for the transfer and assimilation of foreign technology. However, as we have noted above, alternative postures on TNC activity have been identified – one a passive and the other an active approach. The former uses TNC investment to exploit static wage or resource-based cost advantages, whilst the latter directs TNCs into increasingly complex and higher value-added activities and attempts to ensure that they establish a firm technological base in an economy. The former strategy requires a sound macro environment, established property rights and good supporting infrastructure. The latter requires all of these plus skill and education development and encouragement to local R and D. The policy choice is how best to direct the process of globalisation to ensure that a sound technological base can be established through TNC activity. Countries that fail to rise to this challenge risk marginalisation in world trade, which is a fate that has befallen many poor countries, principally, but not exclusively, in sub-Saharan Africa.

Conclusion

Thinking on industrialisation and industrial policy has undergone many shifts over time, although we believe we see some things more clearly now than forty years ago. Openness to trade matters greatly, as does local R and D and FDI. Globalisation provides challenges and risks, but if its opportunities are taken, the expectation must be that more developing countries will experience higher levels of industrialisation and, hence, higher income levels. Rising GDP and industrialisation in themselves do not guarantee development in broader social terms, but they are an important necessary condition.

Notes

1 Industrialisation since 1960

1 See UNIDO (1999: v) for the current United Nations country grouping.
2 Liedholm and Mead (1999) give an indication of the importance of the small scale, largely informal, manufacturing sector in several countries; see also Chapter 5.
3 See Lall (2000a) Table 3. Developing country share in world manufactured exports has risen from 16% in 1985 to 23% in 1998.
4 Developing countries share in world manufacturing value-added rose from just over 8% in 1963 to just under 12% in 1984; see UNIDO (1985: 5). Calculations from the UNIDO database suggest a figure of nearly 20% in 1995; of this, 5% is accounted for by China.
5 See Bairoch (1975: 66–67). From 1938–50, a period of economic dislocation due to the Second World War, manufacturing output in developing countries grew by less than 4% per year.
6 Jalilian and Weiss (2000) examine the relationship between manufacturing share in GDP, income per capita and various other country characteristics. The significant positive relationship between manufacturing share and income per capita found in earlier studies is confirmed. There is also a significant positive relationship with population so that, other things being equal, larger countries tend to have a higher manufacturing share. For their stylised economy, Chenery *et al.* (1986) put the turning point at which the share of manufacturing in national income declines at an income level of approximately US$5500 per capita in 1982 prices.
7 Data come from World Bank (2000).
8 For example, in a cross-country regression analysis explaining the manufacturing share in GDP by income and population, World Bank (1993: 306) finds the share is 26% higher than predicted in Korea, 38% higher in Singapore and 68% higher in Thailand.
9 Employment data are far from complete in the World Development Indicators, hence 1990 is the most recent reference point for regional employment estimates.
10 Comparisons with nineteenth-century data come from Squire (1981: 24–25).
11 These figures are derived from UNIDO (1997) statistical annex.
12 See Katz (2000).
13 See Squire (1981: 25).
14 Within manufacturing the shift away from light industry between 1960 and 1980 was significant; for example, the share of heavy industry in the group of developing countries rose by 14 percentage points, from 43% to 57% between 1963 and 1980; see UNIDO (1983: 62–63).
15 These classifications follow UNIDO (1997: 117). Low technology activities are ISIC categories 311–42, 353–54 and 361–81. They correspond to food products, relatively simple consumer items like clothing and footwear and basic intermediates like paper,

rubber, glass and metals. Medium technology activities are ISIC 351–52, 355–56, 384 and 390, which cover chemicals, plastics and transport equipment and miscellaneous manufactures. High technology activities are ISIC 382–83, and 385, covering electrical and non-electrical machinery and scientific equipment.

16 Data pre-1980 come from World Bank (1986: 26) and post-1980 Lall (2000a). Definitions of manufactured exports can vary. The most common, which is used for the data cited here, is Standard International Trade Classification sections 5 to 8, excluding 68, non-ferrous metals. Lall (2000a) gives data on a value basis and, as noted earlier, shows developing countries accounting for nearly a quarter of world exports of manufactures by the late 1990s, from a very low base forty years earlier.

17 See, for example, the data presented by Patel and Gayi (1997: 5–7).

18 UNCTAD (1999a) Table 6.3.

19 See Lall (2000a) for further details of these four categories.

20 See Lall (2000a) Table A.4.

21 Data from the UNIDO database suggest for 1995 average manufacturing value-added per capita figures of US$225 (in 1990 prices) for developing countries as compared with US$4650 for developed economies. Within the developing country group these figures range from an average of US$32 in Africa to US$728 in East Asia.

22 Data come from the UNIDO database.

23 China is by far the largest exporter of manufactures in total and, together with Taiwan and Korea, it accounts for nearly 40% of all developing country manufactured exports. Data in this paragraph come from Lall (2000a).

24 One set of criteria used to define an industrialised economy was put forward by Sutcliffe (1971: 23–6.) These are:

- a minimum of 25% of GDP originating in the industrial sector;
- at least 60% of industrial output in the form of manufactures;
- at least 10% of the total population employed in the industrial sector.

Together these criteria are intended to exclude those countries which have a large industrial sector due to the importance of mining rather than manufacturing, and those where only a relatively low proportion of the population earn their living from industry.

25 Table 1.6 also includes Colombia in the second tier group, but this is now implausible given its record of industrial decline in the 1990s (see Table 1.11).

26 The countries listed here are similar to the group of 'the rest' that Amsden (2001) cites as the key late industrialisers of the second half of the twentieth century. The differences are that Amsden excludes Hong Kong and Singapore as city states with no agricultural hinterland and includes Chile. She argues that 'the rest' were the economies with a sufficient history of industrialisation pre-1945 to be able to build their industries in the post-war world.

> 'The remainder' comprised countries that had been less exposed to modern factory life in the pre-war period, and failed thereafter to achieve anywhere near 'the rest's' industrial diversification. The dividing line between the two sets of countries was not absolute, as noted later, but countries without robust manufacturing experience tended to fall further behind, and the developing world became divided between those that were excluded from modern world industry and those that were redefining its terms.
>
> (Amsden 2001: 1–2)

27 As a point of comparison from the data in UNCTAD (1996a) for the least developed countries in the early 1990s, manufactures averaged just over 20% of total exports.

28 On the import side, their increasing domestic production of capital goods has meant that several NIEs have been able to reduce their dependence on capital goods imports. As a specific example of this pattern one can note that, by 1980, imports of machine tools provided only around one-third of domestic use in India, Brazil and Taiwan, which is roughly the same proportion as in France and the UK; see UNIDO (1983: 295).

29 Total factor productivity growth is defined formally in Chapter 3; the estimates cited here come from Bosworth and Collins (2000). There is considerable controversy over the exact figures; see Crafts (1999) for a survey of alternative estimates. However, using the simple tests put forward by Sutcliffe (1971), of the four first-tier East Asian NIEs, Singapore and Korea, clearly pass, whilst Taiwan would almost certainly do so if comparable data were available. Hong Kong does not, however, because of the major shift in economic structure that has taken place since the 1980s with manufacturing by Hong Kong firms migrating to the mainland, at least in part, in response to lower labour costs there. Brazil and Argentina pass, despite the latter's poor growth record, whilst Mexico narrowly fails by the employment criteria. All other countries in Table 1.10 fail by the employment criteria.

30 Hong Kong might also be included here, since UN statistics show an absolute fall in manufacturing during the 1990s as industries relocate to the Chinese mainland. However, with the re-incorporation of Hong Kong into China these are within-country relocations not genuine de-industrialisation.

31 Poor overall performance in Africa has been explained by a combination of policy errors, relating to the types of policies discussed in Chapter 3, shocks such as wars, climatic factors and global market trends for particular exports, and weak institutions. Econometric analysis highlights trade policy (with less open economies having slower growth), quality of institutions and macro stability (as proxied by the level of government savings) as key factors; see Sachs and Warner (1997). The authors also find that the share of natural resources in total exports has a negative relationship to growth, although this is open to a number of interpretations. For a more general discussion of slow growth in Africa, see Collier and Gunning (1999). Jalilian *et al.* (2000) has chapters on various aspects of industrialisation in Africa.

32 The analysis uses a panel data approach and covers sixty-five countries. De-industrialisation at the country level is defined as a situation where there is a negative residual – that is, a lower than predicted manufacturing share in GDP given the country's characteristics – and that this residual grows over time. A similar analysis is conducted for rates of manufacturing growth; see Jalilian and Weiss (2000) for details.

33 There is strong evidence that poverty falls with rapid income and employment growth, so that the key role of manufacturing in poverty reduction is in stimulating economic growth; see World Bank (2000b) for a general discussion. Data on poverty reduction in East Asia prior to the 1997–98 crisis are in Ahuja *et al.* (1997).

2 Are there different paths to industrialisation?

1 For example, see the discussion in World Bank (1981).

2 Krueger (1978) defines this situation formally, as one where for year t, $B_t > 1.0$, with B_t defined as:

$$B_t = \frac{(1 + m + n + p)_t}{(1 + r + s)_t}$$

and m is the rate of import tariff;
n is the rate of import surcharge;
p is the rate of scarcity premium created by import licensing;

r is the rate of export encouragement schemes, other than direct subsidies;
s is the rate of export subsidies;
the subscript t refers to year t.

The numerator $(1 + m + n + p)$ gives the degree to which the domestic price of an importable is raised above its world price by a protective system that may involve tariffs, surcharges and licences for imports. Similarly the denominator $(1 + r + s)$ shows the degree to which domestic prices for an exportable are raised above world prices by subsidies or other forms of encouragement. Any export taxes would be treated as a negative subsidy. Where $B_t > 1.0$, domestic prices for importables will exceed world prices for the same goods by more than the domestic prices of exportables exceed *their* world prices, and thus greater incentive will be given for import-substitution than for export. This ratio can be calculated at different levels; for individual commodities, for branches of a sector, for different sectors, or for the economy as a whole. At this last level, one will be aggregating over all importables and exportables, and it is this calculation that will be most relevant for the classification of economies as inward or outward-looking. In contrast, following this approach, outward-looking economies are those where the bias against exports is removed and, in the aggregate, net incentives to domestic sales and exports are equal. In Krueger's formal definition, in outward-looking economies, $B_t = 1.0$. A value of $B_t < 1.0$ implies a pro-export bias in incentives and this is taken as an extreme case of outward-looking policies. An alternative approach to measure anti-export bias is to use effective rate of protection estimates for home and export sales. This approach is discussed in Chapter 3.

3   These figures relate to the late 1960s; see Balassa (1982) Table 2.3.

4   The key role of internal demand, as opposed to external demand, as a source of growth for manufacturing in large countries is demonstrated in Chenery (1979). Here growth of output is broken down into that due to internal demand, export expansion, import-substitution and technical change. Distinctions are drawn between the growth of primary activities, light and heavy manufacturing, and between countries of different income levels. The general conclusion is that, in large economies, the expansion of domestic demand is clearly predominant, providing around 80% of output growth for light industry and 65% for heavy industry across countries at different levels in income. In smaller countries specialising in manufacturing, the role of export demand is greater, but even for these economies internal demand is found to account for around 60% of output growth for light industry and 35% to 40% for heavy industry. Ballance *et al.* (1982), utilising different data to that employed by Chenery, find even stronger support for the view that internal demand 'stands in the forefront of the growth process'. In general they find internal demand to be more important than Chenery's results suggest. In only six out of twenty-eight countries in their sample does export expansion account for more than 10% of total manufacturing growth.

5   For an illustration of one approach, see the definition of the effective rate of protection in Chapter 3 and estimates of its value for different countries in Table 3.3

6   Another approach to the classification of countries is to use cross-sectional international data to compare the pattern of trade and production in an individual country with a typical pattern for a developing country of a similar resource endowment, size and income level. Outward- or inward-orientation can then be defined in terms of a divergence from a typical pattern; see, for example, Leamer (1988). Pritchett (1996) points out some of the complications associated with Leamer's approach. Alternatively, one can construct a single quantitative proxy for the degree of restrictiveness of trade policy and draw comparisons either between countries or within a country over time on the basis of changes in the chosen indicator. An example of this is the openness index of Dollar (1992).

7 It is interesting that an earlier and similar attempt at trade classification World Bank (1987) identified three economies – Hong Kong, Korea and Singapore – as 'strongly outward oriented'. Data on Taiwan were not included. The strong manufactured growth in Korea helped boost the average growth for this group well above the average for less outward oriented and inward oriented economies. This is despite the fact that many observers would date Korea's trade liberalisation as late as the early 1990s, making it a relatively protected economy in the period covered by World Bank (1987). By the Sachs–Warner criteria it is also classed as 'open'.

8 These have been treated with scepticism by some observers. One can cite almost equally scathing comments from major figures writing from quite different positions, for example from the conventional Neoclassical perspective the highly respected Arnold Harberger writes that 'Cross country growth regressions seem hopelessly naïve to long time observers of the growth process like myself. To us there is too much to question in regression lines that draw much of their slope from the difference between Sudan and Switzerland, between Bangladesh and Brazil or between Ceylon and Canada' (1998: 21). In a similar vein Lance Taylor, chief formal critic of Neoclassical macro-economics, writes: 'The regression equations typically leave a substantial part of total variance unexplained, so that even if they point to "modest" positive effects of liberalisation or openness on growth, such conclusions cannot possibly hold for all countries included in the sample' (Ocampo and Taylor 1998).

9 This is demonstrated by Pritchett (1996) who tests for the correlation between measures such as average rate of tariff, share of imports covered by quotas and effective rates of protection.

10 Dollar (1992) developed an openness index as a single quantitative indicator for the classification of trade policy. The indicator is a measure of real exchange rate distortion and variability. The starting point is the recognition that protection will raise a country's price level relative to prices in its trading partners. However domestic prices can also differ from partner's prices due to differences in resource endowments and the differences in factor costs these create. Hence, to capture the impact of protection and trade controls on relative prices, one must also allow for differences in resource endowments. The openness index does this for ninety-five countries over the period 1976–85.

A relative price level (RPL) is calculated for each country using the US as comparator. Hence, for country i:

$$RPL^1 = 100 * e.Pi/Pus$$

where Pi and Pus are domestic and US prices for a given basket of consumer goods and e is the exchange rate to convert Pi to US dollars.

Once the actual RPL is known for country i, this must be compared with the predicted relative price level (RPL[1]) based on the country's resource endowments, which is derived from regression analysis. The trade policy-induced price distortion is measured as 100*(RPL/RPL[1]). The overall openness index is based on both the level of this distortion index and its variability and is calculated as a weighted average of the price distortion index and its coefficient of variation, with the weights determined by regression analysis.

11 It is sometimes argued that within the logic of Neoclassical models moves to a more open trade policy can have only a once-for-all impact, since the underlying or steady state growth of an economy will be determined by labour force growth and technical progress. However, it is argued that the length of time taken to reach this steady state growth rate can vary significantly depending on the policy environment. In a model of this process Gundlach and Nunnenkamp (1998) estimate that closed developing economies (defined in relation to capital rather than trade flows) would be more than thirty years behind open economies in the move to their steady states.

12 Transnationals can be defined as firms investing in more than one country and supplying more than financial capital; for example management, technology or marketing expertise. Investments of this type are direct investments rather than portfolio investment, where shares alone are purchased without the provision of non-financial inputs. Transnationals will have subsidiaries and affiliates (firms with links other than through direct ownership) in a number of host economies.

13 These six countries accounted for nearly 50% of all direct foreign investment to developing and transitional economies 1993–98; see UNCTAD (2000) Table 1.5. Developing countries as a group were the recipients of a little under 20% of total FDI inflows in 2000; cited from the UN by the *Financial Times* 29 June 2001.

14 Data for the early 1990s on US enterprises operating in developing countries shows that foreign firms are important exporters of manufactures in the big Latin American countries, taking over 20% of manufactured exports in Mexico (although this figure must exclude the maquila firms) and 13% in Brazil; see UNCTAD (1996) Table 4.8.

15 Japanese transnationals diverged from this pattern in the past, often investing in mineral processing to secure natural resource supplies. Since the 1980s, however, the key element in Japanese FDI has been the so-called 'flying-geese pattern' whereby Japanese TNCs direct their investment to lower wage sites in East Asia, either to export the final goods back to Japan or to third country markets. If wages rise in one host economy (for example, Thailand) this may set off further migration of investment to another lower wage economy (for example, Vietnam). This movement is likened to a flight of geese.

16 Data on TNC activity from developing countries is uncertain. One adjustment to UN statistics suggests that outward FDI from developing countries as a group rose from $5 billion in 1980 to $108 billion in 1993. Over roughly the same period the share of these countries in total stock of outward FDI rose from around 1% to 5%; see Dunning *et al.* (1998).

17 It is revealing to note the difference in size between the average Latin TNC with annual global sales of around $4 billion and the leading Korean TNCs with sales of over $30 billion; see Chudnovsky and Lopez (2000: 55).

18 For example Balasubramanyam and Salisu (1991) suggest that outward-looking or export-oriented economies are more successful at attracting FDI than are inward-looking economies, since FDI is in part a function of an economy's rate of growth.

19 De Mello (1997) reviews this literature.

20 Although the authors' approach is rigorous, the main uncertainty in this analysis is how to adequately categorise economies. The authors use the rather crude expedient of taking import share in GDP as a measure of the stance of trade policy. Whilst this approach is open to several objections, they also extend their analysis by using a trade classification from the World Bank based on an assessment of actual policies. Their results remain robust to this new analysis.

21 White (1984) does not provide a definition of an 'intermediate regime'. However, his use of the term appears to depart from the original definition of Kalecki (1976), since White writes of 'socialist intermediate regimes'. In Kalecki's original discussion intermediate regimes are transitional, as yet neither capitalist nor socialist.

22 For example, Jameson (1981) classed Guyana and Cuba as intermediate regimes, and Gurley (1979) questioned whether Ethiopia and Benin could be classified as socialist.

23 Weiss (1995b) discusses the transition from statism and an ideology of socialism to a market-oriented system in Mozambique. Perkins (2001) discusses the role of industrial policy in China and Vietnam at present and points to some evidence of improvements in productivity stemming from enterprise reform.

24 It was not always so, however. Gurley (1979: 188) calculated the average annual growth of GNP per capita 1960–74 for a group of thirteen 'Marxian socialist countries'. The average for this group, of 3.7% per annum, can be compared relatively

favourably with 4.2% for the advanced capitalist economies, and 3.1% for non-socialist developing countries. The thirteen covered included the East European Soviet bloc countries and China, Cuba and North Korea, but excluded several of the then more recently established socialist countries. However, such comparisons were obscured by poor and sometimes fictitious data, which were often not constructed on a directly comparable basis to non-socialist economies. Data on North Korea appear to have been particularly misleading.

25 India is the most obvious example of the first pattern and Tanzania is an example of the second.

26 See Amsden (2001: 214) for statistics on the size by sales of the fifteen largest manufacturing state enterprises in the NIEs in 1993. She points out that detailed studies suggest that management competence varied greatly in such enterprises between countries and branches and even within branches in the same country. She suggests that in steel, for example, state enterprises were highly efficient in Korea and Taiwan, but not in general in Mexico and Brazil, although in the latter, efficiency varied considerably between the three public sector steel mills.

27 For a discussion of privatisation of industry in Mexico, see Weiss (1995c); Cook and Kirkpatrick (1995) contains other case studies on privatisation. Data on the extent of privatisation specifically in manufacturing are not recorded in the World Bank World Development Indicators database, which shows only total proceeds from privatisation. By this criteria the top five privatising economies over the 1990s are Brazil (total proceeds $70 billion), Argentina ($45 billion), Mexico ($29 billion), China ($20 billion) and Malaysia ($10 billion).

3 Neoclassical orthodoxy dominant

1 See Little (1982: 25). Little *et al.* (1970) can be seen as the seminal text putting forward the Neoclassical position on industrialisation and trade and was arguably one of the most influential academic works ever published on development issues. Reidel (1991) is a clear, more recent, statement of the Neoclassical case on trade policy.

2 This broad policy package is often described as 'Neoliberalism'; see Colclough (1992) for definitions of Neoliberalism and, more generally on reform programmes, see Weiss (1995a).

3 There are exceptions to these propositions under conditions not specified in the model; see Bhagwati (1991) for a fuller statement of the model.

4 Strictly in the figure a new production frontier should be added reflecting economic not private production possibilities.

5 This is the 'policy hierarchy' argument, which implies that measures to correct a distortion should be targeted as directly as possible at the source of the distortion to minimise by-product costs; for example, if wages for labour are kept above their scarcity level by institutional means, this implies using a labour subsidy targeted at the groups of workers affected rather than attempting to compensate employers by means such as subsidised credit or tariff protection, which both create further costs in terms of distortions of economic incentives; see Corden (1974: 28–31).

6 Curry and Weiss (2000) provide a detailed discussion of the concepts and procedures involved with economic pricing.

7 See, for example, the survey by Solow (1970).

8 Here 'new' can be defined as either new in a generic sense or as a higher quality version of an existing product; see the analysis of Romer (1994).

9 A formal statement and application of this model is in Edwards (1992).

10 Surveys of this approach are by North (1995) and Bates (1995). Williamson (2000) sees Neoclassical analysis, as discussed here, as being concerned with short-term issues of resource allocation. In his view the New Institutional Economics addresses

both medium-run issues (one to ten years) of governance, relating to rules for economic activity, as well as long-run questions (ten to 100 years) of the institutional environment.

11 For example, see Hall and Jones (1999). As a specific illustration, Clague *et al.* (1997) use three alternative proxies in a cross-country regression model to test the hypothesis that differences across countries in property relations and contract enforcement lead to high transaction costs and thus have a negative impact on growth. The three proxy measures of institutional development used are the share of non-cash money in total money supply (in a risky environment cash holdings will be greater), an indicator of investor risk (including likelihood of expropriation) and an indicator of business environment risk (based on contract enforceability, infrastructure quality and bureaucratic delays). All three indicators are significant with the expected signs, although it is concluded that institutions affect growth through their impact on the quality of investment rather than independently.

12 This is in the absence of additional external effects that can justify local production even if costs exceed the world price of competing output.

13 See Balassa (1977) for the original statement of this analysis.

14 See, for example, Ranis (1985).

15 See Londero and Teitel (1996) and, earlier, Teitel and Thoumi (1986), who trace the growth of exports from secondary import-substitute activities in Argentina and Brazil and question whether these were simply the result of export incentives. However, regardless of the details of this case, in general, in recent years the growth of manufactured exports from the region has been disappointing. Amsden (2001) also stresses the link between prior import-substitution and later export success.

16 See Curry and Weiss (2000) for a survey of this work.

17 If import tariffs are imposed, once an import reaches its port of entry, its price will be raised immediately by the tariff. Quotas will also work to raise domestic prices above world levels, even if no tariffs are involved, since they restrict the supply of an import. The price of such a good in the domestic market will rise until demand is equated with the limited supply available under the quota. The excess of the domestic selling price above the import price is termed the scarcity premium arising from the imposition of a quota. The ratio of the scarcity premium to the world price is sometimes referred to as the tariff equivalent premium, since a tariff of this rate would create the same domestic price as the quota.

18 In one of the classic surveys of the ERP measure, Corden (1971: 35–40) gives a proof of the equivalence of equations (3.5) and (3.6); see also Greenaway and Milner (1993).

19 For example, Balassa (1982) summarises data on the frequency distribution of NRP and ERP in six economies for the 1960s and 1970s. Data on protection in Korea in the period 1970–90 is in Lee (1997). Ten Kate (1992) discusses protection in Mexico in the 1980s.

20 See Mulaga and Weiss (1996).

21 A particular example of relatively unfavourable treatment for priority items relates to the protection afforded to capital goods as compared with consumer goods producers. Evidence from Mexico in the early 1980s illustrates this point since priority branches such as electrical and non-electrical machinery, and iron and steel, received an ERP below that granted to certain non-priority branches, such as domestic electrical appliances and automobiles. Weiss (1984) discusses protection and government industrial priorities in Mexico at this time.

22 Formally, per unit of activity, i, the cost–benefit estimate of returns can be expressed as:

$$CB_i = PV(P_i + E_i) - PV\left(\sum_j a_{ji}.P_j + \sum_l a_{li}.P_i\right) \tag{3.7}$$

where P_i is the economic price of i;

E_i is the external effect from the production of i
(not captured in the valuation of inputs), which can be positive or negative;

a_{ji} is the number of units of non-labour inputs j per unit of i;

P_j is the economic price of j;

a_{li} is the number of units of labour input l per unit of i,

P_l is the economic wage for labour category l;

PV indicates present values discounted at the economic discount rate.

Economic efficiency requires that $CB_i > 0$.

23 The link between the CB and DRC measures can be demonstrated by adjusting equation (3.7). If i and j are traded goods, there are no external effects, and labour is the only domestic resource, then:

$$DRC_i = \frac{PV\left(\sum_l a_{li}.P_l\right)}{PV\left(P_i - \sum_j a_{ji}.P_j\right)} \tag{3.8}$$

If i and j are valued in foreign currency, so that the denominator is a net foreign exchange figure, efficiency requires that DRC_i is less than the value of an additional unit of foreign exchange to the economy measured either by the official or the shadow exchange rate. Where the denominator of equation (3.8) is in local currency and the net foreign exchange effect is converted to local currency at the economic value of foreign exchange, efficiency requires a DRC of below unity or 100%, if percentages are used.

Any external effects can be incorporated in DRC calculations by adding or subtracting them from the domestic resources in the numerator of equation (3.8). Greenaway and Milner (1993) and Curry and Weiss (2000) both explain the DRC indicator.

24 For some CB studies, see Chitrakar and Weiss (1994) on Nepal, and Jayanthaku-maran and Weiss (1997) on Sri Lanka. In published work on the DRC measure, in many cases the procedures adopted are relatively crude and fall far short of a rigorous analysis. The economic prices used to value domestic resources are little more than a form of sensitivity analysis to test how a different valuation of domestic resources will effect judgements on efficiency. DRC estimates are often carried out for a single year of operations, rather than over the full working life of an investment, and the results are highly sensitive to the degree of capacity working. This means that, where capacity utilisation is determined by short-run factors, such as foreign exchange availability, DRC estimates can fluctuate substantially between years. Furthermore, most DRC studies ignore or do not incorporate quantitative estimates of externalities, and are rarely carried out over a sufficiently long period of time to examine the long-run trend in the DRC.

25 Strictly it is incorrect to rank by the DRC unless foreign exchange is the binding constraint.

26 In Tanzania in the 1980s, a World Bank study on DRCs in manufacturing was influential in providing a rationale for trade reform. For the sector as a whole, at current capacity utilisation the average long-run DRC was 291%, with 37% of activities generating negative value-added at world prices; reported in Ndulu and Semboja (1994). Even in economies where modest degrees of trade reform have been introduced DRCs for some firms have remained high. For Nigeria in the late 1980s, a survey of manufacturers found that approximately 60% of firms were inefficient by the DRC criteria, with the majority of these producing consumer goods for which protection remained high; see Danju and Weiss (1997).

27 Formally, the ERS can be expressed in a similar way to equation (3.5), except that VADP now includes the effect of subsidies, as well as tariff and quota protection. Balassa (1982) Table 2.4 showed that, by this measure Korea, Taiwan and Singapore had low or negative anti-export bias at the start of their export booms in the late 1960s.

28 In the Malawi study noted above, if one compares value-added from exports with that from domestic sales, on average protection reduces the former by 6% and raises the latter by 50%; see Mulaga and Weiss (1996: 1274).

29 See Greenaway and Milner (1993) Chapter 7.

30 Other forms of non-trade intervention associated with the import-substitution era such as interest rate controls and investment licensing also created distortions and economic inefficiency; Curry and Weiss (2000) explain how the impact of these measures and their consequences for investment efficiency can be quantified.

31 See Amsden and van der Hoeven (1996). Africa proved to be the major exception to this case, however.

32 See Papageorgiu et al. (1991).

33 For a comprehensive critique of this study, see Greenaway (1993).

34 Three factors are identified as explaining this apparent puzzle. The first is that real exchange rate depreciation, which accompanied trade reform in both cases, cushioned firms by replacing tariff and quota protection by exchange rate protection; in other words, the price of competing imports falls due to lower import tariffs but rises if the exchange rate is devalued. The latter effect can offset the former either wholly or partially. The second is that firms in both countries increased productivity and thus maintained both output and employment in the face of import competition. The third is that output was also maintained by either cutting profit margins or real wages; see Harrison and Hanson (1999).

35 See Milner and Wright (1998).

36 See, for example, Fields (1994) and Athukorala and Menon (2000).

37 See Reinhardt and Peres (2000). A possible explanation for this employment trend is the growth of resource-based and relatively capital-intensive manufactures in much of the region.

38 For Chile, Meller (1994) points out that job losses in manufacturing averaged around 2% annually over the liberalisation period 1976–81. He asserts that the absolute reduction in manufacturing jobs due to liberalisation is 10% of the pre-liberalisation level. The precise basis for this number is not explained, however. Also, Mexico experienced a decline in manufacturing employment during the 1980s at the time of liberalisation, although precisely how much of this decline can be attributed to trade reform as opposed to demand deflation is unclear; see Ros (1994). For Brazil, employment in manufacturing fell by 14% over 1991–97 during the period of trade reform, with the bulk of job losses concentrated in capital-intensive activities; see Mesquita and Najberg (2000), who suggest that the episode supports the contention that trade reform can have negative short-run employment effects followed by longer-term growth as labour-intensive exports expand.

39 See Aswicahyono et al. (1996).

40 See Peres and Stumpo (2000).

41 The seminal work here is Edwards (1989).

42 For example, Mody and Kilmaz (1997) show that, after allowing for the impact of income and price elasticities there are country specific effects, which explain why some NIEs have been persistently successful exporters. Countries such as Indonesia, Korea, the Philippines and Turkey have had consistent success with manufactured exports due primarily to country effects. The authors stress their investment in export infrastructure, principally telecommunications, but, equally, country effects may be due to policy reform. This is certainly the conclusion of the multi-country study of Papageorgiu et al. (1991). From their sample data, on a simple 'before and

after comparison', export growth averaged 4.4% for the three years pre-liberalisation and 10.5% for the three years post-liberalisation. However, this result is disputed. Greenaway and Sapsford (1994) took the same sample of countries and tested more formally for the impact of liberalisation on exports. This was done by establishing if, from a growth accounting equation, including exports as an explanatory variable, the intercept or the slope term for exports vary significantly with the introduction of liberalisation policies. In a majority of cases (eight out of twelve) liberalisation is judged to have 'no discernible impact on the export/growth relationship'.

43 In Korea, this early export success was often as a result of government subsidies, direct guidance and export targeting; see Westphal (1998) for a restatement of this view.

44 An example of a cross-sectional study that confirms this result is Nishimizu and Page (1991). This shows that for a sample of economies, where quantitative import restrictions are not used, there is a significant relation between export growth and industrial TFP growth. In protected economies that relied heavily on quantitative restrictions this relation is not significant, however. There is no relation between TFP growth and growth in the protected domestic market.

45 See Aw and Hwang (1995) and Sjoholm (1999).

46 See Akrasanee and Wiboonchutikula (1994).

47 This is the point stressed by the authors; see Clerides *et al.* (1998). However, it should be noted that at a more aggregate level for Colombia, Ocampo and Villar (1995) find a variable for past export experience to be significant in explaining exports 1967–90.

48 This is documented for the US by Harberger (1998).

49 See Pack (1988) and Havrylyshn (1990).

50 For Mexico, see Iscan (1998) and Weiss (1992); for Malawi, see Mulaga and Weiss (1996); for Chile, see Tybout (1992); for Korea, see Kim (1994). Also for Japan using a broadly similar approach, Lawrence and Weinstein (2001) suggest that greater competing imports allowed by trade reform stimulated productivity growth within manufacturing and were far more important than government industrial policy interventions.

51 See the survey of Tybout (2000).

52 For example, for Morocco, see Currie and Harrison (1997) and for Brazil, see Mesquita and Guilherme (1998). Tybout (2000) surveys this literature and introduces a number of technical qualifications.

53 For example, Ocampo (1994) finds no relation between TFP and alternative measures of trade reform including one that is close conceptually to the nominal rate of protection. Similarly, for Ghana, Teal (1999) suggests that in the more liberal trading environment of the 1990s, firms have achieved little in the way of productivity growth. Similar ambiguity is raised by a detailed study on one branch, the automobile sector, where rates of TFP growth are compared for four economies. The most protected of these four, Argentina, had the second highest TFP growth (behind Korea) and experienced relatively rapid TFP growth in the sector, both before and during its period of trade liberalisation in the late 1970s and early 1980s; see Waverman and Murphy (1992).

4 What remains of the challenges to orthodoxy?

1 See Hirschman (1981: 375).

2 Little (1982) introduced the technical definition of Structuralists as those who believe developing countries are characterised by low elasticities of supply.

3 Arndt (1985) traces the origins of Structuralism under Little's definition. He

suggests that Kalecki and Kaldor may have been particularly influential in linking European and Latin American ideas on inflation. Latin American Structuralists developed a theory of inflation based on an analysis of structural bottlenecks. Jameson (1986) examines their methodology, and several of his observations are valid for the wider group of authors that are linked here with a Structuralist approach. He stresses that in a Structuralist analysis each system must be studied as a set of inter-related elements, and not broken down into individual components to be studied separately. Also he argues that Structuralists do not focus simply on surface phenomena, such as prices, but on the structure that lies behind what is directly observable.

4 Several of the key characteristics of Marxian analysis can be seen as the view of the primacy of the production process in establishing class structures and other social relations, the importance of class struggle in the process of historical change, and often the application of the labour theory of value to explain exchange and trading relationships.

5 As an illustration of many of the volumes on this theme, see Colclough (1992).

6 For example, Baran (1957) wrote of a comprador class interested in trade rather than production. Sunkel (1973: 146) extended this notion to a productive, but externally dependent class representative of foreign capital in domestic society – the 'transnational kernel'; that is, 'a complex of activities, social groups and regions in different countries … which are closely linked transnationally through many concrete interests as well as by similar styles, ways and levels of living and cultural affinities'.

7 One implication is that the state bureaucracy may pursue their own interests at the expense of those of the dominant classes, for example in military adventures or expenditures on economically irrational, but prestigious projects. Alternatively the state may intervene against the interests of particular sections of a dominant class in the interests of the system as a whole. An example of this would be the removal of protection from high cost domestic industries to allow other national producers to use cheaper imported goods.

8 Jenkins (1991) used this concept of relative autonomy to explain the success of government intervention in East Asia as opposed to its failure in Latin America, although caution must be exercised since East Asia is far from monolithic and there are important differences between the East Asian NIEs.

9 These points follow Chang and Rowthorn (1995).

10 See Chang (2000b) who stresses the role of industrial policy as one of the mechanisms for the 'socialisation of risk'. This allows private investment in high risk activities with potentially high economic returns.

11 Influential here is the contribution of Amsden (1989: 11), who, generalising from her work on Korea and Taiwan, argues that '(1) the onset of economic expansion has tended to be delayed by weaknesses in a state's ability to act and (2) if and when industrialisation has accelerated it has done so at the initiative of a strengthened state authority'.

12 Amsden (1989) puts this clearly in writing about the need to get relative prices deliberately 'wrong' to stimulate growth. Examples would be subsidised targeted loans and multiple effective exchange rates (arising from differential protection) for particular activities.

13 Wade (1990: 27) defines a corporatist system as one where 'the state charters or creates a small number of interest groups giving them a monopoly of representation of occupational interests in return for which it claims the right to monitor them in order to discourage "narrow", conflictful demands'.

14 Chang (2000b) points out that the 1997 financial crisis cannot be attributed to cronyism per se, since corruption had been present in Korea for many years. What was new in the late 1990s was the access by local groups, the *chaebol*, to short-term

international finance exposing such firms to the vagaries of investor confidence. He further argues that the industrial policy-developmental state model had been abandoned by the Korean government by around 1993 and that this absence of government influence may have exacerbated the crisis by making it easier for resources to be allocated on the basis of corruption and influence rather than economic rationality.

15 For this purpose the classic article by Scitovsky (1958) remains one of the most helpful starting points. A more recent discussion is Stewart and Ghani (1991). Although externalities are central to the early Structuralist view of industrialisation, others, particularly Neoclassical economists, have been sceptical of their significance. According to Little (1982), Scitovsky himself commented on the misuse of his concept of pecuniary externalities to justify many economically unviable projects by vague references to their effects on the profits of other producers. Little and Mirrlees (1974) also suggested that when considering the appraisal of individual industrial projects, external effects are either very difficult to quantify or relatively minor, where they can be measured. They also challenge the assumption that externalities are more prevalent in industry than in other sectors, arguing that if the spread of learning and know-how is a major externality, this is more likely to be important in agriculture than in industry.

16 Scitovsky's own examples of this situation are: oil wells, where output depends on the number and operation of other wells in the same field; fishing, where the catch of one fisherman reduces that of others; and the use of a public road, where one firm is crowded out by others.

17 For example, Stewart and Ghani (1991) draw attention to the Silicon valley experience in California, where proximity between firms has helped greatly the spread of knowledge.

18 It is this second set of externalities, which Scitovsky (1958: 300) pointed out were seen as widely prevalent in developing countries:

> Interdependence through the market mechanism is all-pervading and this explains the contrast between the exceptional and often awkward examples of externalities cited in discussions of equilibrium theory (i.e. technological externalities) and the impression one gains from the literature on underdeveloped countries that the entrepreneur creates external economies and diseconomies with his every move.

19 It is clear that there are numerous ways in which interdependence can affect profits; for example:

a   expansion of producer A may give rise to additional profits in B if the latter is a user of A's output, and A's production is subject to increasing returns to scale, so that its costs and price fall with expansion;

b   growth of A will create a demand for inputs used in A, and will create higher profits in these supplier industries, unless diseconomies of scale are important;

c   where other products are complementary to the output of A, expansion of A can raise the demand for these goods and thus their profitability, again providing diseconomies of scale are not important;

d   producers whose goods are consumed by those whose incomes are raised by the expansion of A will also find demand for their products increased, and thus they will have the potential for higher profitability.

Profit interdependence can be negative as well as positive. Obvious examples of negative externalities of this type would be:

a   where expansion of producer A substitutes for other goods thus lowering their demand and profitability;

b   where expansion of A creates a demand for factors or inputs in limited supply and either reduces their availability or raises their price to others;

c   where output of A is higher cost or lower quality than that of competitors, but after A's expansion, users are compelled for various reasons to use A rather than alternatives.

20 Linkages were popularised by Hirschman (1958).

21 Hirschman (1958: 109–10), for example, argues that:

> The case for inferiority of agriculture to manufacturing has most frequently been argued on grounds of comparative productivity. While this case has not been shown to be entirely convincing agriculture certainly stands convicted on the count of its lack of direct stimulus to the setting up of new activities through linkage effects; the superiority of manufacturing in this respect is crushing.

22 The argument was set out by Young (1928) and expanded and elaborated upon by Kaldor (1966) and (1967).

23 As a means of testing the hypothesis of dynamic increasing returns in manufacturing, Kaldor (1967) used cross-sectional regression analysis to estimate equations (4.1) and (4.2) below, for a number of different sectors across a sample of developed economies.

$$p_i = a + b.q_i \tag{4.1}$$
$$e_i = a + b.q_i \tag{4.2}$$

where q, p and e are logarithmic growth rates for output, productivity and employment respectively, in different economies, and i refers to a given sector.

Equation 4.1 is the Verdoorn relationship between output growth and productivity growth, which has been found to hold for many branches of economic activity. However, since by definition $q_i = p_i + e_i$ it is possible for spurious correlations between q and p to be found, particularly when changes in employment are small. To allow for this, Kaldor argued that the key test for the existence of dynamic increasing returns is not only that equation 4.1 holds, but that in addition equation 4.2 is statistically significant with a b coefficient of less than 1.0; implying that growth of output results from both productivity and employment effects, but that the growth in employment is less than proportionate to the growth in output. In Kaldor's original analysis, industry was the only sector for which both equations were statistically significant.

24 This is 'the growth of indirect or roundabout methods of production', stressed by Young (1928).

25 Young (1928: 531) cites as an example the printing industry where early in the twentieth century a range of specialist producers took over the tasks previously handled by the printers themselves. The cost reductions, or increasing returns, resulting from this process are described as 'economies of capitalistic or roundabout methods of production'.

26 Whilst the conventional infant-industry argument, discussed below, relates costs and productivity in a producer to time, the engine of growth argument adds the growth of manufacturing in the aggregate as a key explanatory variable. This can be seen as an argument for protection of the whole of manufacturing, so that the productivity of individual producers can grow more rapidly. It can be termed an 'infant economy' rather than a specifically infant-industry case for protection, since it relates to learning and specialisation at the sector level.

27 Nurkse (1958: 262) states the case clearly, arguing for the need to base growth on the home market:

> Does it not mean turning away from the principles of comparative advantage? Why do these developing countries not push their exports of primary products according to the rules of international specialisation, and import the goods they need for a balanced diet...? For fairly obvious reasons expansion of primary production for export is apt to encounter adverse price conditions on the world market, unless industrial countries' demand is steadily expanding as it was in the nineteenth century. To push exports in the face of an inelastic or more or less stationary demand would not be a promising line of development.

28 Little (1982: 75) is probably fair in his summary of the orthodox position in the 1950s on the issue of industrial protection:

> I think that few academics among those who wrote mainly about development ... would have accepted in the 1950s that developing countries should avoid direct trade controls and have at most a modest tariff ... Certainly UN officials were not in this camp, and almost no LDC policy-makers would have endorsed such views.

29 For example, in the paragraph following Nurkse's quotation given above, he makes it clear that although the inward-looking strategy he is recommending may involve import controls, if national income grows, although the composition of exports and imports may differ from the pre-protection situation, the volume of trade is likely to be higher than it would be in the absence of trade controls, but with a lower level of economic activity.

30 Similar conclusions on the terms of trade came from Singer (1950), restated in Singer (1984), and in a Radical version, employing the labour theory of value to international trade from the works of Emmanuel (1972) and Amin (1977, 1980).

31 See Prebisch (1964); a similar argument was made by Singer (1950) with the exception that he placed greater emphasis on technical change in rich countries biased against raw materials exported by poor countries as a reason for declining relative prices. Emmanuel (1972), using the labour theory of value to explain international prices, argued that if countries have different commodity specialisations and wage levels, prices will deviate systematically from values to the benefit of the countries with higher wages. Prices must be high enough to cover costs and give the ruling international rate of return, so that an increase in wages in one group of countries (the rich countries or the centre) is a means of redistributing to that group part of the total value produced in the world economy. Emmanuel argues that low wages are the key to understanding movements in the terms of trade of the periphery and that unequal exchange, in his terms, is a major drain of value, and thus of potential income, since person-hours expended in production go un-rewarded.

32 See Prebisch (1984).

33 See Grilli and Chen Yang (1988).

34 See Kaplinsky (1998).

35 Sapsford and Balasubramanyam (1994). Where contrary results are found, this tends to be due to differences in either data or statistical technique. For a survey of results, see Sapsford *et al.* (1992).

36 See Bloch and Sapsford (1997).

37 The commodity terms of trade is defined as Pp/Pm, where Pp is the export price series for primary goods and Pm is the import price series for manufactures, while the income terms of trade is $Pp.Qp/Pm$ where Qp is an index of primary export volume;

see Grilli and Chen Yang (1988) for this estimate of the aggregate purchasing power of exports.
38 See Kaplinsky (1998).
39 For example, Mrydal (1957) and Lewis (1955), as well as Prebisch.
40 See the discussions in Rodrik (1992) and Ocampo and Taylor (1998).
41 This is the 'import protection as export promotion' case popularised by Krugman (1984).
42 See Rodrik (1992). However, since improved market shares are the key factor stimulating technical change in this model, this cannot apply to all firms, so that this is an argument for selective protection, that is identifying and supporting firms where the stimulatory effect on technical change will be greatest.
43 For a non-technical introduction to this literature, see several of the chapters in Krugman (1988).
44 This is the so-called 'prisoner's dilemma' of Game theory; see Brander (1988).
45 Baldwin (1992) uses this illustration in the context of jet production, arguing that the support of European governments for the Airbus may have pushed McDonnell–Douglas from the market.
46 Baldwin (1992) examines the welfare effects of this policy. Semi-conductor memory chips for computers are often discussed as an area where strategic interventions may apply. However, it has been argued that Korean export success here was due to the initiative of private firms, not to interventions by the state; see Chang (1992).
47 Support that does not create a wedge between domestic and world prices, as do tariffs and quotas, is termed 'promotion' in the Neoclassical literature; examples are financial subsidies, tax credits and interest rate subsidies.
48 Bell *et al.* (1984) is the classic article setting out this argument.
49 See Westphal (1998).

5 Small-scale industry

1 See Haggblade *et al.* (1990) Table 1.
2 Tybout (2000) Table 1 provides evidence of this with employment data for a number of developing countries mostly from the 1970s which are contrasted with the employment structure in the US.
3 The data come from Mead (1994).
4 See Liedholm and Mead (1999).
5 See Peres and Stumpo (2000).
6 Livingstone (1991) has a discussion of the profile of SSE in Kenya. The analysis of the sample of firms from Ghana in Lall *et al.* (1994 Table 4.5) reveals a generally rising share of exports in output and of external finance in total finance as enterprise size increases.
7 Stewart and Ranis (1990: 4), for example, define appropriate technology as 'the technology which makes best use of a country's resources to achieve its development objectives'.
8 See the survey of Stewart and Ranis (1990).
9 See Stewart and Ranis (1990: 6). Pack (1987) is a detailed study of Textiles that finds that older, more conventional equipment has a cost advantage over the most modern equipment in either its highly capital or highly labour-intensive forms.
10 Strictly comparing alternatives by a ratio can be misleading where one is larger than the other, since the larger alternative may have a lower rate of return but still generate a larger absolute benefit. Use of this equation (5.2) implies that one large firm can be compared with a set of small firms each with the same production conditions that can together produce the same output as the large firm.
11 Little *et al.* (1987) Chapter 7 survey this data and point to a few exceptions. They

argue from Korean evidence that the more disaggregated the analysis becomes, the more difficult it is to establish that the smallest firms are always the least capital intensive.

12 With the minor exception that two-person firms are slightly more capital-intensive than three- to five-person firms, this is true even when eleven separate size categories of firm are distinguished.

13 Also at the upper end of the size range, capital intensity does not increase monotonically with size. In Baking, firms with more than 1000 employees have a lower capital–labour ratio than those with 251–500 and 501–1000 employees.

14 Early work on India produced this result; see Dhar and Lydall (1961).

15 The case for such 'collective efficiency' and 'flexible specialisation' amongst small firms is examined further (page 117).

16 Little *et al.* (1987), Chapter 7, discuss Census data from several countries for the 1960s and 1970s.

17 The negative figure for Air-conditioning implies that the wages bill cannot be covered and that the firms are loss-making. This is more likely to be due to data error rather than actual market conditions.

18 The original study is by Liedholm and Mead, and is cited by Stewart and Ranis (1990).

19 See Cortes *et al.* (1987).

20 See Little *et al.* (1987: 216–17).

21 For Ghana, see Mensah *et al.* (2001) and for the Gaza Strip, see Migdad *et al.* (2001).

22 For example, a survey of data from five countries in sub-Saharan Africa found an average rate of around 13% annually in the early 1990s; see Mead and Liedholm (1998: 65).

23 However, of the seven countries compared in the survey, only in India do such graduating firms provide more than 50% of small–medium sized enterprises (11–200 workers); see Liedholm (1992) Table 31.

24 For this group of countries as a whole, from the evidence of recent surveys, nearly three-quarters of small enterprises (10–50 workers) started as micro firms (less than ten workers). These data come from Mead (1994).

25 For these five economies, micro and small enterprises accounted for over 40% of the total increase in the labour force during the 1980s (Mead 1994: 1883).

26 See, for example, Gerry (1978) and Moser (1978).

27 For example, Gerry (1978) in his study of Dakar, writes of a chain of exploitation as capitalist sub-contractors, bureaucrats and suppliers of raw materials handle commodities at different stages prior to their entry into the petty production process. The implication is that, at each stage, market power allows value to be siphoned off.

28 In the framework of the labour theory of value wages paid by capitalists are determined by the cost of reproducing labour power; essentially a cost of living approach.

29 Schmitz (1982) has a perceptive and sympathetic critique of Gerry and others.

30 Clear statements of the arguments are Steel (1993) and Little (1987).

31 Haggblade *et al.* (1990) survey the impact of different market distortions and link these with SSE development.

32 For example, Levy (1993) finds the availability and cost of finance as the most important constraint cited by small firm owners in Tanzania and Sri Lanka. Liedholm and Mead (1999), Chapter 6, provide evidence on the importance of a shortage of credit in a range of countries, which they find to be more important at the time of start-up with its significance diminishing as firms persist in their operations. It appears also to be less important for rural as compared with urban-based enterprises.

33 The formal theoretical case is set out in Stiglitz and Weiss (1981). Weiss (1995a: 242–46) summarises the argument.

34 UNIDO (1997: 90–93) describes this process and points out the much weaker links between formal and informal credit institutions in Africa as compared with Asia.

35 See Little (1987: 233) who argues that 'The lack of institutional credit can be seen as a filter that arguably does more to eliminate dishonest, incompetent and sluggish would-be borrowers than it does to prevent potential climbers from setting foot on the mountain of success'.

36 See Rabellotti (1997) for the relevant definitions.

37 Schmitz (1995) elaborates on the idea of collective efficiency.

38 Nadvi and Schmitz (1994) and Schmitz and Nadvi (1999) survey much of this empirical work. Pedersen *et al.* (1994) contains a number of case studies. Rabellotti (1997), who compares footwear clusters in Mexico and Italy, is perhaps the most detailed study available. McCormick (1999) examines evidence on clusters in Africa.

39 For example, in her comparison of Mexican and Italian footwear clusters, Rabellotti (1997: 137) points to much greater vertical integration amongst Mexican firms, which she attributes to the result of earlier import protection. In an extension of this work, Rabellotti (1999) argues that in response to trade reform, footwear firms in Mexico have increased their collaboration. She also finds some support for a link between improved firm performance (defined in various ways) and links within a cluster.

40 See the survey of evidence in Schmitz and Nadvi (1999). One of the best documented clusters is the Sinos Valley footwear cluster in Brazil, which has been examined in a number of papers by Schmitz; see, for example, Schmitz (1995) and Nadvi and Schmitz (1994).

41 Humphrey and Schmitz (1996) suggest a demand side approach for policy involving the organisation of trade fairs for the products of small firms, giving groups of small firms the chance to bid collectively for public procurement contracts, and, through technical upgrading, supporting small firms in their efforts to win sub-contracting contracts from large firms.

42 MacPherson (1996) provides econometric evidence from Southern African that growth has been higher in small urban firms or those based in commercial districts as compared with rural small firms, which he attributes to externalities associated with their location.

43 It may be significant that Rabellotti (1997) in her detailed study on footwear clusters in Mexico finds that it is the medium size firms who are most dynamic, with the small firms performing relatively poorly.

6 Technology

1 Alternative treatments of technology have been given various labels, such as neo-Schumpeterian and neo-Structuralist; see, for example, the discussion in Schmitz and Cassiolato (1992).

2 Lall, in Lall *et al.* (1994: 5). A distinction sometimes used is between the public knowledge element of technology, which covers known technological blueprints and the underlying scientific theory, and tacit, firm-specific knowledge that forms the basis of firms' own competitive advantage. It is this latter element that defines TC.

3 See Evenson and Westphal (1995).

4 This is the approach in Romijn (1997) who focuses on production capability and measures it by the complexity of product range.

5 See the discussion in Piore and Sabel (1984).

6 The Japanese firm Canon, by redefining the camera as a computer with a lens, is cited as an example of this type of firm; see Best (1998).

7 For example, Alcorta (1994) suggests that whilst optimal scale is reduced by new technology at the product level, this need not be the case at the level of the plant or the firm. This could be because new technologies require higher R and D expenditure that has to be covered by higher total output.

8 See Freeman and Hagedoorn (1994).

9 These statistics on enterprise financed R&D are cited in Lall (2000b).

10 For example, a firm in Singapore has adapted the production process of audio–visual products to small, lower income markets. For television sets, modifications were necessary to design sets able to withstand large voltage fluctuations and to be operated with varying transmission signals. In addition cost-competitive production had to be possible at low output levels; see Hill and Fong (1991). A more general discussion of electronics exports from East Asia is given by Hobday (1995).

11 See, for example, Daniels (1996).

12 Katrak (1997) explains the model and why the slope of TF is expected to be smaller than that of SG.

13 In his formal test of this model, Katrak (1997) finds that the latter case, with imported technology largely unrelated to domestic technological efforts, is the more valid for Indian firms.

14 Their thinking can be summarised by the following quotation:

> The structural approach implies that technology-driven structural change requires explicit and separate attention over and above capital accumulation and that the capacity for generating such change is itself a source of comparative advantage.
>
> Justman and Teubal (1991)

15 This discussion follows Schmitz and Cassiolato (1992), who describe this approach as Neo-Schumpeterian; for an illustration, see Perez and Soete (1988).

16 For a discussion of this concept, see Freeman (1995).

17 The attempt to develop a national aircraft technology in Indonesia in the 1990s is also widely regarded as a clear example of a misguided attempt to leap-frog into a new technology; see Hill (1998).

18 Amsden (1989) and (2001) makes this point clearly.

19 See Lall (1996) for a general discussion of technology policy in the NIEs. The Korean computer sector is a well documented example of technology policy interventions. This involved government concessional loans and the importation of foreign technology by Korean firms. Computer memories are the most successful area and Samsung, whilst initially licensing US and Japanese technology moved rapidly to develop its own design capacity; see Ernst *et al.* (1998).

20 This is the so-called TRIPs agreement – Trade Related Intellectual Property – which imposes a uniform patent life of twenty years and has been described as 'an unrequited transfer of royalties from user (developing) to producer (developed) countries'; see Srinivasan (2001: 5).

21 See Amsden *et al.* (2001).

22 As discussed earlier, the classic survey article on this is Bell *et al.* (1984) which compares productivity growth in protected infant firms with that in competitor economies. If productivity growth in the former cannot keep pace with that in the latter, maturity of infants will never be achieved. The authors conclude: 'few of the infant enterprises studied in less developed economies appear to have demonstrated the high and continuous productivity growth needed to achieve and maintain international competitiveness'.

23 See the survey by Teitel (1984).

24 See Dahlman (1984) and Dahlman and Cortes (1984). The case of the sponge iron technology is a good illustration of a technical change that was only viable due to

the incentives created by government. The technology of direct reduction based on natural gas could not compete with the more conventional blast furnace technology, if gas was priced at the energy equivalent of alternative fuels. The author worked in Mexico in the early 1980s on a cost–benefit assessment of this technology.

25 See Amsden (2001: 243).

26 See Katz (2000). There is some anecdotal evidence of successful Latin American exporting firms 'learning by exporting' as in East Asia; see Macaria (2000).

27 This discussions draws heavily on Schmitz and Hewitt (1992).

28 See Schmitz and Hewitt (1992: 29–30).

29 Schmitz and Hewitt (1992: 35–36) cite data showing that national firms employed a considerably higher proportion of staff in R and D than foreign owned firms. In the post-trade liberalisation period some national firms survived, so that six Brazilian-branded PC manufacturers had 26% of the domestic market in 1997. This is more than double the share of local Mexican firms in their domestic market; see Dedrik *et al.* (2001).

30 See Lall *et al.* (1994); earlier evidence on technical change in African firms is in Langdon (1984) on Kenya, and Mytelka (1985) on textile production in the Ivory Coast, Nigeria and Kenya.

31 See Kaplinsky (1994). Production pulling involves the transfer of work in progress through a plant so that each workpoint only manufactures when it observes that the subsequent stage of production has no accumulated work in progress beyond that planned for. To illustrate the extent of gains, labour productivity rose by 80% in waste bin production and by over 300% in book-end production after re-organisation.

32 In the developed country context, Cowling and Sugden (1998) suggest that R and D tax credits boost only large corporations with formal R and D units and that, in theory, once one allows for oligopolistic rivalry between such corporations, the net impact of such credits might actually be to reduce total R and D. This paradoxical result follows if subsidies to a rival reduce the marginal return to further R and D in a firm sufficiently. Hence, whilst for any individual firm a tax credit will raise its R and D, when a rival receives the credit, the firm's R and D may be negatively affected. There is empirical evidence to suggest that this is not an implausible real world case, although it will only be relevant for developing countries with highly oligopolistic industrial sectors, dominated by a few firms.

33 Lall has argued consistently for a selective approach to technology support; see, for example, Lall (1996).

34 It has been argued, for example, that the medium size and smaller Japanese com-panies would have been unwilling to borrow to finance new robotic technology, hence the government's decision to set up a leasing company, as a means of diffusing the technology; see Ernst *et al.* (1998: 26).

35 See Teubal (1996).

36 See Cowling and Sugden (1998).

37 See Freeman (1995).

38 See Amsden (2001: 244–45).

39 These projects include next-generation semiconductors, high definition televisions and environmentally-conserving motor vehicle technology; see Amsden (2001: 279).

7 Globalisation and industrialisation

1 See Department for International Development (2000).

2 See Temin (1999).

3 As evidence of this, world exports were roughly 9% of world income in 1913, 7% in 1950 and nearly 14% in the early 1990s; cited in Temin (1999: 84). Eatwell and

Taylor (2000) provide an overview of the significance of international capital flows under globalisation.

4 UNCTAD (2000) Tables 1.1 and 1.2.

5 How this will affect internal income distribution within a country will depend on whether a country's traded goods are labour or capital intensive. If globalisation leads to a rise in traded relative to non-traded goods prices within a country, in Neoclassical theory, labour income will gain at the expense of capital income provided traded goods are labour-intensive relative to non-traded goods. For a further discussion, see Weiss (1995a) Chapter 5.

6 Evidence on this global divergence is in UNCTAD (1997) part 2. There it is pointed out that much of the global income convergence in the pre-1914 period was due to labour migration from Europe to resource-rich economies such as the USA, Canada, Australia and Argentina.

7 Sklair (1994) contains several revisions to and re-assessments of this literature.

8 This follows Porter (1990).

9 The system of 'lean production' is discussed in Womack *et al.* (1990). The development of merchant networks has led to references to the 'virtual' corporation based on sub-contracting rather than vertical integration; see Davidow (1992). The growing tendency towards regional trade and investment blocs is influencing the geographical spread of these relationships; for example, since the formation of the North America Free Trade Area (NAFTA) in the early 1990s, there has been a major reduction in apparel exports to the US from East Asia and a corresponding rise from Mexico. Similarly, the share of car components sourced from Mexico as compared with those supplied from within the US has risen significantly.

10 This discussion draws heavily on Gereffi (1995).

11 This is the major technological dichotomy in global industry discussed in Chapter 6 between what was termed a 'Fordist system' of mass production and smaller scale, specialised batch production, termed 'flexible specialisation'.

12 The commodity chain approach has been used most widely in the study of apparel exports and the processing of some primary products; see the discussion in Gibbon (2001).

13 See Lall (2000b).

14 There were of substantial differences between Asia and Latin America and, in general, policy was much less restrictive in the latter region; the role of TNCs in manufacturing in the large Latin American economies has always been relatively high; see Tables 2.7 and 2.8, for example.

15 The benefits to a country from the establishment of an export processing zone are principally the higher income for those who obtain jobs in the zones. Other effects tend to be weak, since firms there will pay few taxes and establish few linkages with local suppliers; for a quantification of the net benefits from the Sri Lankan zone, see Jayanthakumaran and Weiss (1997).

16 Curry and Weiss (2000) set out the methodology required for the application of this approach to FDI projects.

17 The degree to which national firms are actually stimulated to improve productivity by foreign entry into the domestic market has been the subject of numerous empirical studies, which have often produced mixed results. For example, positive effects from FDI were found for Mexico by Blomstrom (1986), but negative initial effects on domestically owned competitors were reported for Venezuela by Aitken and Harrison (1999) and for Côte Ivoire and Morocco by Harrison (1996a). Kokko *et al.* (1996) find a positive spillover to labour productivity from FDI in the manufacturing sector of Uruguay.

18 See Lall (2000b).

19 The requirement for TNCs in the Latin American automobile sector to achieve local content targets for parts and components is the best known (and probably

most successful) illustration of this policy. Local content requirements are now prohibited under the WTO agreement on Trade Related Investment Measures (TRIMS).

20 See UNCTAD (1997: 93).

21 This evidence is not totally unambiguous since causation is an issue. Whether participation in world trade raised GDP growth rates or growth stimulated expansion of imports and exports is still a cause for debate. In general, as we have noted in Chapter 2, there is an ongoing debate in the literature as to how far trade reform positively stimulates growth.

22 However, it should be noted that this result is strongly influenced by the performance of China and India, both of whom are in the globalising group. If a non-population weighted result is used, average GDP per capita growth in this group drops to below 3% in the 1990s, which is only modest by historical standards.

23 See Lall (2000a: 345).

24 This is calculated as $(w/v)_i/(w/v)_{us}$, where w is wage cost per worker in US$ and v is value-added per worker in US$ and i refers to country i and us to the USA.

25 In so far as there are quality differences between US and other producers, the expectation must be that US goods are of higher quality, reducing still further the competitiveness of low-income competitors relative to the US.

26 Theoretically, given the relative low human skills to land ratio in Africa, one would not expect as high a share of manufactures in total exports as in other regions. The formal analysis that brings out this point is Wood and Mayer (1998), who use a regression model incorporating resource and factor endowments to explain export share. Lack of infrastructure and misaligned exchange rates are the key factors in explaining a lower than predicted share of manufactures in total exports. Another explanation is that manufacturing is a relatively transactions-intensive sector, as evidenced by its relatively high share of intermediates to value-added. The costs of doing business in Africa are seen as high due to poor infrastructure, poor contract enforcement and volatile economic policies, and these costs are more important for manufacturing than for resource extraction or agriculture. This may provide another explanation for Africa's weak performance in manufacturing; see Collier (2000).

27 See Wangwe (1995).

28 The labour cost advantage of these locations in this sector is evidenced by the fact that in the early 1990s, it is estimated that, in Vietnam, unit labour costs were only 10% of those in Korea and Hong Kong; see Hill (2000).

29 This success is despite the not particularly competitive wage cost position evidenced in Table 7.2; see Lall (1995) for a discussion of government policy in Malaysia and its role in building up these exports.

30 For example, by 1998, manufactures had reached 85% of total exports compared with only just over 40% at the start of the decade, and of these Table 7.4 shows 30% to be in the high technology category; see Macaria (2000: 22).

31 The main indicator of the importance of this form of manufacturing is the statistic that, in 1998, 42% of manufacturing employment was in this type of firm. Similar statistics of the importance for manufacturing employment of such firms geared to the US market are found for the small Central American economies of El Salvador, Costa Rica and Dominican Republic; see Buitelaar and Padilla (2000).

32 The country studies in Helleiner (1995) confirm the importance of the real exchange rate for manufactured exports. Londero and Teitel (1996) chart the shift from the import substitute to export markets for goods from Colombia, Venezuela and Brazil.

8 Creating competitive advantage

1 The term 'market friendly' was popularised in World Bank (1991).

2 For a discussion of the differences and similarities between East Asian NIEs see, for example, Alyuz *et al.* (1998) and Evans (1998). For a succinct discussion of the Korean system in its heyday, see Chang (1993).

3 Public goods can be defined as those whose use by one user does not reduce supply to others, and where direct charging of individual users is not possible.

4 See, for example, Lall (1994). An authoritative voice from the region describes the East Asian model as 'fundamentally a traditional model of the mixed economy where the government plays an important role', where 'policy-makers were intent on complementing markets rather than replacing them'. He then goes on to highlight a series of interventions that operated through 'multiple channels to encourage savings, promote exports and to achieve the desired allocation of resources'; see Park (2001). If spelled out in detail the list is long enough to justify Lall's original rejection of the market-friendly classification. It is interesting, however, that advocates of the two alternative versions of industrial policy both try to claim Korean policy from the 1960s to the early 1990s for their version; presumably because most people agree that it worked.

5 As we discuss in Chapter 4, Amsden (2001) develops this argument in detail.

6 See, for example, Lall (1995), Rock (1995) and Hill (1995). Jomo (1997) surveys the position in the follower NIEs of Malaysia, Thailand and Indonesia and documents their use of various forms of intervention, although the effectiveness of industrial policy in these economies is unclear. In Malaysia in particular, efforts to develop heavy industry and to spread industrial ownership to native Malays appear to have created economic inefficiencies.

7 Amsden (2001) feels the industrial policy of Argentina never got off the ground and rapidly degenerated into corruption. This is a major part of her explanation for Argentina's industrial decline; see Table 1.11.

8 Weiss (1986) examined Japanese industrial policy where the term 'administrative guidance' originated. Central to this policy was the concept of 'excessive competition', which can be interpreted as a market situation where too many firms compete in such a way as to lower long-run profits below normal levels for all participants. Industrial policy aimed to avoid this by restricting entry to particular sectors and encouraging mergers. In Neoclassical terms, excessive competition is an oxymoron, since competition cannot be excessive.

9 World Bank (1993a) stresses this point.

10 Amsden (2001) Chapter 6 points to the similarity in behaviour of development banks across a very diverse set of economies in the post 1945 period.

11 This has been described as a system of 'relational banking' in which banks had close ties, often of ownership, with enterprises rather than arm's length commercial relationships. The *chaebol* in Korea are the clearest illustration of this system at work and this form of banking explains the very high debt–equity ratios in Korean manufacturing, which became a focus for concern during the 1997 financial crisis.

12 In listing these various criteria, Amsden (2001) points out that conventional economic efficiency indicators of the type discussed in Chapter 3 were applied nowhere. In the author's experience, for example with Nacional Financiera in Mexico, this is not quite true, but it is certainly the case that key investment decisions would often not have involved standard cost–benefit analysis.

13 For a discussion of Japan, see Weiss (1986); for Korea, see Amsden (1989); and for Taiwan, see Wade (1990).

14 Technology transfer agreements were scrutinised by the bureaucracy in these countries to protect national interests. This involved attempting to avoid the import of

duplicate technology, limiting royalty payments and removing what were judged to be excessively restrictive clauses on the use to which the technology could be put. For details of how this was done in Japan, which provided the model for the others to follow, see Ozawa (1974).

15 See Lall (1995).

16 See Hill (1995).

17 In describing the Thai system in some detail, Amsden (2001: 23–28) reveals that 'on average the BOI (Board of Investment) annually withdrew benefits from 7% of its clients for non-compliance with agreed terms'. This is a very low withdrawal rate and suggests that the control mechanism was not very tight.

18 See Lall (1987).

19 See Ros (1994). Weiss (1984) explains the system of incentives and industrial priorities in Mexico in the 1976–82 period.

20 In general, for several of the East Asian NIEs, above one-third of total growth is explained by increasing total factor productivity. The productivity-driven economies from amongst this group are Korea, Hong Kong, Taiwan and Japan, all with annual TFP growth (1960–90) averaging over 3%. As a comparison, one can note the corresponding averages for Latin America of 0.1% and sub-Saharan Africa of −1%; see World Bank (1993a: 64). How far industrial policy can be held responsible for such productivity growth is not wholly clear (and Hong Kong must be exempted from the discussion as a largely market-driven economy). Total factor productivity estimates are also subject to considerable uncertainty. Chapter 1 has already cited slightly lower estimates at 2% annually for some of these economies, from Bosworth and Collins (2000). However, the general point is that in these economies productivity was higher than elsewhere.

21 This analysis has been extended by Pack (2000) who, in focussing on Japan and Korea, does find a difference in industrial structure between these economies and similar comparators with a much higher share of the promoted sectors, metal products, machinery and electrical equipment, in both countries and also of transport equipment in Korea. Again, however, he finds no significant difference in productivity growth between promoted and non-promoted sectors. Using simulations that allow for the impact of industrial policy in changing industrial structure, and in accounting for a proportion of the modest differences in productivity growth between favoured and non-favoured sectors, he concludes that, at best, industrial policy through its productivity effect may have had an impact of no more than 0.2%–0.3% of GDP annually (that is, without industrial policy, growth would have been lower by this amount). Allowing for secondary effects on investment might push the final figure to 0.5%. In the words of Pack (2000: 64) this is 'hardly trivial, but not the secret of success' in economies where 8% annual growth has been common.

22 See, for example, Westphal (1998).

23 This the logic of the high profit-high investment nexus identified by Alyuz *et al.* (1998).

24 Lee (1997: 1274) finds that eight out of twelve infant industries either matured (that is, reached international competitiveness) or tended to mature (that is, moved towards competitiveness), with four showing no sign of maturing.

25 This follows Park (2001). For further discussions on the Korean case, see Shin (2000) and Chang (2000a).

26 There is an acerbic comment on this issue that recommending countries follow the Korean model is like telling a young basketball player to follow the Michael Jordan model; world class but can they do it!

27 Ranis (1989) points to the key ingredients of secularism, egalitarianism and, above all, nationalism in explaining the success of government action in fostering institutional change for economic growth.

28 In Korea, for example, the new President, Park Chung Hee dismissed more than 35,000 civil servants in 1961 to create a new system; see Evans (1998: 73).
29 For the author's earlier discussion of this modified form of industrial policy, see Cody *et al.* (1990).
30 Information on the WTO comes from World Trade Organisation (1999).

Bibliography

Agarwala, R. (1983) 'Price Distortions and Growth in Developing Countries', *World Bank Staff Working Paper*, no. 575, World Bank, Washington, DC.

Ahuja, V., Bidani, B., Ferreira, F. and Walton, M. (1997) *Everyone's Miracle: Revisiting Poverty and Inequality in East Asia*, World Bank, Washington, DC.

Aitken, B. and Harrison, A. (1999) 'Do Domestic Firms Benefit from Foreign Direct Investment? Evidence form Venezuela', *American Economic Review*, vol. 89, no. 3.

Akrasanee, N. and Wiboonchutikula, P. (1994) 'Trade Policy and Industrialisation in Sri Lanka', in G. Helleiner (ed.) *Trade Policy and Industrialisation in Turbulent Times*, Clarendon, Oxford.

Alcorta, L. (1994) 'The Impact of New Technologies on Scale in Manufacturing Industries: Issues and Evidence', *World Development*, vol. 22, no. 5.

Alyuz, Y., Chang, H.-J. and Kozul-Wright, R. (1998) 'New Perspectives on East Asian Development', *Journal of Development Studies*, vol. 34, no. 6.

Amin, S. (1977) *Imperialism and Unequal Development*, Monthly Review Press, New York.

Amin, S. (1980) *Class and Nation, Historically and in the Current Crisis*, Heinemann, London.

Amsden, A. (1989) *Asia's Next Giant*, Oxford University Press, New York.

Amsden, A. (2001) *The Rise of the Rest: Challenges to the West from Late-Industrializing Economies*, Oxford University Press, New York.

Amsden, A. and van der Hoeven, R. (1996) 'Manufacturing Employment and Real Wages in the 1980s', *Journal of Development Studies*, vol. 32, no. 4.

Amsden, A., Tschang, T. and Goto, A. (2001) 'Do Foreign Companies Conduct R and D in Developing Countries?', *Asian Development Bank Institute*, Working Paper no. 14, ADBI, Tokyo.

Arndt, H. (1985) 'The Origins of Structuralism', *World Development*, vol. 13, no. 2.

Aswicahyono, H., Bird, K. and Hill, H. (1996) 'What Happens to Industrial Structure When Countries Liberalise? Indonesia since the mid-1900s', *Journal of Development Studies*, vol. 32, no. 3.

Athukorala, P. and Menon, J. (2000) *Liberalisation and Industrial Transformation: Sri Lanka in International Perspective*, Oxford University Press, Delhi.

Aw, B. and Hwang, A. (1995) 'Productivity and the Export Market: a Firm Level Analysis', *Journal of Development Economics*, vol. 47, 313–33.

Bairoch, P. (1975) *The Economic Development of the Third World since 1900*, Methuen, London.

Balassa, B. (1977) 'A Stages Approach to Comparative Advantage', *World Bank Staff Working Paper*, no. 256, World Bank, Washington, DC.

Balassa, B. (1982) *Development Strategies in Semi-Industrialised Economies*, John Hopkins for the World Bank, Baltimore.

Balasubramanyam, V. and Salisu, M. (1991) 'EP, IS and Foreign Direct Investment in LDCs', in A. Koekkoek and L. Mennes (eds) *International Trade and Global Development*, Routledge, London.

Balasubramanyam, V. and Sapsford, D. (1996) 'Foreign Direct Investment and Economic Growth in EP and IS Countries', *Economic Journal*, vol. 106, Jan.

Baldwin, R. (1992) 'High Technology Exports and Strategic Trade Policy in Developing Countries: the Case of Brazilian Aircraft', in G. Helleiner (ed.) *Trade Policy, Industrialisation and Development: New Perspectives*, Clarendon Press, Oxford.

Ballance, R., Ansari, J. and Singer, H. (1982) *The International Economy and Industrial Development*, Wheatsheaf, Brighton.

Baran, P. (1957) *The Political Economy of Growth*, Monthly Review Press, New York.

Bates, R. (1995) 'Social Dilemmas and Rational Individuals: an Assessment of the New Individualism', in J. Harriss, J. Hunter and C. Lewis (eds) *The New Institutional Economics and Third World Development*, Routledge, London.

Behrman, J. (1976) *Foreign Trade Regimes and Economic Development: Chile*, Ballinger, Cambridge, Massachusetts.

Bell, M., Ross-Larson, B. and Westphal, L. (1984) 'Assessing the Performance of Infant Industries', *Journal of Development Economics*, vol. 16, no. 1/2.

Best, M. (1998) 'Production Organisation and Management', in J. Michie and J. Grieve Smith (eds) *Globalization, Growth and Governance*, Oxford University Press, Oxford.

Beyer, J. (1975) 'Estimating the Shadow Price of Foreign Exchange: an Illustration from India', *Journal of Development Studies*, vol. 11, no. 4.

Bhagwati, J. (1991) 'Is Free Trade Passe After All?', in A. Koekkoek and L. Mennes (eds) *Trade Protection and Political Economy; Essays in Honour of Jagdish Bhagwati*, Routledge, London.

Bhagwati, J. and Srinivasan, T. (1975) *Foreign Trade Regimes and Economic Development: India*, Colombia University Press, New York.

Bloch, H. and Sapsford, D. (1997) 'Some Estimates of Prebisch and Singer Effects on the Terms of Trade between Primary Producers and Manufacturers', *World Development*, vol. 25, no. 11.

Blomstrom, M. (1986) 'Foreign Investment and Productive Efficiency: the Case of Mexico', *Journal of Industrial Economics*, vol. 35, no. 1.

Blomstrom, M., Lipsey, R. and Zejan, M. (1994) 'What Explains Growth in Developing Countries?', in W. Baumol, R. Nelson and E. Wolff (eds) *Convergence of Productivity: Cross-National Studies and Historical Evidence*, Oxford University Press, New York.

Borensztein, E., de Gregorio, J. and Lee, J.-W. (1998) 'How Does Foreign Investment Affect Economic Growth?', *Journal of International Economics*, vol. 45, 115–35.

Bosworth, B. and Collins, S. (2000) 'From Boom to Crisis and Back Again: What Have We Learned?', *Asian Development Bank Institute*, Working Paper no. 7, ADBI, Tokyo.

Brander, J. (1988) 'Rationales for Strategic Trade and Industrial Policy', in P. Krugman (ed.) *Strategic Trade Policy and the New International Economics*, MIT Press, Cambridge, Massachusetts.

Buitelaar, R. and Padilla, R. (2000) 'Maquila, Economic Reform and Corporate Strategies', *World Development*, vol. 28, no. 9.

Chang, H.-J. (1993) 'The Political Economy of Industrial Policy in Korea', *Cambridge Journal of Economics*, vol. 17, no. 2.

Chang, H.-J. (2000a) 'The 1997 Korean Crisis – Three Years On: the Crisis, the Recovery, the Future', Paper delivered at the workshop on Brazil and South Korea, Institute of Latin American Studies, London.

Chang, H.-J. (2000b) 'The Hazard of Moral Hazard: Untangling the Asian Crisis', *World Development*, vol. 28, no. 4.

Chang, H.-J. and Rowthorn, R. (1995) 'Role of the State in Economic Change: Entrepreneurship and Conflict Management', in H. Chang and R. Rowthorn (eds) *The Role of the State in Economic Change*, Clarendon Press, Oxford.

Chang, H.-Y. (1992) 'International Competition and Market Penetration: a Model of the Growth Strategy of the Korean Semi-Conductor Industry', in G. Helleiner (ed.) *Trade Policy, Industrialisation and Development: New Perspectives*, Clarendon Press, Oxford.

Chenery, H. (1979) *Structural Change and Development Policy*, Oxford University Press for the World Bank, New York.

Chenery, H., Robinson, S. and Syrquin, M. (1986) *Industrialisation and Growth: a Comparative Study*, Oxford University Press for the World Bank, New York.

Chitrakar, R. and Weiss, J. (1995) 'Foreign Investment in Nepal in the 1980s: a Cost–Benefit Evaluation', *Journal of Development Studies*, vol. 31, no. 3.

Chudnovsky, D. and Lopez, A. (2000) 'A Third Wave of FDI from Developing Countries: Latin American TNCs in the 1990s', *Transnational Corporations*, vol. 9, no. 2.

Clague, C., Keefer, P., Knack, S. and Olson, M. (1997) 'Institutions and Economic Performance: Property Rights and Contract Enforcement', in C. Clague (ed.) *Institutions and Economic Development*, John Hopkins, Baltimore.

Clerides, S., Lach, S. and Tybout, J. (1998) 'Is Learning by Exporting Important?: Micro Dynamic Evidence from Colombia, Mexico and Morocco', *Quarterly Journal of Economics*, Aug.

Cody, J., Kitchen, R. and Weiss, J. (1990) *Policy Design and Price Reform in Developing Countries*, Harvester, London.

Colclough, C. (1992) 'Structuralism versus Neoliberalism: an Introduction', in C. Colclough and J. Manor (eds) *States and Markets: Neoliberalism and the Development Policy Debate*, Oxford University Press, New York.

Collier, P. (2000) 'Africa's Comparative Advantage', in H. Jalilian, M. Tribe and J. Weiss (eds) *Industrial Development and Policy in Africa*, Edward Elgar, Cheltenham.

Collier, P. and Gunning, J. (1999) 'Why Has Africa Grown Slowly?', *Journal of Economic Perspectives*, vol. 13, no. 3.

Cook, P. and Kirkpatrick, C. (eds) (1995) *Post-Privatization Policy and Performance*, Wheatsheaf, London.

Corden, W. (1971) *The Theory of Protection*, Clarendon Press, Oxford.

Corden, W. (1974) *Trade Policy and Economic Welfare*, Clarendon Press, Oxford.

Cortes, M., Berry, A. and Ishaq, A. (1987) *Success in Small and Medium Scale Enterprises: Evidence from Colombia*, Oxford University Press for the World Bank, New York.

Cowling, K. and Sugden, R. (1998) 'Technology Policy: Strategic Failures and the Need for a New Direction', in J. Michie and J. Grieve Smith (eds) *Globalization, Growth and Governance*, Oxford University Press, Oxford.

Crafts, N. (1999) 'East Asian Growth Before and After the Crisis', *IMF Staff Papers*, vol. 46, no. 2.

Currie, J. and Harrison, A. (1997) 'Trade Reform and Labour Market Adjustment in Morocco', *Journal of Labour Economics*, vol. 15, no. 3, part 2.

Curry, S. and Weiss, J. (2000) *Project Analysis in Developing Countries*, revised second edition, Macmillan, Basingstoke.

Dahlman, C. (1984) 'Foreign Technology and Indigenous Technical Capability in Brazil', in M. Fransman and K. King (eds) *Technological Capability in the Third World*, Macmillan, London.

Dahlman, C. and Cortes, M. (1984) 'Mexico', *World Development*, vol. 12, nos. 5/6.

Daniels, P. (1996) 'Technology Investment and Growth in Economic Welfare', *World Development*, vol. 24, no. 7.

Danju, D. and Weiss, J. (1997) 'Manufacturing Performance During Adjustment: Evidence from Nigeria', *Development Policy Review*, vol. 15, no. 4.

Davidow, W. (1992) *The Virtual Corporation: Structuring and Revitalizing the Corporation for the 21st Century*, Harper, New York.

de Mello, J. (1997) 'Foreign Direct Investment in Developing Countries and Growth: a Selective Survey', *Journal of Development Studies*, vol. 34, no. 1, Oct.

Dedrik, J., Kraemer, K., Palacios, J., Bastos, P. and Junqueira, A. (2001) 'Economic Liberalisation and the Computer Industry: Comparing Outcomes in Brazil and Mexico', *World Development*, vol. 29, no. 7.

Department for International Development (2000) 'Eliminating World Poverty: Making Globalisation Work for the Poor', *White Paper on International Development*, Cm 5006, Dec. 2000.

Dhar, P. and Lydall, H. (1961) *The Role of Small Enterprises in Indian Economic Development*, Asia Publishing House, Bombay.

Dollar, D. (1992) 'Outward-Oriented Developing Economies Really Do Grow More Rapidly', *Economic Development and Cultural Change*, vol. 40, no. 3.

Dollar, D. and Kraay, A. (2001) 'Trade, Growth and Poverty', Paper presented at the Asia Pacific Forum on Poverty, ADB, Manila.

Dunning, J., van Hoesel, R. and Narula, R. (1998) 'Third World Multinationals Revisited: New Developments and Theoretical Implications', in J. Dunning (ed.) *Globalisation, Trade and Foreign Direct Investment*, Elsevier, Amsterdam.

Eatwell, J. and Taylor, L. (2000) *Global Finance at Risk*, The New Press, New York.

Edwards, S. (1989) *Real Exchange Rates, Devaluation and Adjustment*, MIT Press, Cambridge, Massachusetts.

Edwards, S. (1992) 'Trade Orientation, Distortions and Growth in Developing Countries', *Journal of Development Economics*, vol. 39, no. 1.

Edwards, S. (1998) 'Openness, Productivity and Growth: What Do We Really Know?', *Economic Journal*, vol. 108, March.

Emmanuel, A. (1972) *Unequal Exchange: a Study of the Imperialism of Trade*, New Left Books, London.

Enos, J. (1995) *In Pursuit of Science and Technology in Sub-Saharan Africa*, Routledge, London.

Ernst, D., Ganiatsos, T. and Mytelka, L. (eds) (1998) *Technological Capabilities and Export Success in Asia*, Routledge, London.

Evans, P. (1998) 'Transferable Lessons? Re-examining the Institutional Prerequisites of East Asian Economic Policies', *Journal of Development Studies*, vol. 34, no. 6.

Evenson, R. and Westphal, L. (1995) 'Technological Change and Technology Strategy', in J. Behrman and T. Srinivasan (eds) *Handbook of Development Economics*, vol. 3A, Elsevier, Amsterdam.

Fields, G. (1994) 'Changing Labour Market Conditions and Economic Development in Hong Kong, Republic of Korea, Singapore and Taiwan', *World Bank Economic Review*, vol. 1, no. 1.

Frankel, J. and Romer, D. (1999) 'Does Trade Cause Growth?', *American Economic Review*, vol. 89, no. 3.

Freeman, C. (1995) 'The National System of Innovation in Historical Perspective', *Cambridge Journal of Economics*, no. 19.

Freeman, C. and Hagedoorn, J. (1994) 'Catching-up or Falling Behind: Patterns in International Inter-firm Technology Partnering', *World Development*, vol. 22, no. 5.

Gereffi, G. (1994) 'Capitalism, Development and Global Commodity Chains', in L. Sklair (ed.) *Capitalism and Development*, Routledge, London.

Gerry, C. (1978) 'Petty Production and Capitalist Production in Dakar: The Crisis of the Self Employed', *World Development*, vol. 6, nos. 9/10.

Gibbon, P. (2001) 'Upgrading Primary Production: a Global Commodity Chain Approach', *World Development*, vol. 29, no. 2.

Government of Mexico (1989) *Censo Industrial 1986*, Instituto Nacional de Estadistica Geografica y Informatica, Mexico DF.

Government of Mexico (1995) *Censo Industrial, Censos Economicos 1994*, Instituto Nacional de Estadistica Geografica y Informatica, Mexico DF.

Government of Nepal (1988) *Manufacturing Census 1986–87*, Kathmandu.

Greenaway, D. (1993) 'Liberalising Through Rose-Tinted Glasses', *Economic Journal*, Jan.

Greenaway, D. and Milner, C. (1993) *Trade and Industrial Policy in Developing Countries: a Manual of Policy Analysis*, Macmillan, Basingstoke.

Greenaway, D., Morgan, D. and Wright, P. (1998) 'Trade Reform, Adjustment and Growth: What Does the Evidence Tell Us?', *Economic Journal*, vol. 108, Sept.

Greenaway, D. and Sapsford, D. (1994) 'What Does Liberalisation do for Exports and Growth?', *Weltwirtshaftliches Archiv*, vol. 130, no. 1.

Grilli, E. and Chen Yang, M. (1988) 'Primary Commodity Prices, Manufactured Goods Prices, and the Terms of Trade of Developing Countries: What the Long-Run Shows', *World Bank Economic Review*, vol. 2, no. 1.

Gundlach, E. and Nunnenkamp, P. (1998) 'Some Consequences of Globalisation for Developing Countries', in J. Dunning (ed.) *Globalisation, Trade and Foreign Direct Investment*, Elsevier, Amsterdam.

Gurley, J. (1979) 'Economic Development: a Marxist View', in K. Jameson and C. Wilber (eds) *Directions in Economic Development*, University of Notre Dame Press, New Jersey.

Haggblade, S., Liedholm, C. and Mead, D. (1990) 'The Effect of Policy and Policy Reforms on Non-agricultural Enterprises and Employment in Developing Countries: a Review of Past Experiences', in F. Stewart, H. Thomas and T. de Wilde (eds) *The Other Policy*, Intermediate Technology Publications, London.

Hall, R. and Jones, C. (1999) 'Why Do Some Countries Produce So Much More Output Per Worker Than Others?', *Quarterly Journal of Economics*, February.

Harberger, A. (1998) 'A Vision of the Growth Process', *American Economic Review*, vol. 88, no. 1.

Harrison, A. (1996a) 'Determinants and Direct Effects of Direct Foreign Investment in Côte Ivoire, Morocco and Venezuela', in M. Roberts and J. Tybout (eds) *Industrial Evolution in Developing Countries*, Oxford University Press, Oxford.

Harrison, A. (1996b) 'Openness and Growth: a Time Series, Cross Country Analysis for Developing Countries', *Journal of Development Economics*, vol. 48, no. 2.

Harrison, A. and Hanson, G. (1999) 'Who Gains From Trade Reform: Some Remaining Puzzles', *Journal of Development Economics*, vol. 59, no. 1.

Havrylyshn, O. (1990) 'Trade Policy and Productivity Gains in Developing Countries', *World Bank Research Observer*, vol. 5, no. 1.

Helleiner, G. (ed.) (1995) *Manufacturing for Export in the Developing World*, Routledge, London.

Hill, H. (1995) 'Indonesia from "Chronic Dropout" to "Miracle"?', *Journal of International Development*, vol. 7, no. 5.

Hill, H. (1998) 'Introduction', in H. Hill and T. Kian Wie (eds) *Indonesia's Technological Challenge*, Institute of South East Asian Studies, Singapore.

Hill, H. (2000) 'Export Success Against the Odds: A Vietnamese Case Study', *World Development*, vol. 28, no. 2.

Hill, H. and Athukorala, P. (1998) 'Foreign Investment in East Asia', *Asian–Pacific Economic Literature*, vol. 12, no. 2.

Hill, H. and Fong, P. (1991) 'Technology Exports From a Small Very Open NIC: the Case of Singapore', *World Development*, vol. 19, no. 5.

Hirschman, A. (1958) *The Strategy of Economic Development*, Yale University Press, New Haven.

Hirschman, A. (1981) 'The Rise and Decline of Development Economics', in M. Gersovitz, C. Diaz Alejandro, G. Ranis and M. Rosenzweig (eds) *The Theory and Experience of Economic Development*, Allen and Unwin, London.

Hobday, M. (1995) 'East Asian Late-Comer Firms: Learning the Technology of Electronics', *World Development*, vol. 23, no. 7.

Humphrey, J. and Schmitz, H. (1996) 'The Triple C Approach to Local Industrial Policy', *World Development*, vol. 24, no. 12.

Iscan, T. (1998) 'Trade Liberalisation and Productivity: a Panel Study of the Mexican Manufacturing Sector', *Journal of Development Studies*, vol. 34, no. 5.

Jalilian, H., Tribe, M. and Weiss, J. (2000) (eds) *Industrial Development and Policy in Africa*, Edward Elgar, Cheltenham.

Jalilian, H. and Weiss, J. (2000) 'De-Industrialisation in Sub-Saharan Africa: Myth or Crisis', *Journal of African Economies*, vol. 9, no. 1.

Jameson, K. (1981) 'Socialist Cuba and the Intermediate Regimes of Jamaica and Guyana', *World Development*, vol. 9, nos. 9/10.

Jameson, K. (1986) 'Latin American Structuralism: a Methodological Perspective', *World Development*, vol. 14, no. 2.

Jayanthakumaran, K. and Weiss, J. (1997) 'Export Processing Zones in Sri Lanka: a Cost–Benefit Appraisal', *Journal of International Development*, vol. 9, no. 9.

Jenkins, R. (1991) 'The Political Economy of Industrialisation: a Comparison of Latin America and the East Asian Newly Industrialising Countries', *Development and Change*, vol. 22, no. 2.

Jomo, K. (1997) *South East Asia's Misunderstood Miracle*, Westview Press, Boulder.

Justman, M. and Teubal, M. (1991) 'A Structuralist Perspective on the Role of Technology in Economic Growth and Development', *World Development*, vol. 19, no. 9.

Kaldor, N. (1966) *Causes of the Slow Rate of Economic Growth of the United Kingdom*, Cambridge University Press, Cambridge.

Kaldor, N. (1967) *Strategic Factors in Economic Development*, Cornell University Press, Ithaca, New York.

Kalecki, M. (1976) 'Observations on Social and Economic Aspects of Intermediate Regimes', in M. Kalecki (ed.) *Essays on Developing Economies*, Harvester Press, Hassocks.

Kaplinsky, R. (1989) 'Technological Revolution and the International Division of Labour in Manufacturing: a Place for the Third World?', in C. Cooper and R. Kaplinsky (eds) *Technology and Development in the Third Industrial Revolution*, Frank Cass, London.

Kaplinsky, R. (1994) *Easternisation: the Spread of Japanese Management Techniques to Developing Countries*, Frank Cass, London.

Kaplinsky, R. (1998) 'Globalisation, Industrialisation and Sustainable Growth', *IDS Discussion Paper* 365.

Katrak, H. (1997) 'Developing Countries' Imports of Technology, In-house Technological Capabilities and Efforts: an Analysis of the Indian Experience', *Journal of Development Economics*, vol. 53, no. 1.

Katz, J. (2000) 'Structural Change and Labour Productivity Growth in Latin American Manufacturing Industries 1970–96', *World Development*, vol. 28, no. 9.

Kim, K. (1994) 'Trade and Industrialisation Policies in Korea', in G. Helleiner (ed.) *Trade Policy and Industrialisation in Turbulent Times*, Clarendon, Oxford.

Kokko, A., Tansini, R. and Zejan, M. (1996) 'Local Technological Capability and Productivity Spillovers from FDI in the Uruguayan Manufacturing Sector', *Journal of Development Studies*, vol. 32, no. 4.

Krueger, A. (1974) *Foreign Trade Regimes and Economic Development: Turkey*, Colombia University Press, New York.

Krueger, A. (1978) *Liberalisation Attempts and Consequences*, Ballinger for National Bureau of Economic Research, Cambridge, Massachusetts.

Krueger, A. (1984) 'Trade Policies in Developing Countries', in R. Jones and P. Kenen (eds) *Handbook of International Economics*, vol. 1, Elsevier Science, Amsterdam.

Krugman, P. (1984) 'Import Substitution as Export Promotion', in H. Kierzkowsky (ed.) *Monopolistic Competition and International Trade*, Clarendon Press, Oxford.

Krugman, P. (1988) (ed.) *Strategic Trade Policy and the New International Economics*, MIT Press, Cambridge, Massachusetts.

Lall, S. (1987) *Learning to Industrialise: the Acquisition of Technological Capability in India*, Macmillan, London.

Lall, S. (1994) 'The East Asian Miracle Study: Does the Bell Toll for Industrial Policy?', *World Development*, vol. 22, no. 4.

Lall, S. (1995) 'Malaysian Industrial Success and the Role of Government', *Journal of International Development*, vol. 7, no. 5.

Lall, S. (1996) *Learning From the Asian Tigers*, Macmillan, London.

Lall, S. (1998) 'Technology Policies in Indonesia', in H. Hill and T. Kian Wie (eds) *Indonesia's Technological Challenge*, Institute of South East Asian Studies, Singapore.

Lall, S. (2000a) 'The Technological Structure and Performance of Developing Country Manufactured Exports 1985–98', *Oxford Development Studies*, vol. 28, no. 3.

Lall, S. (2000b) 'Transnational Corporations and Technology Flows', Mimeo, Queen Elizabeth House.

Lall, S., Navaretti, G., Teitel, S. and Wignaraja, G. (1994) *Technology and Enterprise Development: Ghana under Structural Adjustment*, Macmillan, Basingstoke.

Langdon, S. (1984) 'Indigenous Technological Capability in Africa: the Case of Textiles and Wood Products in Kenya', in M. Fransman and K. King (eds) *Technological Capability in the Third World*, Macmillan, London.

Lawrence, R. and Weinstein, D. (2001) in J. Stiglitz and S. Yusuf (eds) *Rethinking the East Asian Miracle*, Oxford University Press for the World Bank, New York.

Leamer, E. (1988) 'Measures of Openness', in R. Baldwin (ed.) *Trade Policy Issues and Empirical Analysis*, University of Chicago Press, Chicago.

Lee, J. (1997) 'The Maturation and Growth of Infant Industries', *World Development*, vol. 25, no. 8.

Levy, B. (1993) 'Obstacles to Developing Indigenous Small and Medium Enterprises: an Empirical Assessment', *World Bank Economic Review*, vol. 7, no. 1.

Lewis, W. (1955) *The Theory of Economic Growth*, Allen and Unwin, London.

Liedholm, C. (1992) 'Small-scale Industry in Africa: Dynamic Issues and the Role of Policy', in F. Stewart, S. Lall and S. Wange (eds) *Alternative Development Strategies for Africa*, Macmillan, London.

Liedholm, C. and Mead, D. (1999) *Small Enterprises and Economic Development*, Routledge, London.

Lipsey, R. (2000) 'Inward FDI and Economic Growth in Developing Countries', *Transnational Corporations*, vol. 9, no. 1.

Little, I. (1982) *Economic Development: Theory, Policy and International Relations*, Basic Books, New York.

Little, I. (1987) 'Small Manufacturing Enterprises in Developing Countries', *World Bank Economic Review*, vol. 1, no. 2.

Little, I., Majumdar, D. and Page, J. (1987) *Small Manufacturing Enterprises: a Comparative Analysis of India and Other Economies*, Oxford University Press for the World Bank, New York.

Little, I. and Mirrlees, J. (1974) *Project Appraisal and Planning for Developing Countries*, Heinemann, London.

Little, I., Scitovsky, T. and Scott, M. (1970) *Industry and Trade in Some Developing Countries*, Oxford University Press, London.

Livingstone, I. (1991) 'A Re-assessment of Kenya's Rural and Urban Informal Sector', *World Development*, vol. 19, no. 6.

Londero, E. and Teitel, S. (1996) 'Industrialisation and the Factor Content of Latin American Exports of Manufactures', *Journal of Development Studies*, vol. 32, no. 4.

Macaria, C. (2000) 'The Behaviour of Manufacturing Firms Under the New Economic Model', *World Development*, vol. 28, no. 9.

Macaria, C. (2000) *Export Growth in Latin America*, Lynne Rienner, Boulder.

McCormick, D. (1999) 'African Clusters and Industrialisation: Theory and Reality', *World Development*, vol. 27, no. 9.

McPherson, M. (1996) 'Growth of Micro and Small Enterprises in Southern Africa', *Journal of Development Economics*, vol. 48, no. 2.

Mead, D. (1994) 'The Contribution of Small Enterprises to Employment Growth in Southern and Eastern Africa', *World Development*, vol. 22, no. 12.

Mead, D. and Liedholm, C. (1998) 'The Dynamics of Micro and Small Enterprises in Developing Countries', *World Development*, vol. 26, no. 1.

Meller, P. (1994) 'The Chilean Trade Liberalisation', in G. Helleiner (ed.) *Trade Policy and Industrialisation in Turbulent Times*, Routledge, London.

Mensah, V., Tribe, M. and Weiss, J. (2001) 'The Small-scale Manufacturing Sector in Ghana: a Source of Dynamism or of Subsistence Income?', Mimeo, DPPC, University of Bradford, UK.

Mesquita, M. and Guilherme, P. (1998) 'A First Look at the Impact of Trade Liberalisation on Brazilian Manufacturing Industry', *World Development*, vol. 26, no. 10.

Mesquita, M. and Najberg, S. (2000) 'Trade Liberalisation in Brazil: Creating or Exporting Jobs?', *Journal of Development Studies*, vol. 36, no. 3.

Migdad, M., Jalilian, H. and Weiss, J. (2001) 'Small Scale Industry in the Gaza Strip', in O. Morrissey and M. Tribe (eds) *Economic Policy and Manufacturing Performance in Developing Countries*, Edward Elgar, Cheltenham.

Milner, C. and Morrissey, O. (1997) *Measuring Trade Liberalisation in Africa*, Credit Research Paper, 97/3 University of Nottingham.

Milner, C. and Wright, P. (1998) 'Modelling Labour Market Adjustment to Trade Liberalisation in an Industrialising Economy', *Economic Journal*, vol. 108, March.

Mody, A. and Kilmaz, K. (1997) 'Is There Persistence in the Growth of Manufactured Exports? Evidence from Newly Industrialising Countries', *Journal of Development Economics*, vol. 53, no. 2.

Moser, C. (1978) 'Informal Sector or Petty Commodity Production: Dualism or Dependence in Urban Development', *World Development*, vol. 6, nos. 9/10.

Mrydal, G. (1957) *Economic Theory and Underdeveloped Regions*, Methuen, New York.

Mulaga, G. and Weiss, J. (1996) 'Trade Reform and Manufacturing Performance in Malawi', *World Development*, vol. 24, no. 7.

Mytelka, L. (1985) 'Stimulating Effective Technology Transfer: the Case of Textiles in Africa', in N. Rosenberg and C. Frischtak (eds) *International Technology Transfer: Concepts, Measures and Comparisons*, Praeger, New York.

Nadvi, K. and Schmitz, H. (1994) 'Industrial Clusters in Less Developed Countries: Review of Experiences and Research Agenda', *IDS Discussion Paper* 339, IDS, Brighton.

Ndulu, B. and Semboja, J. (1994) 'Trade and Industrialisation in Tanzania', in G. Helleiner (ed.) *Trade Policy and Industrialisation in Turbulent Times*, Routledge, London.

Nishimizu, M. and Page, J. (1991) 'Trade Policy, Market Orientation and Productivity Change in Industry', in J. de Melo and A. Sapir (eds) *Trade Theory and Economic Reform*, Blackwell, Oxford.

North, D. (1995) 'The New Institutional Economics and Third World Development', in J. Harriss, J. Hunter and C. Lewis (eds) *The New Institutional Economics and Third World Development*, Routledge, London.

Nurkse, R. (1958) 'Some International Aspects of the Problem of Economic Development', reprinted in A. Agarwala and S. Singh (eds) *The Economics of Underdevelopment*, Oxford University Press, Oxford.

Ocampo, J. (1994) 'Trade Policy and Industrialisation in Colombia', in G. Helleiner (ed.) *Trade Policy and Industrialisation in Turbulent Times*, Clarendon, Oxford.

Ocampo, J. and Taylor, L. (1998) 'Trade Liberalisation in Developing Countries: Modest Benefits but Problems with Productivity Growth, Macro Prices and Income Distribution', *Economic Journal*, vol. 108, September.

Ocampo, J. and Villar, L. (1995) 'Colombian Manufactured Exports 1967–91', in G. Helleiner (ed.) *Manufacturing for Export in the Developing World*, Routledge, London.

Ozawa, T. (1974) *Japan's Technological Challenge to the West*, MIT Press, Cambridge, Massachusetts.

Pack, H. (1987) *Productivity, Technology and Industrial Development: a Case Study in Textiles*, Oxford University Press for the World Bank, New York.

Pack, H. (1988) 'Industrialisation and Trade', in H. Chenery and T. Srinivasan (eds) *Handbook of Development Economics*, vol. 1, North Holland, Amsterdam.

Pack, H. (2000) 'Industrial Policy; Growth Elixir or Poison?', *World Bank Research Observer*, vol. 15, no. 1.

Papageorgiu, D., Michaely, M. and Choksi, A. (eds) (1991) *Liberalising Foreign Trade*, Blackwell, Oxford.

Park, Y. C. (2001) 'A Post Crisis Paradigm of Development for East Asia', Mimeo, Asian Development Bank Institute, Tokyo.

Patel, C. and Gayi, S. (1997) *Trade Diversification in the Least Developed Countries*, Edward Elgar, Cheltenham.

Pedersen, P., Sverrisson, A. and van Dijk, M. (eds) (1994) *Flexible Specialisation: the Dynamics of Small-scale Industries in the South*, Intermediate Technology Publications, London.

Peres, W. and Stumpo, G. (2000) 'Small and Medium-sized Enterprises in Latin America and the Caribbean under the New Economic Model', *World Development*, vol. 28, no. 9.

Perez, C. and Soete, L. (1988) 'Catching-up Technologies: Entry Barriers and Windows of Opportunity', in G. Dosi (ed.) *Technical Change and Economic Theory*, Pinter, London.

Perkins, D. (2001) 'Industrial and Financial Policy in China and Vietnam', in J. Stiglitz and S. Yusuf (eds) *Rethinking the East Asian Miracle*, Oxford University Press for the World Bank, New York.

Piore, M. and Sabel, C. (1984) *The Second Industrial Divide: Possibilities for Prosperity*, Basic Books, New York.

Porter, M. (1990) *The Competitive Advantage of Nations*, Macmillan, London.

Prebisch, R. (1964) 'Commercial Policy in the Underdeveloped Countries', reprinted in G. Meier (ed.) *Leading Issues in Development Economics*, Oxford University Press, New York.

Prebisch, R. (1984) 'Five Stages in the Development of My Thinking', in G. Meier and D. Seers (eds) *Pioneers in Development*, Oxford University Press, New York.

Pritchett, L. (1996) 'Measuring Outward Orientation: Can It Be Done?', *Journal of Development Economics*, vol. 49, no. 2.

Rabellotti, R. (1997) *External Economies and Co-operation in Industrial Districts: a Comparison of Italy and Mexico*, Macmillan, London.

Rabellotti, R. (1999) 'Recovery of a Mexican Cluster: Devaluation Bonanza or Collective Efficiency?' *World Development*, vol. 27, no. 9.

Ranis, G. (1985) 'Employment, Income Distribution and Growth in the East Asian Context: a Comparative Analysis', in V. Corbo, A. Krueger and F. Ossa (eds) *Export Oriented Development Strategies*, Westview Press, Boulder, Colorado.

Ranis, G. (1989) 'The Role of Institutions in Transition Growth: the East Asian Newly Industrialising Countries', *World Development*, vol. 17, no. 9.

Reidel, J. (1991) 'Strategy Wars: the State of the Debate on Trade and Industrialisation in Developing Countries', in A. Koekkoek and L. Mennes (eds) *Trade Protection and Political Economy; Essays in Honour of Jagdish Bhagwati*, Routledge, London.

Reinhardt, N. and Peres, W. (2000) 'Latin America's New Economic Model: Micro Responses and Economic Restructuring', *World Development*, vol. 29, no. 9.

Rock, M. (1995) 'Thai Industrial Policy: How Irrelevant was it to Industrial Success?', *Journal of International Development*, vol. 7, no. 5.

Rodrik, D. (1992) 'Closing the Productivity Gap: Does Trade Liberalisation Really Help?', in G. Helleiner (ed.) *Trade Policy, Industrialisation and Development: New Perspectives*, Clarendon Press, Oxford.

Roemer, M., Tidrick, G. and Williams, D. (1976) 'The Range of Strategic Choice in Tanzanian Industry', *Journal of Development Economics*, vol. 3, no. 3.

Romer, P. (1994) 'New Goods, Old Theory and the Welfare Costs of Trade Restrictions', *Journal of Development Economics*, no. 43, no. 1.

Romijn, H. (1997) 'Acquisition of Technological Capability in Development: a Quantitative Case Study of Pakistan's Capital Goods Sector', *World Development*, vol. 25, no. 3.

Ros, J. (1994) 'Mexico's Trade and Industrialisation Experience Since 1960', in G. Helleiner (ed.) *Trade Policy and Industrialisation in Turbulent Times*, Routledge, London.

Rosenstein-Rodan, P. (1943) 'The Problems of Industrialisation in Eastern and South Eastern Europe', *Economic Journal*, vol. 53, nos. 2/3.

Sachs, J. and Warner, A. (1995) 'Economic Reform and the Process of Global Integration', *Brookings Papers on Economic Activity*, no. 118.

Sachs, J. and Warner, A. (1997) 'Sources of Slow Growth in African Economies', *Journal of African Economies*, vol. 6, no. 3.

Sapsford, D. and Balasubramanyam, V. (1994) 'The Long-run Behaviour of the Relative Price of Primary Commodities: Statistical Evidence and Policy Implications', *World Development*, vol. 22, no. 11.

Sapsford, D., Sarkar, P. and Singer, H. (1992) 'The Prebisch–Singer Terms of Trade Controversy Revisited', *Journal of International Development*, vol. 4, no. 3.

Schmitz, H. (1982) 'Growth Constraints on Small-scale Manufacturing in Developing Countries: a Critical Review', *World Development*, vol. 10, no. 6.

Schmitz, H. (1995) 'Collective Efficiency: Growth Path for Small-scale Industry', *Journal of Development Studies*, vol. 31, no. 4.

Schmitz, H. and Cassiolato, J. (1992) 'Fostering Hi-Tech Industries in Developing Countries: Introduction', in H. Schmitz and J. Cassiolato (eds) *Hi-Tech for Industrial Development*, Routledge, London.

Schmitz, H. and Hewitt, T. (1992) 'An Assessment of the Market Reserve for the Brazilian Computer Industry', in H. Schmitz and J. Cassiolato (eds) *Hi-Tech for Industrial Development*, Routledge, London.

Schmitz, H. and Nadvi, K. (1999) 'Clusters and Industrialisation: Introduction', *World Development*, vol. 27, no. 9.

Scitovsky, T. (1958) 'Two Concepts of External Economies', reprinted in A. Agarwala and S. Singh (eds) *The Economics of Underdevelopment*, Oxford University Press, Oxford.

Shin, J.-S. (2000) 'Globalisation and Industrial Restructuring: the Case of South Korea', Paper delivered at the workshop on Brazil and South Korea, Institute of Latin American Studies, London, December.

Singer, H. (1950) 'The Distribution of Gains Between Investing and Borrowing Countries', *American Economic Review*, vol. 40.

Singer, H. (1984) 'The Terms of Trade Controversy and the Evolution of Soft Financing', in G. Meier and D. Seers (eds) *Pioneers in Development*, Oxford University Press, New York.

Sjoholm, F. (1999) 'Exports, Imports and Productivity: Results from Indonesian Establishment Data', *World Development*, vol. 27, no. 4.

Sklair, L. (ed.) (1994) *Capitalism and Development*, Routledge, London.

Solow, R. (1970) *Growth Theory: An Exposition*, Clarendon Press, Oxford.

Spath, B. (1993) 'Small firms in Latin America: Prospects for Economic and Socially Viable Development', in B. Spath (ed.) *Small Firms and Development in Latin America*, Institute for Labour Studies, ILO, Geneva.

Squire, L. (1981) *Employment Policy in Developing Countries*, Oxford University Press for the World Bank, New York.

Srinivasan, T. (2001) *Policy Issues in International and Regional Trade: an Overview*, Paper presented to Trade Policy Issues seminar, Asian Development Bank Institute, April, Singapore.

Steel, W. (1972) 'Import Substitution and Excess Capacity in Ghana', *Oxford Economic Papers*, vol. 24, no. 2.

Steel, W. (1993) 'Analysing the Policy Framework for Small Enterprise Development', in A. Helmsing and T. Kolstee (eds) *Small Enterprises and Changing Policies*, Intermediate Technology Publications, London.

Stewart, F. and Ghani, E. (1991) 'How Significant are Externalities for Development?', *World Development*, vol. 19, no. 6.

Stewart, F. and Ranis, G. (1990) 'Macro Policies for Appropriate Technology: a Synthesis of Findings', in F. Stewart, H. Thomas and T. de Wilde (eds) *The Other Policy*, Intermediate Technology Publications, London.

Stiglitz, J. and Weiss, A. (1981) 'Credit Rationing in Markets with Imperfect Information', *American Economic Review*, vol. 71, no. 3.

Sunkel, O. (1973) 'Transnational Capitalism and National Disintegration in Latin America', *Social and Economic Studies*, vol. 22, no. 1.

Sutcliffe, R. (1971) *Industry and Underdevelopment*, Addison Wesley, London.

Sutcliffe, R. (1984) 'Industry and Underdevelopment Re-Examined', *Journal of Development Studies*, vol. 21, no. 1.

Tambunan, T. (1991) 'The Role of Small-scale Industries in the Indonesian Economy: an Analysis of 1970s and 1980s Data', in H. Thomas, F. Uribe and H. Romijn (eds) *Small-scale Production: Strategies for Industrial Restructuring*, Intermediate Technology Publications, London.

Teal, F. (1999) 'The Ghanaian Manufacturing Sector 1991–95: Firm Growth, Productivity and Convergence', *Journal of Development Studies*, vol. 36, no. 1.

Teitel, S. (1984) 'Technology Creation in Semi-industrialised Economies', *Journal of Development Economics*, vol. 16, nos. 1/2.

Teitel, S. and Thoumi, F. (1986) 'From Import Substitution to Exports: the Manufacturing Exports Experience of Argentina and Brazil', *Economic Development and Cultural Change*, vol. 34, no. 3.

Temin, P. (1999) 'Globalization', *Oxford Review of Economic Policy*, vol. 15, no. 4.

Ten Kate, A. (1992) 'Trade Liberalisation and Economic Stabilisation in Mexico: Lessons of Experience', *World Development*, vol. 20, no. 5.

Teubal, M. (1996) 'R and D and Technology Policy in NICs as Learning Processes', *World Development*, vol. 24, no. 3.

Tybout, J. (1992) 'Trade and Productivity: New Research Directions', *World Bank Research Observer*, vol. 6, no. 2.

Tybout, J. (2000) 'Manufacturing Firms in Developing Countries: How Well Do They Do and Why?', *Journal of Economic Literature*, vol. 38, no. 1.

UNCTAD (1996) *World Investment Report*, UN, Geneva.

UNCTAD (1996a) *The Least Developed Countries 1996*, UN, Geneva.

UNCTAD (1996b) *Trade and Development Report 1996*, UN, Geneva.

UNCTAD (1997) *Trade and Development Report 1997*, UN, Geneva.

UNCTAD (1998) *Trade and Development Report 1998*, UN, Geneva.

UNCTAD (1999a) *Trade and Development Report 1999*, UN, Geneva.

UNCTAD (1999b) *World Investment Report 1999*, UN, Geneva.

UNCTAD (2000) *World Investment Report 2000*, UN, Geneva.

UNIDO (1983) *Industry in a Changing World*, United Nations Industrial Development Organisation, UN, New York.

UNIDO (1985) *Industry in the 1980s: Structural Change and Interdependence*, United Nations Industrial Development Organisation, UN, New York.

UNIDO (1997) *Global Report 1997*, United Nations Industrial Development Organisation, UN, New York.

UNIDO (1999) *Global Report 1999*, United Nations Industrial Development Organisation, UN, New York.

Wade, R. (1990) *Governing the Market: Economic Theory and the Role of the State in East Asian Industrialisation*, Princetown University Press, Princetown.

Wangwe, S. (ed.) (1995) *Exporting Africa: Technology, Trade and Industrialisation in Sub-Saharan Africa*, Routledge for United Nations University and INTECH, London.

Waverman, L. and Murphy, S. (1992) 'Total Factor Productivity in Automobile Production in Argentina, Mexico, Korea and Canada: the Impacts of Protection', in G. Helleiner (ed.) *Trade Policy and Industrialisation and Development*, Clarendon, Oxford.

Weiss, J. (1975) *The Use of Project Appraisal Techniques in the Indian Public Sector*, University of Sussex, unpublished D.Phil. thesis.

Weiss, J. (1984) 'Alliance for Production: Mexico's Incentives for Private Sector Industrial Development', *World Development*, vol. 12, no. 7.

Weiss, J. (1986) 'Japan's Post-War Protection Policy: Some Implications for Developing Countries', *Journal of Development Studies*, vol. 22, no. 2.

Weiss, J. (1992) 'Trade Policy Reform: Performance in Mexican Manufacturing', *Journal of Development Studies*, vol. 29, no. 1.

Weiss, J. (1995a) *Economic Policy in Developing Countries: the Reform Agenda*, Prentice Hall, Hemel Hempstead.

Weiss, J. (1995b) 'Mozambique: the Market and Transition', in P. Cook and F. Nixson (eds) *The Move to the Market? Trade and Industry Policy Reform in Transitional Economies*, St Martin's Press, Macmillan, Basingstoke.

Weiss, J. (1995c) 'Mexico: Comparative Performance of State and Private Industrial Corporations', in P. Cook and C. Kirkpatrick (eds) *Post-Privatisation Policy and Performance*, Wheatsheaf, London.

Westphal, L. (1998) 'The Pendulum Swings: an Apt Analogy?', *World Development*, vol. 26, no. 12.

White, G. (1984) 'Developmental States and Socialist Industrialisation in the Third World', *Journal of Development Studies*, vol. 21, no. 1.

Williamson, O. (2000) 'The New Institutional Economics: Taking Stock Looking Ahead', *Journal of Economic Literature*, vol. 38, Sept.

Womack, J., Jones, D. and Roos, D. (1991) *The Machine that Changed the World; the Story of Lean Production*, Harper, New York.

Wood, A. and Mayer, J. (1998) *Africa's Export Structure in a Comparative Perspective*, UNCTAD, African Development in a Comparative Perspective, study no. 4, UN, Geneva.

World Bank (1981) *World Development Report 1981*, World Bank, Washington, DC.

World Bank (1986) *World Development Report 1986*, World Bank, Washington, DC.

World Bank (1987) *World Development Report 1987*, World Bank, Washington, DC.

World Bank (1991) *World Development Report, 1991*, World Bank, Washington, DC.

World Bank (1993a) *East Asian Miracle*, World Bank, Washington, DC.

World Bank (1993b) *World Development Report 1993*, World Bank, Washington, DC.

World Bank (1997) *World Development Report 1997*, World Bank, Washington, DC.

World Bank (2000a) *World Development Indicators 2000*, CD-ROM, World Bank, Washington, DC.

World Bank (2000b) *World Development Report 2000/2001*, World Bank, Washington, DC.

World Trade Organisation (1999) *Trading Into the Future*, WTO, Geneva.

Yagci, F. (1984) 'Protection and Incentives in Turkish Manufacturing', *World Bank Staff Working Paper*, no. 606, World Bank, Washington, DC.

Young, A. (1928) 'Increasing Returns and Economic Progress', *Economic Journal*, vol. 38, no. 152.

Young, A. (1995) 'The Tyranny of Numbers: Confronting the Statistical Realities of East Asian Growth Experience', *Quarterly Journal of Economics*, vol. 110, no. 3.

Index

Printed in the United States
by Baker & Taylor Publisher Services